Little Washington

100 Towns
POPULATION 48–3,500

A NOSTALGIC LOOK
AT THE EVERGREEN STATE'S
SMALLEST TOWNS

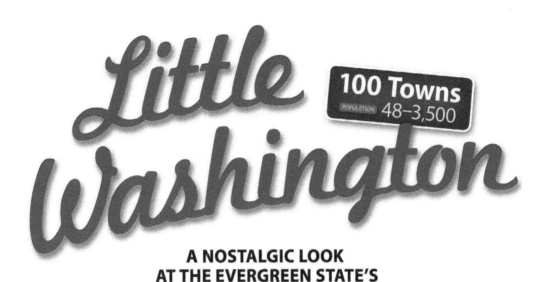

Nicole Hardina

Adventure Publications
Cambridge, Minnesota

Dedication

This book is for everyone who takes the shortcut when they know darn well it's the long way around.

Acknowledgments

Gratitude and admiration to Gail Kihn of Sumas, Louise Lindgren of Index, Charles Fattig of McCleary, Mayor Dan Rankin of Darrington, all of Shorty Long's kids in Entiat, and many others who shared with me their time, stories, and love for their towns. Thank you for your generosity and your important work.

Thank you to Brett Ortler at Adventure Publications for giving me this project, which came along when I needed it, and thank you to everyone on the team who helped see it through.

Many thanks to Arne, Chelsea, and all the Till writers, and to Smoke Farm for the community, the cold river, and the retreat.

Finally, endless appreciation to those who accompanied me on the journey: Ford Nickel, Laura Krughoff, Cheri Gries, and my parents, Pat and Blake Hardina. Most especially, thank you, Mom. As always, you were with me for the longest miles.

Photo Credits

Photographs by Nicole Hardina except as follows:

Inset photos identified by page in a left to right order using a, b, c, d.

202d, U.S. Forest Service-Pacific Northwest Region: This image is licensed under Public Domain Mark 1.0, which is available at https://creativecommons.org/publicdomain/mark/1.0/

116c, Edmund Lowe Photography/Shutterstock.com

Cover and book design by Jonathan Norberg

Edited by Brett Ortler and Ritchey Halphen

10 9 8 7 6 5 4 3 2 1

Little Washington: A Nostalgic Look at the Evergreen State's Smallest Towns
Copyright © 2020 by Nicole Hardina
Published by Adventure Publications
An imprint of AdventureKEEN
330 Garfield Street South
Cambridge, Minnesota 55008
(800) 678-7006
www.adventurepublications.net

ISBN 978-1-59193-845-3 (pbk.); ISBN 978-1-59393-846-0 (ebook)

Table of Contents

Introduction

Dear Reader,

I grew up in an Alaskan town where back roads connected to a few state routes running along a narrow peninsula. Since I moved to Washington in 1997, most of the traveling I've done in this state has been on its biggest freeways. That changed for me when I began writing this book.

Now I've traveled the length of the Columbia Gorge and the glacial-cut valleys of the Colville National Forest. After all this time living here, I finally visited the Palouse Falls, in my research, I learned that they are Washington's official state waterfall, thanks to the advocacy of nearby Washtucna's schoolkids. I talked to farmers, local historians, mayors, librarians, business owners, and some kids eating Popsicles, wondering why I was taking pictures of their town. I stood on Kamiak Butte, listening to birdsong over a green ocean of wheat. I learned about the provenance of phrases like "jerkwater town" and the namesakes of counties, roads, and monuments, controversial and otherwise. I learned that some towns celebrate the Indigenous contributions to their existence, while others push them to the background or bury them altogether. I did my best to approach each community with open eyes and a spirit of curiosity.

What can you really know about a community from the outside? Not enough, I readily admit. There is more to each of these places than I am able to offer here. Still, I know so much more than I did before. The library in Darrington offers classes in the Lushootseed language. The Farmer's Daughter in Kahlotus is owned and run by an actual farmer's daughter. Mount Index existed on a map well before Persis Gunn said she named it.

I live on the traditional land of the Duwamish, the first people of Seattle, whose case to restore federal recognition began in 1978 and remains pending today. With each visit, conversation, and hour of research, I understood and appreciated Washington State more.

This project began with a list of incorporated towns with fewer than 1,000 residents, but that approach provided a limited perspective. Jefferson County is more than Port Townsend; it's also home to the Hoh Rainforest and a dozen or so unincorporated towns like Quilcene, with a few hundred people and an enormous oyster hatchery, and Mount Walker, the only mountain facing Puget Sound that visitors can summit on foot or in a car. In the end, the project expanded to include communities spanning all 39 counties.

Little Washington is my attempt, a 100 times over, to get to know the state I call home. It's part history, part travelogue, and all love letter to the Evergreen State. When I tell people about this book, they almost always ask me which town is my favorite. I could tell you mine, but I hope that after reading this, you'll want to find your own answer.

—*Nicole*

Locator Map

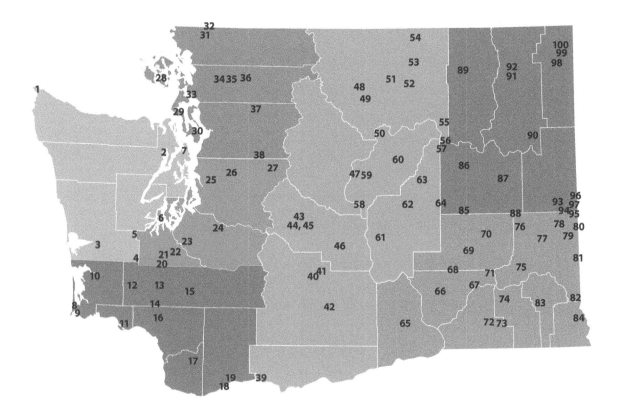

1	Neah Bay	**21**	Tenino	**41**	Naches	**60**	Mansfield	**81**	Palouse
2	Quilcene	**22**	Rainier	**42**	Harrah	**61**	George	**82**	Uniontown
3	Cosmopolis	**23**	Roy	**43**	Roslyn	**62**	Soap Lake	**83**	Pomeroy
4	Oakville	**24**	South Prairie	**44**	Cle Elum	**63**	Coulee City	**84**	Asotin
5	McCleary	**25**	Beaux Arts Village	**45**	South Cle Elum	**64**	Krupp	**85**	Odessa
6	Harstine Island	**26**	Carnation	**46**	Kittitas	**65**	Benton City	**86**	Wilbur
7	Port Gamble	**27**	Skykomish	**47**	Entiat	**66**	Mesa	**87**	Davenport
8	Long Beach	**28**	Lopez Village	**48**	Winthrop	**67**	Kahlotus	**88**	Sprague
9	Ilwaco	**29**	Coupeville	**49**	Twisp	**68**	Hatton	**89**	Republic
10	South Bend	**30**	Langley	**50**	Pateros	**69**	Lind	**90**	Springdale
11	Cathlamet	**31**	Nooksack	**51**	Conconully	**70**	Ritzville	**91**	Kettle Falls
12	Pe Ell	**32**	Sumas	**52**	Riverside	**71**	Washtucna	**92**	Marcus
13	Napavine	**33**	LaConner	**53**	Tonasket	**72**	Prescott	**93**	Spangle
14	Vader	**34**	Lyman	**54**	Oroville	**73**	Waitsburg	**94**	Waverly
15	Mossyrock	**35**	Hamilton	**55**	Nespelem	**74**	Starbuck	**95**	Latah
16	Castle Rock	**36**	Concrete	**56**	Elmer City	**75**	LaCrosse	**96**	Rockford
17	Yacolt	**37**	Darrington	**57**	Grand Coulee Dam	**76**	Lamont	**97**	Fairfield
18	North Bonneville	**38**	Index	**58**	Rock Island	**77**	St. John	**98**	Ione
19	Stevenson	**39**	Bingen	**59**	Waterville	**78**	Rosalia	**99**	Metaline
20	Bucoda	**40**	Tieton			**79**	Oakesdale	**100**	Metaline Falls
						80	Tekoa		

Population: 994
Unincorporated

INSETS L to R: Boardwalks protect the forest floor on the hike to Shi Shi Beach. • Erosion continues to shape Cape Flattery's coastline. • Fort Núñez Gaona-Diah honors Makah veterans and remembers Spain's early attempt to colonize the area. • Neah Bay offers fishing charters for several species of fish, including salmon, halibut, and lingcod.

TOP: The Makah symbol shows Thunderbird carrying a whale.

Neah Bay

People of the Cape

The community of Neah Bay is home to the Makah Tribe and located on the Makah Reservation. The Makah, whose name variously translates as "people of the cape" and "people who are generous with their food," inhabit their traditional lands, minus the 300,000 acres they lost in the 1855 Treaty of Neah Bay. But unlike treaties between Washington's territorial governor, Isaac Stevens, and other Indigenous groups, the Treaty of Neah Bay affirmed the Makah people's rights to maintain their villages and lifeways, including whaling, sealing, and fishing, on land the Makah did not cede.

Sixty years prior to the treaty, Salvador Fidalgo established the first non-Native settlement in Neah Bay, but it failed within a year after conflict with the British. The area now known as Neah Bay was at the time called Deah (or *Di·ya* in Makah), named for Makah Chief Dee-ah. Deah was one of five permanent Makah villages that stretched along the northern and western coasts of what became Washington State.

Pre–European contact, as many as 4,000 Makah lived in these villages. Cedar longhouses 30 feet wide and 70 feet long housed multiple generations of extended families. Summer brought travel to Tatoosh Island, Ozette Lake, and other seasonal camps, fishing grounds, and gathering places. The Makah designed canoes made from western red cedar for whaling, fishing, and war. Selling baskets woven from cedar and grasses became a source of income for the Makah after the treaty and remained important into the 20th century.

From the late 1700s through the time of the Treaty of Neah Bay, diseases introduced by non-Native settlers ravaged the Makah population, and by 1877 the Makah numbered fewer than 1,000 people. Neah Bay was home to an Indian Agency, a reservation trading post, a school, and a lifeboat station. One hundred years had passed since Captain James Cook sailed to Tatoosh Island, and 80 years since a lighthouse went up on the island to guide non-Native sailors through the Strait of Juan de Fuca to and from Puget Sound, to the east. white people began homesteading in Neah Bay in the 1890s. One of the first, a man named W. W. Washburn, established a general store which, after a fire and rebuilding, still stands today as the only store in Neah Bay.

Despite significant losses of both population and land, Makah culture remains vibrant today. The tribe welcomes visitors to their reservation to learn about their past and present.

The Buried Village

Makah legend tells of a great landslide long ago in Ozette, one of the tribe's ancient villages. In 1969, a winter storm shifted the land again, uncovering preserved artifacts and proving the oral history true, and more than 4,000 hours of painstaking excavation began. In a combined effort between the Makah and Washington State University, archaeologists worked without shovels, using only water from a hose to rinse delicate artifacts clean. Their efforts recovered more than 55,000 artifacts, some of which are now on display at the Makah Museum. Radiocarbon dating of the artifacts demonstrated that the slide that buried Ozette happened 500 years ago. In modern times, the last full-time Makah resident of Ozette left in 1917.

In the Beginning

In the historical imagination, the edge of the land is often said to be the geographical end of the world. The Makah orientation to the land is the opposite. "Welcome while you are in Neah Bay, the beginning of the world and the home of the Makah," reads their website, translated into English.

Visitor permits are available at several locations in town, including the Makah Museum and Washburn's General Store. The museum is part of the larger Makah Research and Cultural Center, which encompasses a Makah language and education department, a library and archive, and a historic-preservation office. A full-size gray whale skeleton hangs in the central gallery, the effort of more than 1,000 hours of work by museum staff and Neah Bay High School students after the whales were removed from the endangered species list in 1999. That year marked the first time the Makah had harvested a whale in more than 70 years.

Despite the Treaty of Neah Bay guaranteeing the Makah the right to practice whaling—a deeply spiritual and community-based practice for them—the tribe hadn't hunted since the 1920s, when commercial whaling nearly drove many species to extinction. In recent years, however, whale populations have made a strong recovery, and the tribe has moved toward recovering the whaling rights

A 2-mile trail over boardwalks and bridges and through a typically muddy creekbed yields a reward: Shi Shi Beach, at the edge of the Pacific. Hikers can continue along the beach to Point of Arches or connect with the Cape Alava Trail. Bring a tidebook to avoid getting stranded.

first granted to them more than 160 years ago. A decision by the US Court of Appeals for the Ninth Circuit mandated that the Makah file a waiver to the Marine Mammal Protection Act before they harvested any more whales. The Makah did so in 2005, and studies by the National Oceanic and Atmospheric Association (NOAA) determined that population levels could sustain some harvesting, though not the four whales per year that the Makah requested. In 2019, NOAA proposed terms for a waiver valid for 10 years. Until a judge rules on the proposal, whaling remains illegal, but NOAA's proposal moves the Makah closer to their goal.

As a tourist destination, Neah Bay is popular with fishermen and hikers alike. Just a few miles from the center of town, a short hike through coastal forest leads to Cape Flattery, the northwesternmost point in the contiguous United States. Turning left at the bridge to Hobuck Road leads to Hobuck Beach, a popular campsite and the location of an annual surfing competition. A few more miles down the road, the short but demanding Shi Shi Beach Trail leads hikers through a muddy creekbed to a cliff, recently improved with a set of steps down to a quiet and beautiful beach where rock formations called seastacks weather the waves and wind, and bedrock angles out of the earth like wrecked ships.

Lava flows accumulated for millions of years to form the basalt cliffs of Cape Flattery, the northwesternmost point of the contiguous United States. Tatoosh Island, just off the coast, is of historical importance to the Makah Tribe. The island is the subject of intense study by climate scientists and wildlife biologists.

Population: 596
Founding: 1889

INSETS L to R: Chefs prize Quilcene oysters for their crisp brine, borne of the pristine waters of Quilcene Bay. • Since 1991, Quilcene's museum has served as a home for preserving area history and ongoing community organizing. • The name of Quilcene's pioneering family graces this mansion and park in town, as well as one of the Olympic peaks. • Quilcene's historical museum is just around the bend from the giant oyster.

TOP: The summit of Mt. Walker offers a bird's-eye view of Puget Sound.

Quilcene

The Olympians

In 1788, John Meares, a British mariner, named Mount Olympus for its resemblance to the celestial realm of Greek mythology. When 34-year-old George Vancouver sailed into the Strait of Juan de Fuca a few years later, he followed suit, naming the range of mountains the Olympics. He named 75 features, from all of the visible mountains to the Olympic Peninsula, Hood Canal, Deception Pass, and Whidbey Island. In his record of his discoveries, Vancouver noted, "I could not possibly believe that any cultivated country had ever been discovered exhibiting so rich a picture."

Jefferson County, named for Thomas Jefferson, who sent Lewis and Clark on their journey in 1804, spans 2,200 square miles, 350 of which are water. Port Townsend, the peninsula's only city, developed in the years just before local Indigenous tribes lost their lands in the Treaty of Point No Point and the Quinault Treaty, which relegated several tribes to reservations. Around the same time, other communities evolved, mostly around mills.

The community of Quilcene sits on land once occupied by the people who bore its name. The first settler, Hampton Cottle of Maine, came in 1860 and worked digging stumps for shipbuilders. Within a few decades, about 50 people had moved to the area to take advantage of the Homestead Act, and in 1881 they established a post office and named the town Quilcene, after the Quil-ceed-a-bish, or "saltwater people."

With plans for a railroad to run from Port Townsend to Quilcene, the community platted the town into 20 blocks. When the railroad came, the town was already both a thriving community and a resort destination.

Millard Fillmore Hamilton, a prominent businessman who'd moved to the area from Indiana in the 1880s, platted Quilcene with his business partner. In 1890, Hamilton purchased a large parcel of land, naming it Hamilton's Addition. He paid an architect to build a mansion, by far the largest home in the area. In the Panic of 1893, Hamilton lost his money, and William Worthington, known to be Hamilton's rival, purchased the house. Though the fortunes of its citizens rose and fell, Quilcene settled into an identity as a tourist destination, which it remains today.

Southwestern Jefferson County: The Hoh Rainforest

Begin at the beaches strewn with ancient trees turned massive driftwood, and move inland through temperate old-growth rainforest, straight through to glaciers. Geothermal springs and waterfalls bubble and burst from the dense vegetation. In the Hoh Rainforest, named for the Indian tribe who once lived along the Hoh River, branches drip chartreuse moss over Jurassic-size ferns. Forest like this once ran from southeastern Alaska all the way to central California. Before Olympic National Park became a national monument in 1909, the Hoh, Quinault, Quileute, and others lived here.

To visit the Hoh Rainforest is to experience a living cathedral. Half a million people visit annually. The 17-mile Hoh River Trail follows the riverbed, gaining little elevation for 10 miles before surging up toward Glacier Meadows and the summit of Mount Olympus. More-accessible hiking options include the Hall of Mosses and the Spruce Nature Trails, both of which educate visitors in the species of flora and fauna that reside in this indescribably beautiful place. Herds of Roosevelt elk wander through campsites to gravel bars amid the rushing Hoh River. Eagles nest overhead. Here, visitors will find One Square Inch of Silence: The Hoh is the quietest place in the entire country.

From a Single Grain of Sand . . .

In 2011, the town of Quilcene declared a new slogan for itself: "Pearl of the Peninsula." Coming up with the nickname was a community event, from voting to celebrating the results. A gala and awards ceremony were held to recognize local efforts to beautify the town and engage the community. From scrubbing moss from sidewalks to tidying the totem pole garden, Quilcene's citizens made sure the town lived up to its shiny new moniker. Public

events like this happen at Worthington Park, on 10 acres just behind the Quilcene Historical Museum. The Hamilton-Worthington House is available to rent for public and private events.

Visitors can drive or hike to the summit of Mount Walker, the only peak facing Puget Sound that is accessible by vehicle. Seattle is visible to the south across the Hood Canal, and the Olympics and North Cascades can be seen to the north.

Just outside of Quilcene, from the top of Mount Walker—the only peak facing Puget Sound with a summit visitors can reach by car—the water so thoroughly divides the land that it seems impossible to travel the area by car. The gaze drops down lush slopes, taking in the specific coastline of each island, the depth of the valleys. Seattle emerges from the cloud banks like a distant Oz, just visible. Somehow, it's just two hours by car from the Emerald City to the Pearl.

The Hamilton-Worthington House, listed on the National Register of Historic Places, was home to two of Quilcene's early settlers. Millard Fillmore Hamilton built the house in 1892 and sold it to William Worthington in 1907.

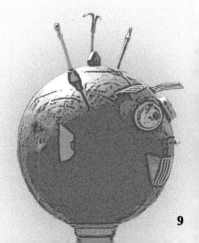

Population: 1,649
Founding: 1861

INSETS L to R: Cosmopolis has been a mill town since its early days. • A bridge over the Chehalis River links Cosmopolis to greater Grays Harbor County. • Hoquiam artist Jenny Fisher painted this mural, part of an ongoing project to create 40 murals in Grays Harbor. • Industry has left its mark on the banks of the Chehalis River in Cosmopolis.

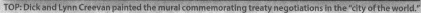

TOP: Dick and Lynn Creevan painted the mural commemorating treaty negotiations in the "city of the world."

Cosmopolis

The Western Pen

Washington's first highways were its rivers. Before Grays Harbor had a name, the Chehalis people traveled the rivers from the base of the Cascades to the Pacific Ocean, trading goods and sharing cultures with other tribes. When whites began settling in the area, they rapidly industrialized the same riverine highways. By 1924, Grays Harbor became the first port in the world to ship 1 billion feet of lumber by water. James Pilkington filed the first donation land claim in the area that would become Cosmopolis in 1852, 60 years after Robert Gray sailed into the harbor where five rivers run to the Pacific. Pilkington sold his claim a few years later, and settlers organized the town of Cosmopolis—"City of the World" and Grays Harbor's first city—in 1861.

Early attempts at industry focused on grist milling, but the wheat was far away and expensive to transport. In the 1880s, the Pope and Talbot Company, which had already found success farther north at Port Gamble, sent a manager to buy Cosmopolis's fledgling shingle mill operation and trading company. They established the Grays Harbor Commercial Company, and Cosmopolis—or Cosi to locals—quickly gained a reputation as a company town.

Production ramped up quickly, and Grays Harbor became the largest harbor-based shipping port for lumber worldwide. Immigrants flocked to Grays Harbor for work. Finnish settlers established Hoquiam and Aberdeen just downriver from Cosmopolis. Though jobs were plentiful and the supply of timber seemingly endless, workers endured terrible conditions.

Neil Cooney was born in 1860, just as Cosmopolis became a city. In his forties, he became the manager of the Grays Harbor Commercial Company (GHCC), and in 1920, he bought it. As an employer and manager, Cooney had a reputation for ruthlessness. Despite considerable pressure from the Industrial Workers of the World (IWW), the GHCC never unionized. The IWW, known locally as the Wobblies, branded Cosmopolis as the "Western Penitentiary" and Cooney as its warden. As documents for the National Register of Historic Places note, "Cosmopolis was the mill, and the mill was Cooney."

Even so, Cooney's legacy wasn't altogether negative. Under his ownership, the GHCC improved the water system and housing in Cosmopolis. For himself, Cooney built a mansion of spruce, cedar, and other woods endemic to the Pacific Northwest. "The showplace of Grays Harbor," as people called the mansion, is today a bed-and-breakfast. Cooney, who died in 1943, bequeathed money to the county for a hospital and to the school district for scholarships. His will offered 500 acres and $100,000 to anyone who would build a sulfate pulp plant. Weyerhaeuser did just that in 1957.

Enduring Through Strength

In 1855, fresh from brokering the Treaty of Neah Bay with the Makah to the north, territorial governor Isaac Stevens attempted treaties with several other Indigenous nations living in permanent villages along the Chehalis River watershed. Negotiations took place in Cosmopolis. While several nations signed, including the Quinault, Hoh, Queets, and Quileute, several more refused, including the Chinook, Chehalis, and Cowlitz. Signing nations gave up more than 1 million acres. Allotments further reduced the amount of Indigenous-held land dramatically. The Chehalis eventually relocated to a reservation in the southeastern corner of the county. In their own words, "The Chehalis people have endured through self-reliance and determination."

Just Cosi

Cosmopolis feels like a place where everything is running somewhere else. The highway runs through town past the few businesses, the police station, and city hall. The Chehalis River runs parallel to the highway, and in any direction you look, industry is moving downriver.

Though its profits declined precipitously, Weyerhaeuser continued to produce wood pulp, an ingredient used to make everything from toothpaste to cigarette filters. In 2005, the company gave notice of its intent to close the pulp mill, citing "poor markets, aging machinery, high operating costs, and small-scale operations." The closure cost nearly 350 jobs in the area, and Weyerhaeuser shuttered not only the pulp mill in Cosmopolis but also the lumber mill in Aberdeen, to the tune of 245 and 97 jobs, respectively. A small log mill continued to operate in Aberdeen, but the closure represented a significant and negative impact county-wide.

Five years later, Weyerhaeuser sold the pulp mill to Gores Group from California, which opened Cosmo Specialty Fibers. The opening created 200 jobs, many of which, Gores says, went to former Weyerhaeuser employees. Labor in the area got another boost in 2010 when Governor Chris Gregoire designated Grays Harbor as the construction site for the pontoons needed to replace Seattle's aging Highway 520 bridge across Lake Washington.

Weyerhaeuser, a timber company influential in the region since 1900, sold its cellulose mill to a California-based private equity firm in 2010.

While Cosi may have had its own services once upon a time, it now seems clear that most people who live there cross into Aberdeen, Hoquiam, Montesano, and beyond for everything from groceries to high school. Just over the bridge in Aberdeen, a local mural pays tribute to the immigrants who came to Grays Harbor from around the world, representing dozens of countries by their flags.

The eras of Cooney and Weyerhaeuser are over in this southwestern corner of the Olympic Peninsula. What happens next isn't clear. Cosmopolis hopes to capitalize on tourism, given its location in the southwestern corner of the Olympic Peninsula. Perhaps ironically, the town isn't far from the Hoh Rainforest, a temperate old-growth forest in Olympic National Park. The park consists of nearly 1 million acres of nationally protected land.

A mural in Cosmopolis commemorates the site of treaty negotiations between Washington's territorial governor, Isaac Stevens, and representatives of at least three Indian tribes. The Quinault Treaty was one of 13 treaties establishing reservations for Native Americans in the Pacific Northwest and declaring United States governmental ownership over most of the state.

4

Population: 684
Founding: 1905

INSETS L to R: Fire District 1 has two paid firefighters and 30 volunteers. • Dine in a restored train car at the Gray Goat, Oakville's only restaurant. • Downtown Oakville is a sleepy place • The Oakville State Bank dates to 1909. Though long-since closed, it's the scene of an annual robbery.

TOP: Local industry greets visitors to Oakville in Grays Harbor county.

Oakville

Histories Lived Side by Side

A 1906 historical account called *The Coast* describes Oakville in glowing terms. Timber was king then, and the Northern Pacific Railroad connected the inland town to the coast. The book records Mrs. D. M. Newton as Oakville's first settler, and J. R. Harris as the first postmaster. The Oakville Lumber Company was a major employer, and there was a glove factory and a creamery. Notes *The Coast*, "The people are enterprising and prosperous and there is a most excellent outlook for an increase and advancement along all lines of pursuit." Any account of the Chehalis people, whose reservation lies adjacent to Oakville, is conspicuously missing.

The Chehalis River begins in the Cascade Mountains and runs to the Pacific. The early Chehalis people, or "people of the sands," spoke a Salish dialect. Both the Upper Chehalis (Kwaiailk) and Lower Chehalis relied on salmon as a dietary staple. Other tribes in the area include the Queets, Quinault, Humptulips, Satsop, Copalis, and Wynoochee. History suggests that early interactions between Euro-American settlers and Indigenous groups were peaceful, and the Chehalis likely helped settlers with fishing and hunting. As with other Indigenous groups, however, the Chehalis experienced massive population loss post-contact.

The Chehalis were among those who refused to sign a treaty with Isaac Stevens in 1855. Though the government created the Chehalis Reservation in 1860, the Chehalis, as nonsigners, weren't entitled to governmental assistance—they did not receive patents for their lands but instead had to apply for homesteads. A century would pass before the Chehalis received any monetary compensation for the loss of their lands.

In 1890, the timber camps became a town: Oakville, named for the garry oaks flourishing in the forests around the town's prairies. The Northern Pacific Railroad had begun construction. Three lumber companies and a mill created and sustained the town's economy until the 1920s when the decline of the timber industry began. In the 1960s, timber sales in Grays Harbor County suffered as Asian markets outbid local mills. In the next two decades, federal regulations restricted logging in order to preserve spotted owl and salmon habitats. Industrial decline and recession have led to higher-than-average unemployment in Grays Harbor County compared with the state average. Still, its proximity to Olympia makes Oakville an inviting bedroom community whose population is slowly increasing.

Oakville and the Case of the Mysterious Rain

In 1994, a strange weather event struck Oakville and sickened many of its residents. On August 7, police officer David Lacey sat in his cruiser when the rain began to fall. He turned on his wipers—but the rain was all wrong. The wipers smeared whatever was falling from the sky all over the glass. Resident Beverly Roberts reported that everyone touched by the strange substance got sick with "a really hard flu." Barn cats started dying. The Washington Department of Health tested the Jell-O-like substance and found two common bacteria capable of causing the illness, but according to Mike McDowell, the state's microbiologist, the samples disappeared and his superiors told him not to ask questions. In three weeks, the strange rain fell six times. McDowell speculates that Oakville was chosen as a "test site" by whomever made the stuff. A competing theory holds that military bomb testing over the ocean hit a patch of jellyfish, which seeded the clouds with goo. The mystery remains unsolved.

Timber Town, USA

At the intersection of Main and State Streets, a single building houses Oakville's City Hall and the Oakville branch of the Timberland Library. Across the street is the fire department, and behind that, the community center and a park. On the remaining corner, there's a house. It's a whole town in a single intersection.

The town sign welcomes visitors to Timber Town, USA, and as though to verify the claim, stacks of cut trees are ready for transport in the industrial yard just beyond the sign. Logging trucks stack the fallen trees by the dozen and haul them to mills. The timber industry, it seems, is way, way down, but it's not out. Willis Enterprises has operated a wood chip facility for 40 years, though only a handful of people work at the Oakville location, which focuses on exporting.

Oakville used to have a tavern in a historic hotel, but after discovering asbestos, the city had to demolish the building. A row of closed businesses on the main drag through town includes a bank that's famous as the last in the state to suffer a horseback robbery, which locals reenact each year in a show of civic pride. The annual Zucchini Jubilee provides another opportunity for community togetherness and fun, including games, an obstacle course, and a picnic.

The Oakville fire department started in 1909 with four companies. Today, the fire station occupies a prominent piece of downtown real estate.

The few businesses in town include the Holy Lamb organic-bedding company, located in the most prominent building in Oakville. The century-old barnlike building once housed the Little Bit general store. Holy Lamb sells its products in more than 100 stores and has a showroom in Olympia. Harry's Grocery sells food staples in town, and the Gray Goat Bar and Grill recently opened, serving breakfast, lunch, and dinner in an old train car.

Despite its small population, Oakville has both an elementary school and a combined middle school and high school; more than 35% of 220 students in the school district are Native American. The high school mascot is a snarling acorn. It's almost too easy to make the old joke about acorns and trees, but in Oakville, it may be true. Bob Johnson, owner of the Gray Goat, grew up in Oakville. In addition to running the restaurant, he's done maintenance for the school district for two decades.

The Gray Goat Bar and Grill, Oakville's only restaurant, features a train car turned dining room by owner Bob Johnson, who bought the place in 2017.

Population: 1,653
Founding: 1898

INSETS L to R: In 1912, Henry McCleary built this hotel in demonstration of his mill's various wood products. • First owned by McCleary and later bought by Simpson, the factory in Oakville has operated since 1912. • During World War I, the women of McCleary worked in the factory, which began providing lumber for aircraft production. • A park in downtown McCleary displays fire and logging equipment from an earlier era.

TOP: Local historians are doing the important work of keeping McCleary's history alive.

McCleary

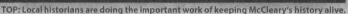

Drop the -*Ville*, Please

In 1890, Henry and Ada McCleary moved from Ohio to Washington. Henry McCleary, who knew his way around a sawmill, got a job at Foy and Son in Tacoma. A handful of years later, McCleary and Edward Foy became business partners and started a mill of their own. McCleary Camp became a town in rapid fashion, though it wouldn't incorporate until 1943. By 1901, the town had a school. Two years later, it had a dance hall. In 1910, it got a post office. When the inevitable fire struck McCleary Camp, a new sawmill was already under construction. Production halted briefly and then surged forward.

Gold rushes from California to British Columbia and the Yukon spiked demand for timber to support startup mining towns and the railroads. In 1910, McCleary bought a failed door factory and moved its operation to his town, by then called McClearyville. Ada McCleary, however, didn't care for the -*ville* at the end, so the town became simply McCleary.

Charles Fattig, a McCleary local and historian, says of Henry McCleary, "He knew how to run a mill and make money." WWI was a source of prosperity for McCleary, whose door company began supplying lumber for aircraft. When local men went to war, women took over their positions and kept the factory producing.

McCleary had a reputation for running a tight ship, and not just when it came to his company. In 1919, Congress passed the Volstead Act, enforcing the recently passed 18th Amendment banning the manufacture, transportation, and sale of alcohol. Cue the forest distilleries. Washington State's bout with Prohibition preceded the national experiment, and Henry McCleary not only allowed but sanctioned illegal distilleries on his land. He exported McCleary Moonshine, transporting bottles of the stuff, labeled with the slogan "Made in the Woods," on the unsuspecting Northern Pacific Railroad. As McCleary historian Ernest Teagle once put it, "When the nation went dry, McCleary went wet."

Even when engaged in illicit activity, McCleary was principled. Charles Fattig says, "If [the moonshine] was good, he allowed it. If it killed anybody, he had you run out of town." Running people out of town was something McCleary earned a reputation for. As Fattig tells it, employees of McCleary's door company sometimes stole lightbulbs, prompting McCleary to pay them a visit at home. If he saw one of his lightbulbs burning—you guessed it.

By the late 1930s, sawmills had all but exhausted Washington's old-growth timber, and the Depression sank every business but the door company. In 1941, McCleary sold the factory, and the entire town, to Simpson Logging Company.

Bear Wars

Marking its 60th anniversary in 2019, the McCleary Bear Festival is an annual weekend similar to a high school homecoming, complete with a court of royalty and a street dance for teens. The festival got its start in 1959, when the McCleary Historical Society decided the town needed a summer celebration. Initially, the winning name for the festival was "Second Growth," reflecting the importance of timber to the local economy.

The timber industry had begun replanting the forests it had logged for decades. Unfortunately, black bears were eating the new saplings—a single bear, in fact, might eat 40 saplings every day. Thus, the Second Growth Festival had a dual purpose. McCleary declared war on the bears, and the festival added McCleary's own version of a chili cook-off: a bear-stew eating contest. Commemorative pins, many of them on display at the McCleary Museum, are a local collectors' item. The Bear Festival takes place annually in mid-July.

Preserving the Past for the Present

When Simpson Logging Company took over McCleary, the town didn't even have sewer facilities, and its water and road systems were in disrepair. McCleary incorporated in 1943, establishing local governance. Though Simpson employed most of the town, the citizens of McCleary took control by incorporating. Still, the company contributed, improving the water supply and electrical grid and assuming administration of the town's power supply. Simpson scaled back its operations in the mid-1980s in response to

new regulations on logging, but the door factory continues to operate and today employs upwards of 300 local workers. The factory dominates the town visually, and a row of neat houses across the street from its entrance embodies McCleary's identity as a factory town. For some workers, the commute is just out the door and across the road. Other residents drive to nearby Olympia for work, dividing McCleary between factory town and bedroom community.

When the men of McCleary went to serve in WWI, the women of McCleary took their place in the door factory. Thanks to local historians like Charles Fattig, we know the names of some of the women who worked there.

The Carnell family donated a house in 1984 for the McCleary Museum. Though the museum may not be open every day, a sign on the door lists the phone numbers of the curators. There's a good chance that if a visitor calls curator Charles Fattig, he'll answer from inside the museum and come to the door. Fattig has been a member of the local historical society for more than 30 years, and he's knowledgeable about McCleary's history in both the general and the specific. Fattig notes that in the first decades of the 20th century, McCleary saw an influx of Greek and Italian immigrants, such that McCleary had its own Little Italy. One immigrant, Angelo Pelligrine, came to McCleary at the age of 13, speaking no English, and went on to become an English professor at UW in 1932.

The museum publishes a quarterly newsletter featuring profiles of local people in the town's history, sharing old photos, and generating interest. But despite the historical society's efforts, the museum faces an uncertain future. In 2019, the Carnell family asked the museum to vacate, citing the building's poor condition. As of this writing, the historical society and the museum are looking for another home. Hopefully, they'll find one. Preserving local history is hard work and a labor of love. Why do people volunteer to do it? As Charles Fattig says, "To keep history from becoming history."

The McCleary Hotel was built in 1912 by the town's founder. The train passed right in front of it. "Only upper-crust people could afford to stay there," says a local historian.

TOP: After nearly 50 years of ferry service, Harstine Island finally got a bridge in 1969.

Population: 1,002
Unincorporated

INSETS L to R: The community center serves as the informational and organizational hub of life on the island. • Jarrell's Cove is a private marina on Harstine Island. • Harstine Island's welcome sign points visitors to businesses and natural features. • Hoodsport Winery is the sole representation of Harstine's own Island Belle grapes in Washington winemaking.

Harstine Island

Third Time's the Charm

Harstine Island takes its name from US Navy Lieutenant Henry J. Hartstene, a member of the Wilkes Expedition of 1838–1842, which explored and mapped Antarctica, the Pacific Ocean, and the northwestern coastline of the US. Disagreement over how to spell the island's name seems to have begun early on. The original spelling used in the late 19th century was *Hartstein;* a US Geological Survey map from 1914 says *Hartstine.* A planned community built on the northern end of the island in 1970 was called *Hartstene,* but the generally accepted spelling today is *Harstine.* In any case, the first non-Native settler on the island wasn't Henry Hartstene but Robert Jarrell.

Jarrell came to the Puget Sound area in the 1850s and made the island his permanent home in 1872. Six years later, he married a woman named Philura, who was the only non-Native woman on the island for another 15 years. When Robert died 20 years later, Philura buried him on their land and deeded the land to the community as a public cemetery, which is still in use today. In homage to Scandinavian burial customs, the shoes of the deceased are left on their graves. A community committee oversees and maintains the cemetery.

Prior to European settlement, the Squaxin people, who spoke the Lushootseed language, inhabited the land. The Squaxin Island Tribe moved onto nearby Squaxin Island after signing the Medicine Creek Treaty in 1854. Today, Squaxin Island is uninhabited, and the tribe lives along several inlets in southern Puget Sound.

Like the Squaxin before them, settlers in Mason County exploited the waterways' rich resources, including oysters. As logging ramped up, its resulting pollutants began to threaten the oyster population. Communities up and down the coast depleted their oyster stocks, and by the 1930s, there wasn't much left to log, either. Boomtowns in Mason and adjacent counties started to go bust. The establishment of a prison in the area and a focus on tourism helped keep struggling communities alive. In 1974, the Boldt Decision upheld the rights of Indigenous tribes to fish in state waters; 20 years later, the law was applied to tidal shellfish. In the 1970s, the Squaxin Island Tribe bought the Harstine Island Oyster Company and renamed it

Salish Seafoods. Today, the Squaxin Island Tribe is the largest employer in Mason County.

In 1914, construction began on the Harstine Island Community Hall. Resident Andrew Johnson donated the land, local men felled easily accessed trees, and area carpenters completed the work.

Electrical lines didn't run to the island until 1947, more than 30 years after the construction of the community hall. According to local news coverage at the time, the cable that electrified the island was more than two years late and cost twice the quoted amount. A journalist noted, "They've been without modern convenience for so many years that they probably won't believe that electricity has been provided for them until they can see the light."

Mason County began operating a ferry to the island in 1922, and in 1969, a bridge connected Harstine to the mainland. In 2019, the bridge's 50th birthday was marked with a parade led by the Pioneer Middle School Marching Band.

Crankster Gangsters

Imagine a line passing through three points. Point A is the drug abuse problem facing many parts of rural America. Point C is purveyors of high-end musical instruments, such as guitar maker Gibson. How is Harstine Island the point B that connects these two seemingly disparate points?

The answer: maple trees. Though commercial logging has declined in Washington by nearly 70%, the market for figured maple—a rare and beautiful variety that carries sound well—has increased dramatically. Local wood buyers, law enforcement, and park employees agree that a population of meth-addled thieves is taking chainsaws to hundred-year-old maples under the cover of darkness and the invisibility provided by Harstine Island's nearly 12,000 acres. Though multiple groups of stakeholders work to nab the thieves, successful prosecution depends on catching them in the act. More often, enforcement encounters the aftermath: a graveyard of trees, each a century or more in the making. Don Van Orman, a local wood supplier, calls the thieves "crankster gangsters." *Seattle Weekly* reporter Ellis E.

Conklin asked another local why anyone, addicted or not, would go to such lengths to steal. "It's real easy to do this," the man replied. "Real easy."

A ferry connected Harstine Island to the Key Peninsula and the mainland until a bridge was built in 1969. In 2019, the annual Bridge Parade marked 50 years of connectivity.

Primitive. No Warning.

Shortly after crossing the bridge to Harstine Island, the road comes to an intersection that offers a simple choice: north or south? The main roads are paved, but turn down any side road and the pavement will likely turn to gravel. A novice in the wilderness will find her bearings by paying attention to the signs. The road ahead is PRIMITIVE, with NO WARNING. Another sign advises, NO COMMERCIAL MUSHROOMING. Cue the jokes about how one knows one is in the Pacific Northwest.

Harstine's residents live scattered across the island's 19 square miles. At the end of many roads, a sign lists the names of the residents, creating a feeling of microcommunities. Properties range from gated mansions to ramshackle dwellings. There's evidence of clear-cutting, but the chartreuse moss clinging to maples and Jurassic wood ferns belie Harstine's proximity to old growth. A marina at Jarrell Cove, on the western side of the island, sells gas and provisions, but don't be too surprised to find a sign on the door that says, GONE TO TOWN. Town, in this case, means Shelton or Allyn, each a 25-minute drive away.

From the trailhead at Harstine Island State Park, you can't see the ocean, but you can smell it. Marine air mingles with the scent of cedar and pine, and the trail's steady descent promises an oyster-strewn beach, calm water, and a peaceful spot to contemplate. Signs suggest activities from badminton to boating, but all you may really want to do is listen to the sound of the boats rocking in the water, birdsong and insect hum, and the sound of your own thoughts. Maybe pick up a barnacle. Or maybe become one for a day.

The Island Belle, a hybrid grape, was developed in Puget Sound.

Population: 920
Founding: 1853

INSETS L to R: Five miles of motorists lined up to cross the Hood Canal Bridge at its opening in 1961. • In Port Gamble, historic preservation isn't just a major effort, it's the town's identity. • The General Store building holds a restaurant, a gift shop, and a museum of sea creatures. • White picket fences divide front yards from Highway 104.

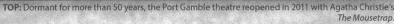

TOP: Dormant for more than 50 years, the Port Gamble theatre reopened in 2011 with Agatha Christie's *The Mousetrap.*

Port Gamble

From Homeland to Company Town

The way Port Gamble in Kitsap County tells its story, William Talbot, a lumber merchant from San Francisco, and Andrew Pope, of the Puget Mill Company, arrived in the area in 1853 and established a sawmill that same year. Prolific industrialists, the two managed to ship their product as far as Australia, Peru, and England. "Fewer than 1,000 settlers lived on the Sound in 1853," the town's website notes, and while "the last whistle blew" at the mill in 1995, Pope Resources still owns the town, administered by Olympic Property Group, honoring "the long-term commitment the founding fathers made" in the "glory days" of this "company town."

Visitors to Port Gamble may indeed feel that the town sprang up out of whole cloth. Signage on historic buildings extols their architectural importance and contributions to town life. Beneath the preserved clapboard exterior, one finds a second Port Gamble, created in the Treaty of Point No Point, fully two years after Talbot and Pope made their claims on S'Klallam Indigenous land.

S'Klallam, derived from the Salish phrase *Nux Sklai Yem,* means "strong people." The tribe's habitation of the Hood Canal and San Juan de Fuca Strait areas predates Euro-American exploration and settlement of those lands by more than 500 years. By the time Talbot and Pope arrived in what would be Port Gamble, disease introduced by Euro-Americans had reduced the S'Klallam population by as much as 90%. Still, they persevered. The Port Gamble S'Klallam Tribe's recounting of the same history notes one settler as complaining that "our whole territory is alive with Indians."

The Point No Point Treaty, signed in 1855 by territorial governor Isaac Stevens and representatives of the S'Klallam, Chemakum, and Twana Tribes, stripped these groups of their lands in a process rooted in both language and concepts foreign to the very people whose homelands Stevens set out to take. The treaty terms maintained that the S'Klallam retained fishing rights in their traditionally inhabited land, but they also required the tribe to relocate to a reservation more than 100 miles away. The S'Klallam refused to go.

While "the record is silent," S'Klallam oral history holds that new mill owner William Talbot asked the S'Klallam to relocate just across the water at Point Julia, guaranteeing them mill jobs and lumber in exchange. According to the S'Klallam's own record, Talbot kept his word: the S'Klallam relocated but stayed nearby, and Talbot built them a trading post. A Euro-American named the new settlement "Little Boston." In the 1930s, the tribe sought and received federal recognition, and the US government purchased some of the Puget Mill Company's land to add to Point Julia, creating the Port Gamble S'Klallam Reservation.

These details are not unimportant—they mean just as much to the development of Port Gamble as does the fact that the Talbot built the town in the image of his hometown in Maine, where so many of his workers would come from, and that explorer Charles Wilkes named the town for naval officer Robert Gamble, wounded in the War of 1812. One can't talk about the movement from the muley saw, which cut 2,000 board feet per day, to the sash saw, which cut 10 times as much, without also talking about the pole-and-thatch construction that the S'Klallam used during the warmer months spent gathering resources, or about how many generations sheltered together during the long, wet winters, which were a time of religious and ceremonial activities.

Port Gamble cares about its history—its concern is evident in every carefully manicured lawn—but visitors have to work hard to discover a fuller truth. Otherwise, what is there to know about a place, really, besides that it's a nice place to stop in for a beer on a sunny day?

Bridging the Gap

In the mid-20th century, getting from the Olympic Peninsula to the Kitsap Peninsula meant taking a ferry. Though some rural residents resisted its construction, the Hood Canal Bridge opened in 1961. Building it represented a significant engineering challenge: salt water, tidal conditions, and a geography that tended toward enhanced wind action threatened the bridge's structural integrity. The bridge rests on floating pontoons, unusual for a saltwater bridge. In fact, the Hood Canal Bridge is the longest such bridge in salt water in the world.

The Hood Canal Bridge opens by raising and retracting three hydraulic spans. The process takes from 10 to 45 minutes, according to the Washington Department of Transportation. Due to post-9/11 security regulations, WSDOT no longer publicizes when military submarines pass through the canal.

Engineers constructed a pontoon bridge because the depth of Hood Canal (as much as 340 feet), as well as the soft subgrade on the canal floor, made supportive structures impossible. These vulnerabilities proved true in 1979, when the bridge sank after hours of 120-mph winds and 15-foot waves. The reconstructed bridge opened in 1982, with the provision that it close anytime winds of 40 mph blow for at least 15 minutes. The current structure is a drawbridge that opens to marine traffic—which has the right-of-way—including nuclear submarines at the Bangor Trident naval base nearby.

Pleasantville

It's been said that Fort Gamble looks like a movie set, and it indeed feels unreal—it seems that the people who work here come and go each day but no one really lives here. (The population listed at the beginning of this profile reflects the numbers of the Port Gamble S'Klallam Tribe.)

The lumber mill's 1995 closure coincided with the end of Talbot and Pope's lease. Pope Resources bought the town, enabling it to begin a new life as a tourist attraction. St. Paul's Church is a popular wedding venue, commanding a fee of nearly $4,000, including access to the pavilion and the use of a large reception tent.

Port Gamble has also been designated as a Rural Historic Town. Its antiques shops and general store, along with a restaurant that affords a gorgeous view of Hood Canal, make it a popular stop for tourists crossing the bridge to the Kitsap Peninsula on their way to Port Townsend, Port Angeles, and destinations on the Olympic Peninsula.

Port Gamble, like Hershey, Pennsylvania, is one of America's last remaining examples of a company town. And because it's a nationally recognized landmark, residents can't have things like mailboxes and satellite dishes.

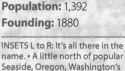

TOP: Go see Ed and browse his perfectly curated collection of used offerings at Banana Books.

Population: 1,392
Founding: 1880

INSETS L to R: It's all there in the name. • A little north of popular Seaside, Oregon, Washington's Long Beach today is a seaside playground, complete with a small amusement park. • The longest beach in the world. • Downtown Long Beach.

Long Beach

Tinkerville, a Tourist Town

Visitors to Long Beach today might notice that the town seems to be exclusively a tourist destination, and they might wonder how that came to be. The truth is, it's always been that way. Long Beach started as a recreational haven and resort for the wealthy residents of Portland, about 100 miles inland.

The history of Long Beach is awash with famous names. Between the end of the 18th century and the turn of the 19th, everyone from James Cook to George Vancouver to Robert Gray visited Long Beach. The early explorers sought a riverine passage to the West, finally established by Lewis and Clark, who visited Long Beach in 1805 after discovering the point at which the Columbia River meets the Pacific. Before these exploratory efforts, the area now called Long Beach was home to the Shoalwater Bay Tribe, a Chinookan people.

The Chinook inhabited both sides of the peninsula separating Willapa Bay from the Pacific Ocean. Coastal Chinook were adept traders who mediated for diverse tribal groups to the north and south, as well as inland along the Columbia River.

Early Euro-American explorers who traded with the Chinook picked up some of their language, leading to the creation of a pidgin dialect called Chinook Jargon, also known as Tsinuk Wawa.

After Lewis and Clark's success, Midwesterners, largely of Scandinavian descent, began colonizing the area. Settlements developed to the south of Long Beach on both sides of the mouth of the Columbia, in present-day Astoria and Ilwaco. In 1880, Henry Harrison Tinker purchased and built Tinkerville, a resort town, which was renamed Long Beach in 1887. The resort centered around the hotel, where for about $10 per week visitors got room and board, including three meals per day. A few years later, the Ilwaco Navigation Company, whose "Clamshell Railroad" operated according to the tidal schedule, extended the line right up to Tinker's hotel. By then, the well-developed boardwalk had gained the nickname "Rubberneck Row." Meanwhile, the Clamshell Railroad became infamous as the "Never Get There Railroad" and the "Irregular Rambling." Logging, seafood harvesting, and agriculture, particularly cranberries, made significant contributions to the local economy until the 1960s, by which time the first-growth timber mill and clam fishery were in clear decline. Though Long Beach still leads the country in cranberry production, its economy has always relied on tourism.

Tsinuk Wawa

Documented use of a Creole language blending English with coastal Chinookan stretches back to 1805. As explorers, traders, and colonizers interacted with Indigenous people in the mid-18th–19th centuries, as many as 10,000 people adopted Chinook Jargon. Also known as Chinook Wawa and Tsinuk Wawa, the dialect spanned as far north as southeastern Alaska and as far south as northern California. Notably, Chief Seattle resisted the language, insisting that anyone wanting to trade with him could learn to use his language, Duwamish. In common use until the 1950s, Chinook Jargon began to lose prominence in the era of Indian boarding schools operated by the Bureau of Indian Affairs, during which white school officials often physically punished Indigenous children for using their native languages. Today, websites like chinookjargon.com and immersion programs led by tribal members seek to restore Tsinuk Wawa and other Indigenous languages, preserving both their use and their enduring importance as a part of a living history.

Choose Your Own Adventure

While tourism has always been central to life in the area, legislation such as the Boldt Decision, which granted 50% of all fishing rights to tribes across Washington, along with environmental-protection efforts pitting erosion control against private-land ownership, have led to shifts in the tourism-based economy over time. Still, recent census data shows that the greatest number of Long Beach residents employed in the area work in accommodation and food service—in other words, tourism.

As it became necessary to redirect tourist dollars from activities like sport fishing, Long Beach found new ways to capitalize on its reputation for relaxation. Local kite enthusiasts opened the World

Kite Museum in 1989, aided by a single donation of more than 700 kites, mostly from Malaysia, Japan, and China. Kite flying is a popular activity on the beach, and with 28 miles of sand, the beach can accommodate as many kites as show up to fly. Every year, the museum hosts a festival, drawing hundreds of fliers for a week of competition.

In the early days of the Razor Clam Festival, Long Beach residents worked together to cook the world's largest clam fritter. The 15-foot pan used for the task until 1948 stands downtown, next to a wooden sculpture of a spitting razor clam.

Other area attractions include the Pacific Research Foundation's Cranberry Museum, offering an education in the century-long influence of cranberry farming in the region and a walking tour of a working cranberry farm. There's also an event called Splash-Dash-Geocache each fall. If none of these strike your fancy, there's always Jake the Alligator Man at the Marsh Museum on the downtown strip.

For nature seekers, a long boardwalk built in 1990 offers an accessible way to enjoy the beach while protecting it, and an eight-mile Discovery Trail extends through the wetlands all the way to Ilwaco and Cape Disappointment. To the layperson's eye, Chinook culture is less visible in Long Beach than in neighboring towns like Ilwaco, where drawings, sculptures, and exhibits foreground the importance of the Chinook heritage in the area. However, the Chinook Indian Nation, comprising five Chinookan tribes, still inhabit their native lands, including the Long Beach area.

From across the parking lot at the beginning of the boardwalk, visitors can pick up the Discovery Trail, leading four miles to Cape Disappointment in Ilwaco.

TOP: Jessie's Fish Co., one of Pacific County's largest employers, faces an uncertain future.

Ilwaco

Where the Trail Comes Out

Though Ilwaco's European heritage is predominantly Finnish, it's Chinook culture that dominates Ilwaco's retelling of its history. Before Ilwaco was given its name, after Elwahko Jim, son-in-law of Chief Comcomly of the Chinook Confederacy, it was called *No' Squalakul'*, which translates from Chinookan as "where the trail comes out"—a reference to the town's location at the end of a traditional portage route between Chinook villages on the Columbia River and Shoalwater Bay.

Though the Chinook people have never been officially recognized as a tribe by the US government, their story is front and center at the Columbia Pacific Heritage Museum in downtown Ilwaco, which details the story of the Chinook from pre-contact in the late 18th century to epidemics that devastated 90% of the population to ongoing efforts to achieve federal recognition as the Chinook Indian Tribe. Recognition was promised by the Tansey Point Treaty, which was signed in 1851 but never ratified. In 2002, the Assistant Secretary for Indian Affairs denied the Chinook federal recognition, concluding that the tribe had "failed to prove historical continuity." The Chinook continue to fight for recognition and rights to their homeland, which they call the *Chinuk Illahee*.

The museum in Ilwaco also details the journey of Lewis and Clark, beginning with a display of Thomas Jefferson's instructions to Meriwether Lewis in June of 1803, including specific advice about keeping journals and maps, recording natural science and ethnographic information, practicing diplomacy, and finally, returning safely. Jefferson left it to Lewis and Clark to draw the line when it came to how much they would risk in pursuit of their goal of finding a path through the waterways from Louisiana to the Pacific Ocean, stressing the importance of erring on the side of safety. "In the loss of yourselves, we should lose also the information you will have acquired," he wrote. "By returning safely with that, you may enable us to renew the essay with better calculated means."

The thread of Ilwaco's past is connected to its present at the museum. Exhibits feature Lewis Alfred Loomis, who revolutionized transportation on the peninsula after the Civil War; the Clamshell Railroad, famous for its dependence on the tides; and detailed histories of local industry, including fishing, logging, and cranberries.

In 1968, the US Coast Guard instituted a National Motor Lifeboat School and commissioned a new steel-hulled motorboat after several marine disasters resulted in the loss of both lives and wooden motor lifeboats in the area just outside of Ilwaco, known as "the graveyard of the Pacific" for its notoriously difficult-to-navigate waters. Lifesaving has been an important part of the area's marine presence since the establishment of the Klipsan Beach Station, built in 1889, and continues with the National Motor Lifeboat School at Cape Disappointment. It is the "only heavy weather training school for coxswains in the Coast Guard, and it draws surfmen-in-training from all over the world," as well as tourists, who can watch the Coast Guard perform lifesaving drills from Cape Disappointment State Park.

Cape Disappointment

Just outside of Ilwaco on historically Chinook land lies Cape Disappointment, which is anything but disappointing. In 1788, English captain John Meares named the cape Disappointment after he failed to find an entrance from the cape to the Columbia River. Today, tourists visiting this majestic site where river meets ocean will find the oldest lighthouse in the Pacific Northwest, as well as the only two lighthouses in the US that stand just 2 miles apart. The Lewis and Clark Interpretive Center offers an educational experience, and miles of trail are accessible to everyone. The paved Discovery Trail runs all the way to the town of Long Beach with frequent paths to the beach, offering accessibility for nature seekers of every age and ability.

Making a Comeback

Upstairs at the Salt Pub, Ilwaco seems to wear its industrial heart on its sleeve. Fishermen mingle with tourists over microbrews and fish tacos made from the local catch. Visible from the picture windows overlooking the harbor, commercial and charter boats share space in the marina, and Jessie's Ilwaco Fish Company processing plant dominates the near landscape.

Commercial and charter boats share Ilwaco's marina, and Jessie's Ilwaco Fish Company dominates the near landscape before the harbor gives way to the Pacific. Local resident Bob Schroeder says that in the 1950s he could walk across the boats in the harbor.

Ilwaco's business district is just up the hill from the marina, separated only by a dock ramp and a wide paved path leading to the doors of the Salt Pub and Ole Bob's Seafood Market, as well as Karla Nelson's beautiful Time Enough Books and several art galleries featuring local works. Ilwaco's Saturday outdoor market brings out local artists like wood turner Richard Schroeder, who moved to Ilwaco not long ago with his wife, Diane, after years of city life. Richard says you can tell true city people by the way they start to pace midafternoon. "Then there are the folks who buy a book and curl up at the pub," he says. "Come Sunday afternoon, we have to roll them up and send them home."

Diane Schroeder is on the board of the museum, as is Karla Nelson, owner of Time Enough Books. "The building used to belong to the phone company," Diane says. For a while, the museum accepted anything and everything, but it has truly become valuable under the leadership of its latest executive director, Betsy Millard. Some of the museum's holdings were found to belong to the Chinook people. "They needed to be reappropriated," says Diane. The board reached out to the tribe to return the items but were ultimately allowed to keep them on loan with permission of the Chinook people.

Ilwaco today boasts a thriving local arts scene and a growing tourism industry, centered around its historical roots and mariner lifestyle. "They say small towns like this are making a comeback," Richard says. In Ilwaco, it's easy to see why.

Cape Disappointment is home to the oldest lighthouse in the Pacific Northwest, as well as the only two lighthouses in the US that stand just 2 miles apart.

Population: 1,637
Founding: 1875

INSETS L to R: There's no better welcome to "the oyster capital of the world," than—you guessed it—this giant bivalve mollusk. • The Steam Donkey, invented by John Dolbeer in 1881, transformed the Pacific NW logging industry. • Including its majestic stained glass ceiling, building the courthouse cost $132,000 in 1911. • A carved swing offers a shady seat under an enormous tree in this South Bend yard.

TOP: The Pacific County Courthouse represents South Bend's victory over Oysterville.

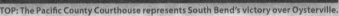

South Bend

Rail, Meet Sail

In 1869, brothers Valentine and John Riddell located a sawmill on a southern bend in the easily navigable Willapa River. Eleven years later, South Bend incorporated. Within 20 years of its founding, South Bend was booming, thanks to the efforts of the South Bend Land Company to promote it as a "City of the Future." In a strategic move intended to create sustainable economic development, the Land Company ceded the right-of-way to half of its considerable holdings to the Northern Pacific Railroad in 1890. In exchange, Northern Pacific promised a line between South Bend and the inland town of Chehalis and eventually all the way to Yakima, east of the Cascade Mountain Range.

Rumors in town held that the railway would construct a terminal in South Bend, making it a hub of rail transport in Washington State. The Hotel Willapa was constructed near the site of the proposed terminal. Advertising hailed South Bend as "The Baltimore of the Pacific" and "The San Francisco of the Pacific Northwest." However, the terminal was ultimately not established

in South Bend, and the industrial boom that had boosted the population from 150 in 1889 to 3,500 in 1894 began to slow.

Eventually, the interstate replaced the railroad. Fishing, oystering, canning, and lumber industries kept South Bend vacillating between boom and bust and formed its economy. Future economic booms in the area redounded not to South Bend but nearby towns such as Raymond, which hadn't ceded land to the railroad in the same manner and thus had more room for civic development.

The introduction of Japanese oysters in the 1930s revitalized a flagging industry, and South Bend survived on the continued economic staples of oysters, timber, and fishing, as well as its position on the Willapa and the railway. Opposing sides of town vied for commercial centrality until fires destroyed much of the east end, securing the west end as the commercial hub of South Bend. In 1892, South Bend became the seat of Pacific County after a contested election, and in 1910, it erected the Pacific County Courthouse, which has been on the National Register of Historic Places since 1977. As the seat of Pacific County, South

Bend is the home of county-wide governance, as well as the Pacific County Heritage Museum and Historical Society.

A Stolen Courthouse

Today, South Bend is the county seat, but that wasn't always so. Pacific County was the third county to be established north of the Columbia River, after Lewis and Clark Counties. Originally, Cape Disappointment, where Lewis and Clark first saw the Pacific Ocean, held the title of county seat. A year later, the federal government claimed that land for a military reservation, forcing residents to vacate and relocating local governance to nearby Chinookville, a Native settlement. Three years later, Oysterville claimed the county seat in an election and held it for nearly 20 years. South Bend boomed, and the population demanded a vote to move the county seat there. Oysterville didn't take the news well and refused to give up the county records until a gang of South Benders went up the river by steamer and took them by force.

In 1975, local historical magazine *The Sou'wester* published the account of John A. Morehead, a county commissioner who witnessed the events of Sunday, February 3, 1893. According to Morehead, 50 men from South Bend, fueled by righteousness over their election win plus a few rounds of drinks, stormed upriver to Oysterville on two steamboats, determined to take the courthouse by relocating the official records. Led by an "egotistical tailor and taxidermist with well-developed biceps," the men seem to have stormed up to Oysterville without a plan. Morehead reported that Phil Barney, the county auditor, took little notice of the shenanigans until he found his office ransacked, at which point, Morehead writes, "Barney grabbed up a chair leg and the execution he did with it on the head of those South Benders would have put Samson of old to shame as he spread carnage among the Philistines with the jawbone of an ass."

At the end of the day, some documents and furniture were removed, and, Morehead writes, "in due time the contents of the courthouse were removed over to South Bend by the usual method of transportation." South Bend faced a challenge to the county seat by the town of Raymond shortly after as that city boomed, which, according to Morehead, provided the impetus for the construction of the beautiful courthouse standing in South Bend today. Known as the "Gilded Palace of Extravagance," the courthouse is now more than 100 years old.

The steam-powered winch was invented in 1881 in California and first used in Washington in Skagit County.

Keeping It Local

Local artists are telling South Bend's history all over town. In murals, drawings, sculptures, and carvings, they draw a through line between the town as it was in its early boom years to now, offering both history and suggestions for fun ways to spend the day, including kayaking the sleepy Willapa, bird-watching, or touring the nearby wildlife refuge. A tour of the courthouse is obligatory, and a stopover at Robert E. Bush Park can be done on foot or by boat; moorage is just $5 per day. Members of the Chinook Tribe welcome the annual salmon run. The Chinook people are not recognized by the federal government, but they are widely recognized in town itself, in local art and by mention.

In the Oyster Capital of the World, the road is paved with—you guessed it—oyster shells. The Chester Club Oyster Bar has the best oysters in town.

Population: 775
Founding: 1907

INSETS L to R: Just off of down-town Cathlamet, a walk through the park leads past the museum and down a path to the marina. • Old dock pilings make a great nursery for opportunistic plants. • Cathlamet's spacious, light-filled library has a great view of the water. • As the seat of Wakhiakum County, Cathlamet is the center of all county business. A sign outside the courthouse gives a brief summary of the town's history but misspells its founder's last name.

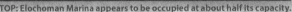

TOP: Elochoman Marina appears to be occupied at about half its capacity.

Cathlamet

A Stone in Tall Timber

Cathlamet is the only incorporated town in Wah-kiakum County, one of the smallest counties in Washington. Both the county's and town's names have Indigenous origins and refer to groups of people who spoke different, mutually unintelligi-ble languages, though both groups spoke dialects of Chinook, a family of languages used by several groups. Chinook Jargon was a lingua franca crucial to trading between the Chinookan groups and trad-ers along the Columbia and on the northwest coast.

Modern-day Cathlamet sits near the mouth of the Columbia River, which once separated these groups; the Kathlamet lived on the south side of the river, in present-day Oregon, and the Wahkiakum lived on the north side. A disease referred to in historical accounts as "gray fever," thought to be Asian flu or smallpox and borne by early trad-ers, decimated both groups, and their languages are now extinct, carried on only by local names. *Cathlamet* means "stone," and *Wahkiakum* means "tall timber" in Chinookan. Chief Wakaiyakam is buried in Cathlamet's Pioneer Cemetery.

In 1792, on an expedition to verify Captain Robert Grey's discovery of the Columbia River, Lieutenant W. R. Broughton spotted the land now called Cathlamet. Fifteen years later, Lewis and Clark camped here and traded with Indigenous tribes during their journey to the mouth of the Columbia; by the time they arrived, however, much of the Native population had already been devas-tated by disease. A few years after Lewis and Clark left the area, the remaining Kathlamet crossed the river and joined the Wahkiakum, forming a new settlement, which eventually became the location of the first white settlement in the area.

Early trade focused on furs, but James Birnie, a Scot who worked for the Hudson's Bay Company, began trading for preserved fish in the 1830s. Soon James; his wife, Charlotte, who was part Kootenay; and their 10 children became the first permanent white settlers in the area, opening a trading post called Birnie's Retreat. The US government created the Washington Territory in 1853, and a year later, the territorial government named Wahkiakum County, with Cathlamet as the county seat.

Early industry in Cathlamet focused on Columbia River salmon. In the 1870s, Scandinavian immigrants began arriving to work donation land claims. Homestead claims were free, but the dense forest made clearing the land difficult. In the early 20th century, harvesting the county's forests was big business and remained so until the mid-1980s. In the 1930s, extensive damming of the Columbia River began to affect the salmon population. The last cannery closed in 1947. In 1925, a ferry service began bringing people across the river; it is still in operation today.

Giants in the Trees

One day, someone posted an open invitation for interested musicians to jam at the Skamokawa Grange. Three people responded to the ad: Erik Friend is a drummer and recent transplant from Seattle to Wahkiakum who dreams of building a treehouse. Ray Prestegard can play any kind of stringed instrument, and his family has lived in the area for generations. Jillian Raye, a banjo player and vocalist, had recently moved to the area to be close to family. The three came together with a remarkable set of musical skills, only to meet the person who'd posted the open call: Krist Novoselic—yes, *that* Krist Novoselic, formerly of Nirvana. The four of them formed Giants in the Trees, with Novoselic on bass. The Giants have played all over the Northwest and have garnered international attention. Despite, or maybe because of, their diverse musical interests and backgrounds, the four have found a harmonious chemistry and a musical style that focuses on traditional song structure and experimentation.

A Unique Welcome

When asked about Cathlamet's original name, Birnie's Retreat, Rick Nelson, publisher of the *Wahkiakum County Eagle*, says, "Cathlamet was the original retirement community." Indeed, with the decline in fishing and logging, Cathlamet is now a draw for those seeking a slower pace and proximity to nature. It has a lot to offer to both

residents and visitors, including a library, a museum, restaurants, a hotel, a brewery, and outstanding views of the Columbia River. As the seat of Wahkiakum County, Cathlamet is the hub of local business, and though fewer than 1,000 residents call the town home, it sustains a newspaper:

From the hill above Elochoman Marina, parts of downtown Cathlamet and the Columbia River are visible, hinting at the promise of the town's welcome sign.

The Wahkiakum County Eagle started in 1846 and has been in continuous production since 1891. It contains sections like "Downriver Dispatches" from the western part of the county, and news from Skamokawa, an unincorporated community nearby whose name, Nelson tells me, in Chinook Jargon means "smoke on the water."

On the way into town, a sign promises that "a unique welcome awaits you in Cathlamet." Descending toward Elochoman Slough Marina, visitors may feel a sense of shift. A marine breeze peels away layers that accumulate in city life. Attention grows languid, landing on an eagle's sentinel silhouette or the pilings of a former dock, now sprouting a green nursery of ferns. People say hello to strangers and locals alike. On one corner of Main Street, a home attached to (and once a part of) the Hotel Cathlamet boasts a colorful flower garden and a large pond full of koi. Caught gazing at the flowers, I found myself in conversation with the home's owner, a woman with rainbow-painted toenails and a laugh that occupies her entire body. When I complimented her garden, she told me she'd been watching the bees; some nosed in but backed out of flowers, while others seemed to make a half-turn in the petals.

Cathlamet's charms are many, and its culture is thriving. Throughout the year, the town marks holidays with community breakfasts and beer gardens, potlucks, and play days. Whether you want to be on the water or near it, whether you're interested in camping, cycling, or checking Washington's farthest-flung breweries off your list, Cathlamet will delight and inspire.

Julia Butler Hansen (1907–1988), a longtime Cathlamet resident, represented Cowlitz and Wahkiakum Counties in the Washington House of Representatives for 22 years and went on to serve in the US House of Representatives until 1974. A wildlife refuge outside of Cathlamet is named in her honor.

Population: 632
Founding: 1906

INSETS L to R: The Chehalis River runs through Rainbow Falls State Park. • Pe Ell's old jail sits on the main road near the veterans memorial. • The 56-mile Willapa Hills Trail is the westernmost part of a system spanning Washington State along old rail lines. • Though its population is 25% lower today than at its founding more than 100 years ago, the town of Pe Ell keeps moving.

TOP: A WWII-era M3 Stuart Light Tank stands in Pe Ell's Veterans Memorial Park.

Pe Ell

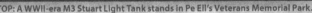

A Sack of Flour and Six Rutabagas

In 1880, Polish immigrant Matthew Kroll was working as a sod buster on a Nebraska farm. When drought hit the area, he and his wife, Regina, made plans to leave. They had a young son, Felix. The Krolls thought about moving to Wisconsin, but Matthew had heard there were too many stumps. Then he saw an advertisement for a "land of milk and honey." That land was Pe Ell.

The Krolls arrived in 1892, lived on a homestead owned by the Kowalsky family, and eventually bought their own acreage. Kroll's grandson, Edwin Kroll, wrote the story of how his family came to Pe Ell. Edwin Kroll died in 2011, but his story and others from Pe Ell's history have been preserved by the USGenWeb Project, a free nonprofit genealogy website that's become part of the constellation of resources keeping local memories alive. According to Edwin Kroll, his grandparents could clear an acre of land "for a sack of flour and six rutabagas."

The Krolls were one of several Polish families to immigrate to the Pe Ell area near the turn of the 20th century. In 1916, Polish immigrants built Holy Cross Church, Washington State's

only congregation of the Polish National Catholic Church, which split from the Vatican in an effort to maintain the Polish language. Nine decades after its construction, the aging and unsafe church was razed, and locals mourned its loss.

Pe Ell incorporated in 1906, and within a year its population topped 1,000 people. The Northern Pacific Railway had arrived about 10 years earlier. In addition to farming, logging and millwork were major employers in the area. Records show schools operating in Pe Ell from as early as 1900, and by 1912, local districts had already consolidated in Pe Ell. In 1913, the town added the Central School. Decades later, local districts consolidated again, and again, Pe Ell kept its schools. School records say that "former students remember carrying their chairs from the old school to the current one in 1952." Remodeling and new construction in the 1990s and 2000s brought Pe Ell School District into the modern era.

Local legend has it that Pe Ell got its name because the Indigenous people couldn't pronounce the name of an early French Canadian settler, Pierre Charles. Another story holds that it's an abbreviation of Charles's first name and his wife's: "P. L." Other accounts say it's the other way around; that is, European settlers adapted an Indian word. Either way, locals seem to embrace the mispronunciation, and maybe it doesn't matter. This beautiful little town gets all the important things right.

Over the Rainbow

Just outside Pe Ell, adjacent to farmland along the Chehalis River, Rainbow Falls State Park offers wide, grassy spaces and plenty of opportunities to explore Lewis County on foot. A short walk on a trail lined with salal and salmonberry descends to the slow-moving river and the brief but beautiful falls.

The park is one access point for the Willapa Hills Trail, and there's another trailhead just a block off of downtown Pe Ell. The trail follows a former rail line and is part of a cross-state trail system created along the old railbed. The Willapa Hills section of the trail runs for 56 mostly flat miles and is great for running, walking, cycling, and even horseback riding. Along the way, check out the Newaukum River Bridge, the oldest bridge in Lewis County. The Northern Pacific Railway ended service in the 1950s, and Washington State Parks purchased and converted it into a trail. The full length of the trail has been open since 2016.

Rails to Trails and Fairy Tales

Highway 6 runs right through the middle of town, and many of Pe Ell's homes stand alongside it, their front porches 50 feet from the road. Though the town's population has decreased since its founding, it has a pub, a café, and a coffee shop, as well as a grocery store, a gas station, a few churches, a veterans' hall, and a few businesses. The farmers' market on Saturdays runs from 8 a.m. to noon. The Pe Ell school is on the highway too; about 300 students from pre-kindergarten through high school are enrolled. In 2019, the school district applied to move to four-day weeks, hoping to save money on substitute teachers and transportation while extending each school day to avoid sacrificing instructional time.

Though small in population, Pe Ell is big on community spirit, its generosity extending well beyond the city limits. Locals Mirinda and Tim Moriarty grew up in California and opened Jones Creek Brewing just outside of Pe Ell in 2017. The next year, the Camp Fire struck California, killing 86 people and displacing 14,000 families. In response, California-based brewery Sierra Nevada created a new beer called Resilience Butte County Proud IPA, and they shared the recipe widely. The goal was to create a fundraising effort to help the survivors. The Moriartys in Pe Ell heeded the call and brewed a big batch. They're donating 100% of the proceeds from their batch of Resilience to the relief effort. If they sell out, they'll contribute $1,500.

Rainbow Falls State Park, just outside of Pe Ell, offers tranquil, reflective moments. Visitors can access the Willapa Hills Trail in the park as well as in downtown Pe Ell.

In addition to reaching out to neighboring states in need, Pe Ell has opened its doors to community events such as the Fairyblossom Festival, which ran for several years in Chehalis before outgrowing its venue. The festival found a new fairy glen in Pe Ell in 2018. If fairies and beer aren't your thing, the annual Tour de Farms bike ride showcases some of the region's most prominent farms, as well as the Willapa Hills Trail system.

Pe Ell is a peaceful place, but it's not without conflict. Regular flooding in the area has led to a proposal for a dam on the Cowlitz River. In 2007, flooding of the Chehalis River Basin caused water to rise 8 feet up the walls of some homes. Residents whose homes suffered this kind of damage support the dam, as do business owners, who hope that it might create additional recreational opportunities and thus more tourism. Representatives of the Quinault Indian Nation, on the other hand, have urged officials to consider the dam's potential impact on the local salmon population and ecosystem. The US Army Corps of Engineers agreed to consider alternatives to the dam, called Alternative One, and began their review in 2019. For now, the future of the Chehalis River floodplain hangs in the balance.

A charming sign beckons visitors to check out Pe Ell's weekend farmers' market, which runs Saturdays until noon.

Population: 1,766
Founding: 1913

INSETS L to R: Frosty's is a true Napavine institution, dating to the turn of the 20th century. • Napavine is a neighborly town. These folks stopped by the open door of the former post office and now boutique to let their pup meet the shop owner's. • A sign beside the Napavine fire department reminds downtown patrons to honor the spirit of service the firefighters demonstrate. • A look through town.

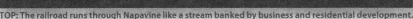

TOP: The railroad runs through Napavine like a stream banked by business and residential development.

Napavine

Little Town on the Prairie

A 1908 history notes Napavine's importance as a town on Northern Pacific's main line. That year, the town had a number of general stores, three hotels, two butcher shops, and other businesses. Farming and dairy drove the local economy, as did timber; still, the record notes, "Napavine has never had a boom." Instead, it grew slowly as part of the texture of the surrounding communities.

Napavine remembers John Cutting as the first to file a land claim in the area, but it was Scottish immigrant James Urquhart who changed the name from Napawyna, chosen by settler Horace Pinto, to Napavine. The word is said to derive from the Indian word, *napavoon*, meaning "small prairie," though it is unclear to which Native dialect the word belongs. An 1893 history of the post office credits Urquhart with starting the Napavine post office, "established in the wilderness," and notes Mr. Urquhart as "the father of eight Republican voters." James and his wife, Helen, had 11 children in all, 9 sons and 2 daughters. In 1873, Northern Pacific accepted the town's name change and officially rechristened its station as Napavine.

That same year, Chehalis, just 8 miles away, became the seat of Lewis County. Soon enough, industry based in Chehalis would provide employment opportunities for residents of Napavine in agriculture, coal, and dairy, but chiefly lumber. In the early 1920s, the lumber market fell hard as the country adjusted to a postwar economy, but the pulp and paper markets soon began to grow. During the Great Depression, lumber production dropped by two-thirds in Washington, and most loggers lost their jobs. Production levels rose during and after WWII, and three decades of housing boom sustained Lewis County for a while longer. Today, the economies of Lewis County towns like Napavine remain mutually interwoven.

The Boy Mayor

In 2008, the first year of his administration, Mayor Nicholas Bozarth wrote in an address to the town, "I am optimistic about the future of our city." He thanked residents for making Napavine "what we expect it to be" and called on them as "valuable teammates." In terms of future planning, Mayor Bozarth described his "Let's Do Business Plan" to attract new companies to the area. He expressed concern over whether the town was adequately supporting the volunteer fire department and talked about plans to investigate rising water costs.

That same year, Bozarth drew ire from the owners of Frosty's, a local bar and grill, when he made a rule prohibiting city workers from entering establishments recognized as bars during working hours. He had to suspend the chief of police, Shelby Clements, after a scandal involving several officers exchanging inappropriate text messages with a county manager.

During his campaign, Bozarth knocked on every door in Napavine and won three-fourths of the vote. He was just 22 years old. Bozarth's stint in local politics is over for now, but he didn't go far. Today, he's a physician who practices family medicine in Chehalis.

Growing Pains

From its early days as a town of just a few hundred people, Napavine has experienced rapid and often exponential growth. The population doubled between 1990 and 2000, and from 2000 to 2010 it increased another nearly 25%. The city council anticipates another doubling of the population by 2025. These periods of explosive growth have brought both opportunities and challenges.

In 2005, two new developments added nearly 100 new homes to Napavine, with almost twice as many approved for construction. The city has been annexing adjacent land, too, and plans to acquire another 630 acres. The city council in Napavine has a history of planning for expansion, starting with their move to build a water and sewer system decades ago. The Cardinal Glass Company located in a nearby 900-acre industrial park, bringing new employment opportunities to the area, and an amphitheater built in 2003 added tourism to the list of reasons to visit Napavine.

Many of the challenges Napavine faces are directly related to these opportunities. The City of Chehalis disputed Napavine's annexation of the land west of I-5, as Chehalis had already made

plans for the same land. Some residents of the annexed area resent the move and have concerns about the water quality. Indeed, Napavine faces water shortages and contention over one of its six wells. Other foreseeable infrastructure shortages include classroom space. Currently, there are fewer than 1,000 students in the Napavine School District. While the elementary school was remodeled in 2001, the high school dates to 1980. The possibility of increased traffic and rising home prices concern other citizens. Then again, some people predict that Napavine will stay small.

According to locals—and the sign outside—Frosty's Saloon & Grill has occupied its current location and held onto its name since 1901. It's a local institution.

In 2013, Napavine celebrated 100 years since its incorporation. As part of its celebration, the town recognized the ways the town has changed, but also "the one factor that has remained constant": Napavine is still a small town. In 2005, *The Daily Chronicle* of Lewis County interviewed Napavine residents about the changes they had seen or saw coming. Some noted that over the long term, Napavine might become a part of the larger towns of Centralia and Chehalis. Others hadn't noticed any change at all. "This town?" one responded. "Not much."

While some buildings in Napavine have faithfully maintained a single business from the outset, others have gone through several iterations, like this former post office, city hall, and now chic clothing boutique.

Population: 621
Founding: 1906

INSETS L to R: Heritage Communities were formed during Washington's territorial period, from 1853 to 1889. • Though few in numbers, Vader's citizens devote considerable resources to preserving their town and interpreting it for visitors. • This home sits just off the main intersection in town. • One Vader home flies the American flag as well as the pine tree flag popularized during the American Revolution.

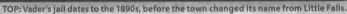

TOP: Vader's jail dates to the 1890s, before the town changed its name from Little Falls.

Vader

Between Rumor and Memory

In the 1870s, Paul Kraft became postmaster in southern Lewis County. As was the fashion, the town took the same name as the county. Three decades later, when enough of a town existed to incorporate, citizens chose to rename it Little Falls, after the falls on Olequa Creek. The Northern Pacific Railway wasn't happy about the change, as the railroad already had a Little Falls stop in Minnesota, so they started referring to the Little Falls in Washington as Sopenah. Locals refused to play along but eventually agreed to change the name, settling on Vader, after one of the town elders, Martin Vader. In 1913, the state recognized the name change.

Some say that Martin Vader objected to having his name used and moved away in protest, while others say he moved simply because he needed care in his advanced age. The assistant to the president of the railroad noted, "The humor of the matter is that we supposed the old gentleman would be highly flattered in having the town named after him but instead of that he took it as a personal indignity and immediately moved to Florida." In any case,

the rumors flourished, as do other rumors. One local resident says that around the time of the name change, 4,000 people lived in Vader, though census records show the population was about the same as it is today. Still, for a time, Vader boasted of being the largest city between Tacoma and Portland.

Vader boomed between 1906 and 1912. The Little Falls Fire Clay Company employed 100 workers, and Stillwater Logging employed 180 more. The town's fortune was short-lived, though. Weyerhaeuser bought Stillwater in 1914 and shut it down, and shortly thereafter, a fire destroyed the Fire Clay Company and the Stillwater Mill. The Depression was just a few short years away. Perhaps the most shocking rumor in Vader's history is that, facing a jobless future, the people of Vader insured their homes only to intentionally burn them down. The crimes remain unproved, but this mystery is a part of the story that Vader seems to want to tell about itself.

Lewis County resident Margaret Hodges Hopp recorded her family's Vader story in a local history published in 1985. L. S. Hodges and his family moved to Vader after buying a farm sight unseen and traveling from Iowa with all of their belongings strapped to their car. Hopp recounted, "When they reached the farm in Vader, they found a house not fit for human occupancy, hardly fit for animals, and no running water." The Depression had just begun. The Hodges found life in Vader just the same as the one they'd left in Iowa: "no work." The family sold the farm and moved to Napavine. "Work was the reason for moving," Hodges wrote. "It always was."

Preserved in Pieces

Though much of Vader's history succumbed to fire and disrepair, three buildings represent its boom era and remain in good condition. The Ben Olsen House, on the National Register of Historic Places since 1976, dates from 1903, making it the oldest house in Vader. Ben Olson came to Vader from Sweden and founded the Stillwater Logging Company.

Grace Evangelical Church, also on the historic register, is an example of the Victorian Gothic architectural style. The church began as a mission outpost in 1891; as the population grew, so did the congregation. Over the decades, the church has remained a community resource throughout Vader's good and hard times. People gathered here to assemble care packages for soldiers during wartime, and during the Depression, the church became a resource for staples like food and clothing.

Finally, Vader has preserved its humble city jail. The small, one-story building sits today next to the picnic shelter beside Werden Park, which holds a small collection of signs telling Vader's story. At the bottom of the steps to the jail, the town has placed a miniature railroad crossing, with a signal light and a small section of track. A basketball court behind the jail completes the park. Instead of inmates, the jail is home these days to the tiny Vader museum. It's volunteer-run, of course.

God's Assembled Realists

Vader once had an opera house, along with two hotels, a hospital, and a city band. Of course, it had a school. But one year after Vader celebrated its centennial, the school district closed for good.

An article in *The Daily News* describing the closure reads like an obituary: "Though planned for several months, the small Lewis County school district formally ceases to exist the first minute of September." Three levies failed to raise the funds necessary to keep the town's school district open, so Castle Rock's school district, 10 miles away, absorbed Vader's student population. The school closure fit a century-long pattern of job loss in Vader. The town had to pay the school superintendent's salary through the end of the year, but teachers and staff lost their salaries immediately.

> Vader's City Jail, more than 110 years old, is a focus of restoration and preservation efforts. A small park next to the jail offers a lesson in local history.

Like the school, most of Vader's Victorian buildings are gone. Today, manufactured homes, trailers, and small houses stand in tall grass at the end of short gravel tracks. One home in Vader flies three flags: the American flag, a black POW-MIA flag bearing the slogan "Don't Tread on Me," and a white flag featuring a simplistic drawing of a tree. The last one is called the Appeal to Heaven flag, first used by the Continental Army during the American Revolution.

A few blocks away, a community center, thrift store, and post office make up the bulk of Vader's downtown. A building that looks like a warehouse is home to Vader's Assembly of God congregation. "Trust God, but lock your car door," reads the sign above the entrance. Vader's history has given its residents plenty of reasons to be realistic.

From a low in the 1970s, Vader's population has rebounded to a level near that at its founding. Still, some refer to Vader as a "semi-ghost" town.

Population: 759
Founding: 1852

INSETS L to R: The outskirts of Mossyrock burst with color, courtesy of DeGoede Bulb Farms and Gardens. • Mayfield Lake is stocked for sportfishing. The former town of Ghosn lies 200 feet below the surface. • The G Theatre, an architectural marriage of art deco and the Old West, opened for business in 1943. • Tacoma Power operates the Mossyrock Dam, Washington's tallest hydroelectric project.

TOP: The road to Mossyrock offers a surreal glimpse of Mt. St. Helen's shorn peak.

Mossyrock

The Mother of All Counties

Modern-day Lewis County lies between Mounts Rainier and Saint Helens. The Cowlitz River runs through the middle on its way to join the Columbia. Lewis County backs up to the Yakama Indian Reservation to the east and Grays Harbor County to the west. There was a time when the county was much bigger.

At the end of the War of 1812, the US and the UK agreed to share the land west of the Continental Divide between the 42nd and 49th parallels. The two governments controlled the territory together for nearly three decades. In 1844, Democratic presidential candidate James Polk campaigned on the slogan "54-40 or Fight!"—a reference the geographical point of 54 degrees and 40 minutes latitude. Polk won the presidency, and Americans soon outnumbered the British in the area six to one.

Not yet formally a territory, Oregon's nascent legislative body was already dividing the land into four districts. A redrawing of the lines in 1845 led to the creation of Lewis County, which spanned all of the land north of the Columbia River to

54 degrees and 40 minutes north and east to the Cowlitz River. Now the sixth largest county in the state, Lewis County comprised fully half of Washington and British Columbia in its earliest iteration. By 1848, negotiations led to the creation of the Oregon Territory, setting the line between America and Canada at 49 degrees north.

Prior to white settlement, the Taitnapam and Lower Cowlitz peoples inhabited Lewis County. By some accounts, the Taitnapam were Upper Cowlitz who merged with the Western Klickitat. The Taitnapam lived on the Cowlitz River at what is now Mossyrock; they were known as prolific hunters and traded horses with other tribes. Taitnapam women were experts in basket making.

The Lower Cowlitz people called the prairie *Coulph.* In 1852, Henry Busie settled the first claim on the prairie, and a settler named Mitchell took a claim at the east end. Local legend holds that when the Klickitat people attempted to drive the white settlers out, Busie killed himself in fear. Shortly thereafter, a settler named Halland named the area Mossy Rock, after a prominent outcropping at the east end of the prairie. An early post office received the mail once every three weeks from Napavine. Mail carriers rode horseback from Napavine to Mayfield and took a ferry across the Cowlitz River at Mayfield to Mossyrock.

Timber and sawmills made up Mossyrock's early economy, as did dairy and cattle; rail access never came to fruition, however. After the Great Depression, plans to dam the Cowlitz River would change communities in the prairie forever.

The Family Secret

Tucked between two of Washington's biggest lakes, Mossyrock is known for its Christmas tree and blueberry farms. You might think it's the kind of place where a kid can't get into much trouble. Gladys Taylor found some, but she was miles away from home at the time.

In May 1917, 23-year-old Taylor hid in the storeroom of the merchant schooner *A. B. Johnson*, setting out from Willapa Bay. Days later, the crew found her hiding, but it was too late to turn back. The ship was bound for Australia, but in mid-June a German ship, the *Seadler*, and its captain, Count Felix "Sea Devil" Von Luckner, captured the *A. B. Johnson*, taking the crew hostage. The captain of the *A. B. Johnson* introduced Taylor as his wife.

With hostages on board, the *Seadler* raided four more ships and then wrecked on a coral reef, stranding 120 men and one woman, Taylor, on the coral atoll of Mopelia. For nearly two months, Taylor and the men made camp. "I was treated like a queen," Taylor recounted. When a rescue ship came, she was disappointed. "I almost wept when Mopelia, the island of my adventure, faded on the horizon."

After the Dams

Everyone knew what a dam would mean: The towns of Riffe, Kosmos, Neskia, and Mayfield would all be under water. As one-time Riffe resident Buddy Rose, author of *Stories from Rife, Washington*, told the community website LewisTalk, "Standing next to the wooden stakes and ribbons and looking down at my house and the rest of the town far below, it did not seem possible that water could fill the valley to the point where we were standing."

Before the dams, Tacoma City Light had to buy power from the Bonneville Power Administration— during WWII, that cost $1 million per year. Tacoma City Light needed to expand its infrastructure. It petitioned for two dams on the Cowlitz River, and in 1951, the Federal Power Commission granted Tacoma a license to begin construction.

The Mossyrock Dam on the Cowlitz River is the largest dam in Washington. Its primary purpose is the production of hydroelectric power. Secondarily, it promotes flood control.

Historian David Wilma notes that "hydroelectric dams were viewed in the Northwest almost as a patriotic act" because of the jobs they created. But in the case of *The City of Tacoma vs. the Taxpayers of Tacoma*, opponents of the dam projects argued to the Supreme Court of Washington that Tacoma was overstepping its bounds. Local fish and wildlife advocates filed an additional complaint, arguing that "irreparable injury will result to the State of Washington in that part or all of the fish runs in the Cowlitz River will be destroyed." Despite the protests, work began on the Mayfield Dam in July 1955. Continued legal challenges delayed its construction, which eventually hinged on agreeing to include a system to transport fish up and over the dam.

The Mayfield Dam is 850 feet long and 185 feet high. Thirteen years after its construction, the turbines began spinning upstream at Mossyrock Dam, the tallest in Washington, at 606 feet from the bedrock to the top. Riffe and Mayfield Lakes, formed by the two dams, are popular recreation sites.

Recently, the US Geological Survey found that Mossyrock Dam may not hold up in the event of a large earthquake, which the Northwest has anticipated for decades. To mitigate the potential impact and provide an opportunity to repair the dam, Tacoma Power lowered the reservoir level by 30 feet. This lowering takes place annually in winter already in order to manage flood capacity, but now the levels will stay reduced all year long. This will limit access to the lake in summer, and the concrete foundations and bridges of long-submerged Kosmos may emerge into view.

Lake Mayfield, a park and resort area just outside Mossyrock, is a reservoir created by the Mayfield Dam on the Cowlitz River, which is part of the Columbia River watershed and dam system.

Population: 1,982
Founding: 1852

INSETS L to R: Salmon navigate three dams on the Cowlitz River, which runs through Castle Rock. • Castle Rock is home to at least 13 churches and one museum-like exhibit proffering a biblical take on Mt. St. Helens' 1980 eruption. • Castle Rock's thriving business district includes doctor's offices, an art and framing store, and a busy bookstore and coffee shop. • The Chester, an early steamboat on the Cowlitz, played an outsized role for its size, connecting people and goods with larger boats in Kelso and Portland.

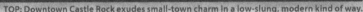

TOP: Downtown Castle Rock exudes small-town charm in a low-slung, modern kind of way.

Castle Rock

Seekers and Settlers

Margaret Huntington arrived in Massachusetts from England in 1633. She traveled with her five children; her husband had died of smallpox. Two hundred years later, one of her descendants, Harry Darby Huntington, moved from Indiana to the newly acquired Oregon Territory. The Oregon Treaty, signed in 1846, resolved the joint ownership of the Oregon Territory between the British and American governments in favor of the Americans, establishing the 49th parallel as the dividing line. The next fall, H. D. Huntington arrived in Oregon. Within a few years, he'd settled in the Cowlitz Valley near the mouth of the river. He hosted a meeting in which he and other Oregon settlers wrote a petition asking Congress to establish a new territory called Columbia. Congress granted their request but called the new territory Washington.

In 1852, more Huntingtons came. William and his wife, Eliza, claimed land adjacent to that of William's cousin H. D. A large, rocky outcrop rose above the claim, which lay between Cowlitz Landing and Monticello. The name for the post office came easily. Huntington dubbed the place Castle

Rock. He became the first postmaster and minister and was a member of the first territorial legislature.

Isaac Stevens's pressure campaign to move Indigenous people from their homelands was in the works, but the Huntingtons weren't the first point of contact for the local people, the Cowlitz. By the time of the Huntingtons' arrival, Europeans had been traveling to the county for more than 50 years, and several thousand people lived along the Cowlitz River in dozens of villages. The Lower Cowlitz people first encountered Euro-American settlers with the Pacific Fur Company in 1811. The North West Company and the Hudson's Bay Company also traded with the Cowlitz. In 1829, a ship captained by American John Domines brought a fever; by contemporaneous estimates, three-fourths of the Cowlitz in the area died in the epidemic, which lasted for several years. The Hudson's Bay Company revised its earlier estimate, claiming that seven-eighths had died. An estimated 500 Cowlitz people remained.

As Cowlitz County grew, farming and logging became the primary industries. Castle Rock had both a shipping port and a shingle mill. By

1886, the *Cowlitz County Advocate* had published its first issue. The timber industry, led by Weyerhaeuser, was a leading employer until its decline. Castle Rock is home to the oldest house in the county, as well as the first clay brick building, constructed in 1889 using clay from the Cowlitz River.

The Greatest Disaster

On May 18, 1980, Mount Saint Helens erupted, 70 miles from Castle Rock in Gifford Pinchot National Forest. A pyroclastic flow 200 feet thick slammed into Cowlitz County, burying bridges, roads, and buildings. The Cowlitz riverbed rose 12 feet, and thick sediment in the Columbia River halted shipping in Portland. Five billion board-feet of timber—enough to build 300,000 homes—burned. Two hundred homes were destroyed. Spirit Lake disappeared under a drastic landslide. Though scientists predicted the explosion, a lack of disaster coordination and imprecise predictions prevented widespread evacuations despite months of warning signs. Fifty-seven people were killed, along with some 7,000 deer, elk, and bears, as well as innumerable smaller animals. It was the most destructive volcanic event in US history.

Over time, however, the landscape recovered, and Mount St. Helens laid claim to being the most active volcano in North America, drawing as many as 750,000 visitors annually. The biggest disaster in Cowlitz County history has become a profitable tourist draw, accounting for $100 million in tourism revenue per year.

150 Years and Counting

In 2002, Castle Rock celebrated its 150th anniversary. As part of the festivities, townspeople held a ribbon-cutting ceremony to open a new walking path to the top of the granite outcrop that was part of Eliza and William Huntington's original claim—the castle rock itself.

Many people encounter the town of Castle Rock on their way to Mount Saint Helens. Several interpretive centers along the Spirit Lake Memorial Highway offer information about the volcano, including one just outside of Castle Rock. Travelers following signs from the highway into the town of Castle Rock may be confused to find themselves at the Mount St. Helens Creation Center, the project of an anti-evolutionist former science teacher.

Downtown Castle Rock has a modern feel with a nod to its historical roots. Low-slung buildings with simple facades recall earlier times, though the buildings now host businesses from bookstores to breweries.

Now at the monument, ecologists work to protect a study zone from recreational damage by snowmobiles, campfires, and dogs. At an advisory meeting on managing the mountain into the future, Castle Rock residents weighed in. *The New York Times* reported that resident Patrice Dick said she was "disgusted" by the continued scientific inquiry into the aftermath. One citizen recommended that the US Forest Service "throw out the study zone and let people recreate." On the other side of the debate, scientist Peter Frenzen argued that researchers must study the entire ecosystem "from ant to elk" to learn how the landscape recovers.

Castle Rock today is a sleepy town. The *Cowlitz County Advocate* has closed along with several other Washington State papers, casualties of the digital age. A quaint downtown offers a variety of restaurants and shops, including Vault Books and Brew, a busy bookstore and coffee shop. Runners and dog walkers share a paved path alongside the Cowlitz River. The town has claimed the title of "Gateway to Mount Saint Helens" since the completion of the road, long before the volcano's 1980 eruption, though with a church on seemingly every block and a so-called creation museum, the town feels more like an ideological cul-de-sac than a trailhead to exploration.

The Cowlitz Tribe has fought for federal recognition since 1912 and finally received it in 2000. They continue to fight for the restoration of their traditional lands. Their tribal offices are 10 miles from Castle Rock in Longview, Washington.

A mural in Castle Rock depicts the *Chester,* a boat used to transport people and goods between Kelso and Toledo at the turn of the 19th century.

CHESTER
The Chester Was. built in 1897. It's 101 foot long hull was light and flexible. Being a shallow draft boat, she barely drew a foot of water when fully loaded. Chester carried passengers and supplies from Kelso, to Castle Rock and Toledo until 1918. A new highway cut into her trade and 21 years on the river had taken it's tole. She was Then stripped and abandoned in 1919.

Population: 1,566
Founding: 1908

INSETS L to R: The Chelatchie Prairie Railroad takes visitors on a free trip through history on the old Vancouver, Klickitat, Yakima line • Lucia Falls is a short walk from the nearby parking lot. Continue on the Bells Mountain Trail for a 4-mile loop to Moulton Falls. • Signage advertising community events functions as a bulletin board that's impossible to miss for citizens and visitors alike • What's a puppicino, you ask? It's a dog bone with peanut butter and whipped cream, obviously.

TOP: Yacolt's welcome sign points to the dual influence of the railroad and logging in the town's development.

Yacolt

What's in a Name?

In Clark County, Yacolt is the only real town, meaning that it had fewer than 1,500 residents at the time of its founding and it doesn't operate under a municipal code. There are 68 such towns in Washington, and under legislation from 1994, no new towns may be created—only cities. Yacolt is in the northeast corner of the county, nearly as far away as possible from the city of Vancouver, Washington, whose significance predates Washington's territorial status.

Lewis and Clark passed through Clark County in 1806, noting an Indigenous population of several thousand people. Within 50 years of contact with European and American settlers, disease reduced the number of Chinookan people to fewer than 100. The British established a post of the Hudson's Bay Trading Company on the Columbia River and named it Vancouver after the British naval captain. When the British and American governments decided on the 49th parallel as the dividing line between territories, the Hudson's Bay Company relocated north to Vancouver Island. Americans began to outnumber the British, and

the county developed as an agriculture and timber producer. The Hudson's Bay Company was long gone by the time the Eaton family became the first non-Native settlers in Yacolt.

Whereas the Chinook occupied the coastal land, the inland groups pre-contact were Klickitat and Cowlitz. Yacolt served as a gathering place for trade between tribes. In the Klickitat language, the word *yalicob* means "haunted place." Though accounts differ, legend has it that a group of children vanished while foraging for berries at the site of what is today Yacolt, perhaps taken by evil spirits. Other explanations hold that Yacolt resides atop a burial ground. In any case, the name predates white settlement.

Charlotte and Joseph Eaton settled in Yacolt after traveling from Wisconsin and losing a previous homestead to flood in Lewis County. They established a post office, but development moved slowly. Thirteen years later, another family arrived. The Garners opened a post office, too, resulting in the unusual situation of a town with two post offices and two names. By 1902, only 50 residents called Yacolt home. That same year, fire came for the town.

Scorching more than 350 square miles across three counties, the Yacolt Burn was the biggest in Washington State history until it was surpassed in 2014 by the Carlton Complex Fire in Okanogan, to the northeast. Two years before the fire, Frederick Weyerhaeuser purchased nearly 1 million acres of timber from the Northern Pacific Railroad with the intention to sell, but not harvest, the timber. The fire ravaged Weyerhaeuser's recently acquired land, but the timber beneath the burn was still valuable, so the company changed tack and got into the business of logging. Weyerhaeuser created hundreds of jobs in the aftermath of the fire and Yacolt bloomed like, well, wildfire. By 1908, the population had increased tenfold. The salvage lasted just a few more years, and Yacolt began to decline, losing half its population in 20 years. Weyerhaeuser remained a regional economic powerhouse well into the 20th century. Yacolt, arguably built by the logging company, seems certain to outlast it.

The Big Burn

The smoke was so thick, the chickens went to roost thinking it was night. Half an inch of ash fell in downtown Portland. People thought Mount Saint Helens or Mount Rainier had erupted. The 1902 Yacolt Burn traveled 30 miles in about as many hours, scorching almost 240,000 acres of timber. Reasons for the fire are obscure, but signs point to a combination of dry, windy conditions and a lack of preparedness. The fire caused an estimated 35–65 fatalities and upwards of $10 million in property damage. Firefighting and fire-prevention efforts followed, but the 90,000-acre Yacolt Burn State Forest still bears the blackened marks of the fire. Though it shares a name with the town, the fire narrowly missed burning Yacolt: A sudden wind shifted the fire north, where it drowned in the Lewis River.

Comeback Kids

Yacolt has grown steadily since the 1970s, aided by its proximity to Portland and Vancouver. Visitors come to ride the Chelatchie Prairie Railroad, a 14-mile tour of the valley on a steam-powered train salvaged from the Northern Pacific Railroad. A one-hour walk through the woods connects 24-acre Lucia Falls Park to nearly-400-acre Moulton Falls Regional Park, which offers volcanic rock formations, waterfalls, and a three-story arch bridge.

While Yacolt's past looms large, the town's concerns are modern. They're holding a contest for sidewalk art and another for a new design of the town seal. The Bigfoot Fun Run brought out more than 100 runners in 2019—not a bad turnout for a town of fewer than 2,000 residents. Community efforts are political as well. In 2018, Washington State voters passed Initiative 1639, expanding background checks on semiautomatic weapons and requiring safe storage methods for firearms.

Moulton Falls and Lucia Falls are two of the numerous park spaces preserved along Yacolt Creek, which is part of the Lewis River watershed.

In response, the Yacolt town council passed a resolution declaring the town a "sanctuary" from the initiative's restrictions. Nevertheless, I-1639 applies to the residents of Yacolt, who contract police services from the Clark County Sheriff's Office.

As elsewhere in Washington State, wine is making an economic impact in Clark County. Near Yacolt, Moulton Falls Winery and Cider House and Pomeroy Cellars combine wine tastings with book clubs, musical performances, and dinners on-site. Local vintners are seeking status as an American Viticultural Area (AVA) for the Southwest Washington area, which would add a 15th AVA to the billion-dollar industry's production and cement Clark County as a wine-tourism destination.

Today, Yacolt's verdant forests and quiet, riverside trails invite a peaceful, not at all haunted, feeling. However, townspeople say they hear things. Some hear children laughing or running up the stairs of their homes. Residents have reported hauntings since 1890, creating a through line of superstition from pre-contact to the present day.

Arrowhead Coffee in downtown Yacolt serves treats for pups and humans alike. Behind the coffeeshop, a cell phone tower cleverly disguises itself as a tree.

Population: 956
Founding: 1935

INSETS L to R: Bonneville's downtown doubles down on Northwestern bigfoot mythology. • The Columbia River Gorge, beloved by winemakers and windsurfers alike. • This petroglyph is thought to come from the Cascades Indians. Its meaning is unknown. • Fort Cascades rose at a natural portage point on the Columbia. Settlers took to the land to navigate around the rapids, used by the Cascades Indians as a fishing and trading site.

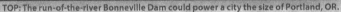

TOP: The run-of-the-river Bonneville Dam could power a city the size of Portland, OR.

North Bonneville

North Bonneville, *Née* Cascades

Thomas McNatt of Tennessee was 21 years old when he married 14-year-old Emily Jane Mark. That same year, they set out with oxen and tents, according to Emily's own words, "bound for the far-west, though we had not yet decided whether our destination should be California or Oregon." After crossing the Missouri River, the young couple joined up with a large group of settlers moving west. Conditions were difficult. Tensions with the leadership of the group led the McNatts to split off, along with the Nales and Sailor families. Cholera and exposure had left fresh graves along their path, and when Mrs. Sailor succumbed, it fell to Emily to care for her four children.

Such was the life of young pioneering emigrants moving west. In 1855, the McNatts moved from Clatsop Plains, where they'd worked a claim for a year, to Cascades. The US Army had recently selected the nascent town for the site of Fort Cascades, intended to protect travelers who had to portage around the rapids. The Army would abandon the site at the start of the Civil War, but by then Emily and Thomas McNatt had established a hotel and tavern as well as a barn and stable. Soon, the town had a blacksmith's shop and a store. A fish wheel caught salmon as they swam upstream. Steamships moved cargo up the river. By 1880, the town boasted 134 residents, nearly all of whom worked for the railroad or the wharf.

Cascades became the seat of Skamania County in 1861. That same year, Thomas McNatt died at the age of 32. Twenty years later, Emily, whom Thomas called Nellie, married W. M. Wallis and moved to Port Ludlow. Genealogical records note that Emily Jane Wallis died in 1911, at the age of 80, but by her own account, she was born in 1836, which means that in 1911 she would have been 75.

In 1893, the town of Stevenson claimed the county seat when residents moved the county's records there from Cascades. One year later, the Columbia River flooded, drowning Cascades, which is now an archaeological site with artifacts and a replica of an ancient petroglyph. Visitors may walk its peaceful perimeter, imagining the lives of Emily and Thomas McNatt and other residents.

Just upstream from the original town site, Bonneville Dam churns the Columbia into electric power. In 1931, the US Army Corps of Engineers recommended the construction of 10 dams on the Columbia River that would provide power and irrigation and aid in navigating the river. Construction began in 1933, turning the Cascades Rapids into a lake. To that point, the rapids had provided the Indigenous population with an easy catch point for salmon and a place for trade while giving the settlers a tremendous headache in terms of navigation and exposure to attack. The dam included a fish ladder, though salmon runs declined as small fish got caught in the turbines and larger fish couldn't find the ladder. By 1999, Columbia River salmon were on the endangered species list.

After the flood in 1894, the community formerly known as Cascades hung on. The Bonneville Dam gave the community a second chance. Hundreds of construction workers arrived, and a town formed to serve their needs. That town, North Bonneville, incorporated in 1935.

Whereas Evidence Continues to Accumulate

In 1969, Skamania County moved to protect the Sasquatch. "Both legends and recent sightings and spoor" supported the evidence for a "nocturnal primate mammal variously described as an apelike creature or subspecies of *Homo sapiens*." Ordinance 1969-1 made slaying Bigfoot a felony punishable by five years in prison. Fifteen years later, Ordinance 1984-2 amended the earlier ruling from felony to gross misdemeanor, punishable by a fine of $1,000, one year in county jail, or both. The ordinance further declared Skamania County a sanctuary for any Sasquatch, Yeti, Bigfoot, or Giant Hairy Ape. The defendant couldn't plead insanity, and if the victim were determined to be "humanoid" rather than "anthropoid," the crime would be elevated to homicide. Bigfoot enthusiasts continue to seek and provide evidence for the existence of the creatures. Their only question is whether the county's Bigfoot-protection ordinance goes far enough.

Big Feet, Big Shoes to Fill

When the Bonneville Dam required a second powerhouse in 1978, the town of North Bonneville moved its site a little to the west. To the tune of $35 million, planning for the new North Bonneville included comprehensive infrastructure that took into consideration the likelihood of future flooding. Both the highway and the railroad relocated. Temporary housing went up for businesses and families.

Native fishing rights allow tribal members to fish from traditional wooden platforms using poles or nets. The landmark case *US vs. Washington* determined that Indigenous populations may take half of all harvestable fish.

The dam consists of three structures spanning nearly 1,500 feet and nearly 200 feet above bedrock. Improvements in the 1990s reduced the time to fill the lock by half, to just nine minutes. Around the same time, the dam, along with the Bonneville Dam Historic District and North Bonneville Archaeological District, took its place on the National Register of Historic Places. The dam supplies electricity to nearly 500,000 homes and costs nearly $10 million per year to maintain. The dam was built with federal loan money, which at the time of this writing has not been fully repaid; nor have Indigenous people received the homes they were promised at the time of the dam's construction. The current administration has floated the idea of selling or privatizing parts of the dam system in the Northwest, an effort that local legislators working at the state and national levels have opposed.

When environmental policies ended logging, the economy of Skamania County neared the point of no return. Today, tourism employs more people in Skamania County than any other sector. North Bonneville has gotten into the game by embracing the Sasquatch. Twelve miles of trails wind through the town, offering four loops with views of mountains, creeks full of salmon, forests, and the pioneer cemetery. Whichever path they choose, visitors will meet many Bigfeet along the way. Don't worry—they're friendly! Stop at the gas station in town for a trail map before you explore North Bonneville's Discovery Trail system.

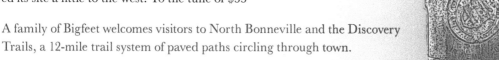

A family of Bigfeet welcomes visitors to North Bonneville and the Discovery Trails, a 12-mile trail system of paved paths circling through town.

Population: 1,465
Founding: 1908

INSETS L to R: All of Stevenson resides between mountain face and river's edge. • The port of Skamania recently added nearly 1,000 feet of paved trail and amenities to its waterfront park. • North Bank Books offers "literary arts in our neck of the woods." • The Bridge of the Gods marks the spot where the Pacific Crest Trail crosses the Columbia River.

TOP: Mount Hood looks like the Pacific Northwest's own Matterhorn from just outside Stevenson.

Stevenson

Swift Water

The Chilluckittequw were people of the river, subsisting on salmon, game, and wapato bulbs. They spoke a dialect of Upper Chinookan, a subset of Chinook Jargon, a Creole language that allowed them to communicate with other tribes along the Columbia River. After the Chilluckittequw had harvested for their own needs, they would rent their fishing sites to other tribes. At the end of the 18th century, nearly 3,000 Chilluckittequw lived between Beacon Rock and the Columbia in what is today Skamania County. A century later, just a few dozen remained.

Lewis and Clark mapped the Columbia in 1805, noting the Cascade rapids. The rapids, created from a landslide four centuries earlier, had benefited Indigenous life by creating a place to easily gather salmon, but they presented an obstacle to others. Unable to navigate the rapids, travelers, fur traders, and shippers had to portage several miles to get around the rapids.

The Chilluckittequw charged tolls for settlers along the Oregon Trail to pass through their land until a road was built in 1844. By 1861, there were three non-Native settlements along the Cascade Rapids, where most settlers found they could go no farther. In 1854, the territorial legislature formed Skamania County from adjacent Clark County, but 11 years later they unmade it, preferring that the tax revenue go to the original county. Congress stepped in a few years later and restored Skamania County, named for the "swift water" of the Columbia.

In 1882, the Shepard family took a donation land claim on the site that became Stevenson. A year later, George Stevenson bought part of that land and platted the town. It seems that Stevenson became the county seat by theft. In 1893, "a suspect crew" moved the county records from the existing county seat of Lower Cascade. A year later, a historic flood wiped out Cascade. Stevenson incorporated 15 years later, the same year that the Spokane, Portland and Seattle Railway arrived.

The town organized itself between mountain and river. Logging camps moved through the forest, sending their harvest downhill to the riverside mills and the railroad. Logging dominated the local economy for the next several decades. Toward the end of the 20th century, the timber industry had eliminated all unprotected old-growth forest. What once seemed an unlimited resource clearly had limits. Public concern for species and habitat loss led to environmental protection legislation, exerting more downward pressure on the industry. By the year 2000, logging in Skamania County was largely over. Tourism rose up to fill the void.

Heaven, This Way and That

North-going travelers cross the bridge on foot. They carry their packs and a sense of exhausted accomplishment. This is the Pacific Crest Trail (PCT), running along the West Coast from Mexico to Canada. Before the PCT hosted some 700–800 hikers a year (60% of whom complete the trek), before Cheryl Strayed made the Bridge of the Gods even more famous by ending her own PCT journey there, and even before the 1,858-foot steel truss bridge existed, a natural dam bridged the river, allowing Indigenous people to safely cross the Columbia Gorge. A landslide between the 12th and 13th centuries created the natural dam, which collapsed in the 17th century, most likely as a result of the last recorded Cascadia Subduction Zone (CSZ) earthquakes. Another cataclysmic CSZ event is decades overdue, and residents of the greater CSZ area, which runs the length of the Juan de Fuca tectonic plate from California to Canada, live on the edge, knowing that any day a massive megathrust earthquake could substantially rewrite the West Coast landscape.

Indigenous legend holds that Manito, the Great Spirit, built the natural Bridge of the Gods out of sympathy for people who needed to cross the river. To watch over the bridge, Manito sent Loo-Wit, a wise old woman. Many people today know Loo-Wit by the name Mount Saint Helens. Today, a $2 toll fee allows motorists to cross the Bridge of the Gods, and foot travelers cross freely. Whether you're in a car or on foot, don't forget to look down.

Our Neck of the Woods

Imagine Disneyland without the mouse ears. Instead of people dressed in animal costumes, they're wearing wetsuits. Instead of roller coasters, they're on kiteboards, and there's no waiting in line for the massive Columbia River Gorge. Mount Hood knifes into the sky like Washington's own Matterhorn. This is Skamania County. At nearly 1,700 square miles, 80% of the county is taken up by Gifford Pinchot National Forest. It's the windsurfing capital of the world, with lakes and rivers for fishing and dozens of gorgeous hikes—no pun intended.

The cantilevered Bridge of the Gods is 35 feet wide and 1,858 feet long, connecting Oregon and Washington from a height of 108 feet above the Columbia River.

This type of landscape attracts a certain kind of person, someone who's likely to place more importance on utility than aesthetics. Stephanie Lillegard has lived in Stevenson since 1995. Her husband's family has lived in the area since 1904. "We live in Great-Granddad's house," she says. Stephanie runs North Bank Books, a well-stocked bookstore offering "literary arts in our neck of the woods." When asked about the people of Stevenson, Stephanie shares that the town is full of outdoors enthusiasts from all over. The result is a community whose shared identity matters more than any of its differences. As her son puts it, "Even the Republicans are nice here."

The town of Stevenson slopes down from the Gorge walls to the water's edge. Stephanie lives about a mile's walk out of town, uphill. "There are a lot of people living in the hills," she says, explaining that veterans and others seeking to live off-grid can inhabit Bureau of Land Management land undisturbed. How do people in town feel about that? Stephanie has a quick answer: "Nobody cares."

Stevenson sits 100 feet up from the river and gets 80 inches of rain each year. Temperatures in the summer hover around 80°F. Recreational sites draw tourists, and Skamania Lodge is the county's largest employer. With restaurants, breweries, resorts, and parks, along with unbeatable views of nature in a peaceful small town tucked between mountain and river, Stevenson invites visitors to eat, drink, learn, and play. Some may even be tempted to stay.

Stevenson Landing is a cruise ship pier adjacent to downtown Stevenson. Six nearby parks offer great places to learn to kiteboard or watch the action.

Population: 589
Founding: 1910

INSETS L to R: Few businesses line Bucoda's main drag, but bright sidewalk art and a community garden brighten up the place. • Chalk art brightens the sidewalk in front of Bucoda's community garden. • This monument marks the Seatco prison lot, now seeded with wild poppies. • The Skookumchuck River flows behind a park at the site of the former Seatco Prison.

TOP: Bucoda tucked itself behind the railroad tracks established by Great Northern in 1872.

Bucoda

A Town by Any Other Name

The first settler recorded in the area that became Bucoda was Aaron Webster, in 1854. He filed a homestead claim and built a sawmill, but he didn't stay long. In the 1860s, Oliver Shead bought Webster's claim, mill and all, and named the nascent settlement Seatco. The word Seatco is an anglicized version of the Coastal Salish word *tsi-at-co,* said to mean "devil" or "ghost place."

It's unclear why Shead thought to give the town such an ominous name, but Seatco lived up to it, becoming the site of Washington's first territorial prison, a privately run institution that would be known for its brutality. By the 1880s, investigations into the prison's living conditions led to its closure. Investors and industrialists J. M. Buckley, Sam Coulter, and J. B. David sought to rebrand Seatco, creating a new name from each of theirs—Bucoda.

The economy of the rebooted town focused on extracting natural resources. The area's forests and coal mines provided employment through the middle of the 20th century. Northern Pacific erected a railroad station in Bucoda in 1872. Thirty

years later, Martin Foord, Frank Stokes, W. W. Whipple, and F. D. Butzer started the Mutual Lumber Company, a mill that employed 300 area men. By the 1920s, Bucoda was known as "the town with the million-dollar payroll." Thirty more years passed before the mill shut down and the payroll stopped. The local Boy Scout troop put up a sign on the spot where the old mill burned, recognizing the mill's founders and employees and their contribution to the area. The mill's location, adjacent to the site of the prison, is now Bucoda's Volunteer Park.

Today, Bucoda is a sleepy place. School-aged children ride the bus to nearby Tenino, where all Bucoda schools had been consolidated by 1967. The prison and the mill are long gone, and there hasn't been a million-dollar payroll since, but Centralia isn't too far south to commute to, and Olympia isn't too far north. Bucoda's population rises and falls in fits and starts, and a subdivision built in the late 1990s testifies to the continued appeal of small-town life in Thurston County. Bucoda keeps on keeping on. It's a small town with, as they say, a big history—and a long memory.

A Town Tries to Forget

The Seatco territorial prison was open for only 13 years, but within 10 years of its opening, investigations had begun into what prisoners described as "hell on Earth." The legislature didn't want to fund the prison, so it was a private business, opened in 1874. Local investors earned $1 per prisoner, per day, plus whatever profit they could make from their prisoners' labor. At the time, prisons had a connection to religious culture; they were meant to be places where reform happened. At Seatco, however, abuse, not reform, was the watchword.

Neither clergy nor family could visit the prisoners, who worked long days making products for the Seatco Manufacturing Company. They reported punishments such as dental extraction and water-based torture, as well as receiving medical treatment without anesthesia. Reports in the *Puget Sound Herald* led the legislature to shut down the prison. In 1887, George Franc was the last inmate to leave, sent with the rest to the new prison in Walla Walla. In 1888, Seatco's prison doors were closed forever.

A mass grave in nearby Tenino marks the place where prisoners who died in custody are buried. Another site, where the old Mutual Mill stood, is purportedly another mass grave, but it's unmarked.

The town that briefly held Washington's first territorial prison changed its name in an attempt to start over, but history remembers. Today in Bucoda, a memorial stone marks the place where the prison once stood. The stone stands in a small field of gravel, surrounded by a chain-link fence. Standing on one side of the fence, the plaque on the stone is readable, paying respect to the memory of Seatco and honoring local historian Neil Corcoran, who helped preserve stories of prison life and worked to get the site on the National Register of Historic Places. The fence around the monument is 6 feet high and padlocked. Beyond the fence is a grassy park and a short path to the Skookumchuck River, with benches for resting and taking in the peaceful scene. Wild poppies have seeded the gravel around the monument, their orange heads nodding in the breeze.

A monument honors former Bucoda mayor and historian Neil Corcoran and commemorates the site of Seatco's territorial prison. Six-foot-high chain-link fencing surrounding the monument hasn't kept out the wildflowers.

Open for Business

As you stroll around Bucoda, the town signs reveal its past. There's Factory Street and Seatco Street, and a subdivision called Old Mill Estates. The train comes through midday, momentarily keeping anyone from coming into town or leaving. A public garden full of pollinators brightens Main Street next to the Brutalist community center, recently restored thanks to the O'Neill families, according to a plaque on the wall. Someone's chalked a cheerful garden of bees, flowers, and caterpillars on the sidewalk outside the community center, as well as a hopscotch grid. The cash register is ringing in Liberty Market, and the neon signs say that Joe's Place is open for business.

After fire destroyed Bucoda in 1930, one building was still standing—Joe's Place, owned and operated by the Wall family for five generations. The original bar, built in 1898, was lost to fire, but a new one went up just before Prohibition in 1919. The wooden bar is original. The walls are hung with a timeline of the bar's ownership, which doubles as a family tree, as well as a list of locals who've gone to prison and their offenses. The town's website says Bucoda is "defined by its history." Joe's Place is doing its part to keep that history alive.

Each year, the friendly town with the dark history transforms into Boo-coda for Halloween, but for now, chalk art brightens the sidewalk in front of Bucoda's community garden.

SKOOKUMCHUCK RIVER

Population: 1,852
Founding: 1851

INSETS L to R: Tenino's downtown is a thriving center for all kinds of business. • Many of Tenino's sandstone structures are on the National Register of Historic Places. • A monument made from local sandstone adorns the entrance to the library in Tenino. • Many of Tenino's sandstone structures are on the National Register of Historic Places.

TOP: The Tenino Depot Museum holds the history of Tenino's railway connections.

Tenino

T-9-O

People have been debating the origins of Tenino's name for more than a century. One theory posits that it's a Native word for "meeting of the ways." This dovetails nicely with the competing theory that the name stems from the early days of the Northern Pacific Railroad: 1090 was a terminal along the railroad, and men working on the line called it "ten ninety" for short. From there, it's a short leap to Tenino, often further abbreviated as T-9-O.

In 1850, Congress passed the Donation Land Claim Act, allowing white male settlers to claim up to 320 acres of land, 640 acres per white married couple. The aim of the act was to promote settlement in the newly acquired Oregon Territory, which then encompassed most of the Northwest. Settlers had to agree to develop the land and live there for at least four years before earning the claim. The DLCA passed years before many treaty negotiations, and as such contained no language recognizing Native sovereignty or land rights. The very next year, Stephen Hodgens, a '49er originally from Maine, filed a claim in the area known today as Tenino. He became the town's first postmaster in 1860.

By 1872, Northern Pacific ran a line through the area, hauling local timber, coal, and sandstone to market. Before concrete became the preferred material of choice for builders, sandstone quarried in Tenino gave the town a commercial identity based on an abundance of the unique natural resource. Sandstone quarrying in Tenino started in the 1880s with discoveries made by S. W. Fenton and George VanTine and took off a few decades later when the Hercules Sandstone Quarry opened in 1903. The company's initial project was to supply stone for breakwaters in Grays Harbor. Within 10 years, the company employed 400 people, exceeding the total number of residents in the town at the time of the company's founding. In 1906, the town incorporated, electing local creamery owner Henry Keithahn as its first mayor.

Almost as soon as the sandstone economy boomed, it went bust. By the 1930s, concrete had replaced sandstone entirely. The prospect of oil briefly spurred hopes for continued economic importance, but early well failures dashed those hopes. Despite the town's economic downturn, the population of Tenino has risen steadily over the years. With proximity to the towns of Rainier, Yelm, Centralia, and Tumwater and the cities of Olympia and Tacoma, Tenino is a self-described tightly knit bedroom community more than a century in the making, "with confidence in the years to come."

Tenino Flips the Scrip

In an economic double whammy, the sandstone quarries closed just as the country plunged into the Great Depression, and Tenino's community bank closed. As depositors rushed to withdraw their money, the Chamber of Commerce began printing "scrips," offering depositors a guaranteed repayment of their account balance, provided they donated up to 25% of their funds to the Chamber. The scrips, printed on spruce and cedar, amounted to nothing less than wooden money. To prevent counterfeiting, the Chamber printed a watermark of sorts on some of the wood slices. It read, "Confidence makes good; money made of wood." More than $10,000 went into circulation in denominations of 25¢, 50¢, and $1. Reportedly, the Chamber collected about $40 from the effort. The scheme, suggested by then–newspaper publisher Don Major, continues to spark interest today. The Tenino Depot Museum has the original money press and collects letters from people hoping to procure a bit of the currency. Rumor has it that collectors have included such figures as King Farouk of Egypt and Italian dictator Benito Mussolini. Locals print new wooden money on the press once a year during their Oregon Trail Days Celebration.

Swimming Through History

The history of many early towns, big and small, follows a common plotline—railroad, sawmill, fire. After losing everything, cities often turned to alternative building materials, such as Tenino's sandstone. Though the industrial-sandstone boom was relatively short-lived, its legacy is still visible everywhere in Tenino. Sandstone marks the pillared entrance to the city park, gives a Flintstones feeling to City Hall, and memorializes those laid to rest in Forest Grove Cemetery. In the park near the Veter-

ans Memorial Wall, sandstone arches bear carvings that tell the story of Tenino's unique swimming pool.

The outdoor swimming pool in Tenino was originally a sandstone quarry. According to local stories, quarrymen were digging just outside downtown when they suddenly hit a natural spring. Water began filling the quarry so quickly that the men had

In a town shaped by sandstone quarrying, an enduring love letter to books greets library patrons with quotes by authors ranging from Dr. Seuss to Jorge Luis Borges. Copy editors doing a close read may notice an unfortunate typo.

no choice but to leave their equipment in place and scramble out of the pit. In 2017, divers discovered a massive steam engine submerged 75 feet down. The quarry, considered a WWII memorial, has been full of swimming kids every summer since 1950.

Today, with over 1,000 school-aged kids, the town has two elementary schools, one middle school, and one high school. In 2015, Tenino's youngest students led an effort to help students in Tongor Attokrokpo, a village in Ghana. The students started a pen pal program between schools in Tenino and the Ghanaian village, and the project soon grew to involve the whole town of Tenino. Thanks to the efforts of the students, Tenino has contributed funds for rice, cows, and school supplies to the famine-stricken African village. Tenino Elementary Principal David Ford has become friends with Principal David Yayravi in Tongor Attokrokpo, and the kids video-chat regularly with their counterparts across the world. The students are so invested in the relationship that they petitioned the city council to make the village Tenino's sister city, a request the council approved. In the past, Tenino shipped its sandstone far and wide to help build towns and cities in need of sturdy building materials. Today, Tenino's elementary students are helping the town to export an even more valuable resource. To an outsider, the project is evidence that just beneath Tenino's stony exterior is a town full of people who care.

From the Veterans Memorial Wall to the First Presbyterian Church to the Tenino Depot Museum Complex, local sandstone is on display in Tenino.

LEST WE FORGET

Population: 1,794
Founding: 1891

INSETS L to R: The Rainier Historical Society formed in 1997 to rescue the 1915 Rainier Schoolhouse, now a volunteer-run library and community center. • The mural on the side of the Main Street Cookie Co. illustrates the town's namesake volcano. • Local history signs at the intersection of Rainier and the Yelm-Tenino trail. • Main Street Cookie Co.

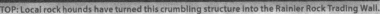

TOP: Local rock hounds have turned this crumbling structure into the Rainier Rock Trading Wall.

Rainier

The Prairie Line

Before 1890, the Northern Pacific Railroad rushed along between Kalama and Tacoma, not stopping on its way through the prairie below Mount Rainier. Settlers on the prairie, called *ten al queth*, or "the best yet" in the Indigenous Lushootseed language, ran alongside the trains, hoping to catch the mail that rail workers threw as the train blew by at speed.

German immigrants Maria and Albert Gehrke were the first non-Indigenous people to settle in Rainier. Along with Albert's two brothers, they established a dairy. In 1890, they established a post office, putting an end to the game of high-speed catch with the train. The railroad, known as the Prairie Line, attracted both settlers and industrialists, who hoped to capitalize on the area's old growth timber. A settler from Binghamton, New York, platted the town the following year, though the town didn't officially incorporate until 1947.

Timber companies became profitable in the area by the turn of the 20th century, and competing mills rose up to meet the demand, driven largely by railway construction but also by the needs of increasing town development. At the same time, rail excursions to national parks were becoming popular tourist attractions. Mount Rainier became a national park in 1899, and the old logging rail known as the Tacoma Eastern Railroad expanded to the western gateway to the park, offering Puget Sound–area residents easy access. By then, non-Indigenous settlers had been living in the area now called Thurston County for 50 years.

Thurston County is one of the first-settled areas in the state, predating territorial Washington by more than 35 years. Settlers first came to the area in 1845. They established early settlements along the Deschutes River and followed Indian trails to the inland prairies, homesteading under the Donation Land Claim Act.

Logging exploded in the late 19th century, and as many as 40 logging camps operated in Thurston County. The town of Rainier sprang up around the mills, and by 1922, Rainier had one of just three schools in the county. Within 20 years, logging was waning and towns began declining. Consolidated school districts were one sign of such decline. The Rainier School escaped this fate. Though a new school was built in 1974, the historic Rainier School building remains an important part of the Rainier community today. Until recently, it held a thrift store and volunteer library, though due to funding limitations, both have closed. In 2004, the Rainier Historical Society succeeded in placing the school on the National Register of Historic Places.

Don't Forget the Water

Mount Rainier National Park is home to 35 square miles of glacier, the largest glacial system in the US outside of Alaska. Within the park are more than 400 lakes and nearly 500 rivers and streams. The Nisqually people, one of many groups descended from the original inhabitants of the valley around the mountain, have long called the mountain *Ta-co-beh*. Six tribes located near Mount Rainier have ties to the mountain, including the Nisqually, Puyallup, Squaxin Island, Yakama, Muckleshoot, and Cowlitz. Other tribal names and spellings for the mountain include Tacoma, Tahoma, and Pooskaus. The name *Rainier* honors a British navy captain. The Alliance to Restore Native Names argues that the name should be changed, a process which could take years. In a Nisqually story, Tacobeh resided with his mother in the Olympic Range a few million years ago. When that range grew too crowded, the two decided to make a new home in the Cascade Range. As they left, the mother said to her son, "Tacobeh: Don't forget the water. Take it along with us." Visitors to the Nisqually Tribe's website can hear the story in English and in Nisqually. "That's why all the rivers come out of that mountain," the narrator says. "The boy didn't forget."

We ♥ Rainier

The majority of Thurston County's 200,000-plus residents live in urban areas, but small towns like Rainier in the southern part of the county have experienced steady growth since the 1960s. Rainier has elementary, middle, and high schools, with more than 800 students enrolled. A 14-mile paved trail links Rainier with the nearby towns of Yelm and Tenino. Visitors hoping to experience life in

the town might attend Rainier Round-Up Days, an annual festival featuring a parade, a car show, and a weekend's worth of the region's best bluegrass music.

More than 30 volunteers have kept the Rainier Volunteer Library open almost 30 hours a week since 2009.

Recently, a group called We Love Rainier WA has been working to inspire community development. The Rainier Arts Commission, a result of the group's efforts, opened a gallery in town to feature work by local artists. The group is currently working to launch a summer market featuring artistic and craft work by local vendors, perhaps pulling in makers from Yelm and Tenino as well. In addition to supporting and promoting local makers, We Love Rainier WA envisions supporting a scholarship fund for local students.

The Northern Pacific Railroad named the town of Rainier for its view of the mountain, and a vibrant mural downtown shows both settlers and Indigenous people pointing toward the mountain together. Ironically, it's possible to visit the town without seeing the mountain at all. As anyone who has lived near mountains can attest, mountains create their own weather. Even on a sunny day, from downtown Rainier in the shadow of Tahoma, the mountain can be as invisible as a god.

A sign for the local barber shop adorns the side of the **Main Street Cookie Company**. Just above, a mural depicts white settlers and Native Salish pointing toward the mountain that George Vancouver called Rainier.

Population: 793
Founding: 1908

INSETS L to R: Roy Elementary School serves 312 students from grades K-5. • Roy, formerly Media, occupies the halfway point between Tenino and Tacoma. • Copper Gables draws a stark contrast to its moss-laden next-door neighbor. • Downtown Roy is home to several businesses from an espresso stand to a general store , a wedding venue and a restaurant.

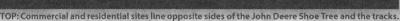

TOP: Commercial and residential sites line opposite sides of the John Deere Shoe Tree and the tracks.

Roy

Of Boom and Bust, of Fathers and Sons

The City of Roy's website claims that the area used to be "Indian country," though "little of their legacy remains to be seen today." Indeed, James McNaught and Dr. C. A. Warren founded the town of Roy in 1894 where the Nisqually people had lived for 10,000 years. The Nisqually homelands encompassed about 2 million acres, from Olympia, on the south end of Puget Sound, all the way to Mount Rainier. The Medicine Creek Treaty of 1854 established the Nisqually Reservation, though history suggests that Chief Leschi's signature was forged. As with other treaties, the Medicine Creek Treaty was less a process of negotiation than coercion: territorial governor Isaac Stevens arrived with a draft of the treaty in hand. The US Senate ratified the treaty the following year.

In 1873, Arthur Denny read a disappointing announcement at the Yesler sawmill in Seattle: Executives from the Northern Pacific Railroad had decided to locate the terminus of the railroad in Tacoma, not Seattle. While Seattle sulked, Tacoma rejoiced. All of Pierce County benefited from the decision. As settlers cleared the timber, sawmills

went up in every town, and the railroad now shipped the lumber as far away as San Francisco. This was boom time for Media, the town smack in the middle of the Tenino–Tacoma line. When Media incorporated in 1908, founder James McNaught decided to rename the town for his son: Roy.

The town ran along both sides of the railroad tracks, and Muck Creek ran thick with salmon. Settlers drove wagons to the river and filled them with fish; what they couldn't eat, they used as fertilizer. Horses wouldn't set foot in the river due to the volume of fish. It was this bounty that drew Northern Pacific Railroad general counsel James McNaught and the train's designated physician, Dr. Samuel Warren. The two men met up in Media to go fishing. McNaught had just purchased the whole place.

By 1912, 20 trains per day passed through Roy, 17 of which stopped in town to pick up or unload goods, or, in the days of the steam train, to refill with water. But while the water tower along the tracks served the rail line, the town itself lacked a water system. For 40 years, firefighters raced from Tacoma to extinguish blaze after blaze. Fire irreparably damaged Roy's economic momentum; to this injury the railroad added insult, when it stopped running the Prairie Line in 1953. In 1917, at the peak of Roy's success, the US Army annexed much of the town for Camp Lewis, erasing the community of Loveland and cutting off Roy from nearby economic opportunities.

Today, Roy's economy centers on farming and raising cattle. Twice a year, the Roy Pioneer Rodeo attracts thousands of visitors. Among their photos of barrel racing and bull riding are sure to be shots of the wooden red water tower from the days of steam trains, from the time when Media went from a whistle stop to an incorporated town with a promising future. No wonder they renamed it after one of their own sons. It would have been as dear to them as their own families.

Reddog's Wild West Town

What's a person to do with a lot of land on his hands? When Johnny Pierce got bored, he started building a ghost town. Pierce, who goes by the nickname Reddog, began by building a shed, fashioning it in the style of an Old West mining town with false fronts and covered porches. Soon, he'd built six structures over an acre and a half. Tourists started knocking on the front door, wanting to have a look around. Reddog went with the flow, and today his ghost town is on its way to being a wedding venue, with two special events already in the books.

No(w) Trespassing

From an outsider's perspective, Roy doesn't feel like a friendly place. Walking the residential blocks just over the railroad tracks from downtown, visitors will notice hostile signs hung on fences and next to front doors. "Can you run 850 feet per second?" one sign asks. "If not, your head best be bulletproof." A few feet away, another reads, "My dog is so lazy he waits for me to shoot trespassers before he mutilates them . . . usually." Moss is gently reclaiming the roof over the modest home's porch, which sits just about 6 inches above the ground. Wind chimes

hang silently in the still air. A green *O* for the University of Oregon adorns the glass window of the front door. All of the shades are drawn.

Copper Gables Barn stands a block off the main drag through downtown, McNaught Road, next to a home that's seen better days. The 10,000-square-foot barn, built in 1915, regularly hosts weddings with up to 200 guests.

Roy is halfway between Tacoma and Olympia against the back of Joint Base Lewis-McChord. Dropping into town is an intentional act. Highway 507 becomes McNaught Road, fronted by City Hall, a small market and gas station, a restaurant and bar, and a drive-through coffee shop. At the back of a gravel parking lot, a hand-painted sign reads JOHN DEERE SHOE TREE PARK. A large maple sprouts as many pairs of shoes as spring leaves. Another sign reads NO TRESPASSING; someone has slyly sprayed a *w* after the "No." A picnic table confuses the issue. Should one sit and stay or walk away?

Many homes here are well kept, but others are in a state of decay. Next to Copper Gables Barn, a wedding venue just off McNaught Road, the roof falls in on a home that looks to have been boarded up 50 years ago. Moss stands 6 inches thick on the shingles, and the grass rises tall around the foundation. It's easy to imagine a day when the grass meets the moss, leaving only a green mound, vaguely house-shaped. The library is next to city hall. There's a sign on the door: PERMANENTLY CLOSED.

On a brief visit, it's hard to know why anyone lives in a place like Roy. Maybe it's that the housing is affordable. Maybe it's the proximity to pasture. Maybe it seems like there's nowhere else to go.

At the bend in the road, where the highway turns into town, Cowgirl's Coffee is lively with customers in cars and trucks heading in and out of town. The young woman working the drive-through window appears to be college-aged. She's from Roy. She doesn't own the coffee shop, but she's enthusiastic at the suggestion that she might. "Gosh, someday!" she exclaims. "I'd love that."

The shoe tree is a peculiarly American roadside attraction. Roy's shoe tree dates to 2003, when the first pair of shoes went up in hopes of creating a point of interest in town. A closer look reveals that while the shoes are of all types and sizes, they are, like the tree, coated in moss.

24

Population: 434
Founding: 1888

INSETS L to R: South Prairie's tiny downtown holds a post office, fire station, community center, park, and two espresso stands in about two city blocks. • The William Bisson House links modern South Prairie to its pioneer roots. • Veterans Park, at the edge of the creek, separates downtown South Prairie from a large recreational space. • Pastoral beauty in South Prairie, Pierce County.

TOP: South Prairie Creek flows to the Carbon River, the Puyallup River, and finally Puget Sound.

South Prairie

The Man Who Left His Mark

Not far from the post office, just a few blocks off State Route 162, known as Pioneer Way as it wends through the town of South Prairie, sits a two-story house on a double lot, facing east, toward Mount Rainier. Built from local fir timber, the house boasts scalloped shakes in pale robin's egg blue with white trim. It's the only home still standing in South Prairie that ties the family who platted the town and drove its early economy to the present day. In 1896, William Bisson wrote his name in black wax on the floorboards.

In 1854, Paul Emery filed a homestead claim for a piece of land in a natural clearing between a creek and the foothills of Mount Rainier. He named his land South Prairie, as Connell's Prairie was just 5 miles to the north. The next year, in the wake of seven treaties signed between territorial governor Isaac Stevens and dozens of Indigenous nations, Emery fled his homestead in fear of the violence erupting all around him, including attacks against settlers and settlements. The following year, the US Army, aided by a group of territorial volunteers, fought with the Klickitat, Nisqually,

and Yakama at Connell's Prairie. Chief Kanasket of the Klickitat was killed during the battle, and the tribes withdrew. Settlers took shelter in blockhouses like the one called Fort McAllister inside the present-day town limits of South Prairie. The Fort McAllister blockhouse is long gone. Francis Bisson settled on Emery's old claim and platted the town of South Prairie in 1888.

Bisson came to Washington in 1876 to work on the railroad. He became the first businessman in South Prairie in 1884 when he built the first general store. At the time, a general store was more than just a place to pick up supplies; Bisson's store would have been a center of town life and a place to get news and gossip as well as staples. Bisson went on to contribute much to the town, serving on the city council and later the Washington state legislature. Meanwhile, William Bisson moved to the area, following his brother's footsteps. Like Francis, William contributed much to the town. He organized South Prairie's first Episcopalian Sunday school and served as treasurer and postmaster, while his wife, Maria, earned money working as a seamstress.

John Flett, contracted by the government to interpret in negotiations with Indigenous nations, had settled in South Prairie to farm. Flett's sons discovered coal nearby, and the railroad sprang up to support the burgeoning mining industry, cutting right through South Prairie. In the 1920s, when Northern Pacific wanted to buy and develop more land, Bisson refused to sell. The railroad left within a decade, taking a chunk of South Prairie's economy with it. As the coal and timber industries depleted those resources, South Prairie ceased to be a major regional supply hub.

JBLM

Any story about Pierce County has to include a brief description of Joint Base Lewis-McChord. As early as 1902, the American military used the land near American Lake as a summer training camp. Then called Camp Weisenberger, the camp was renamed for Meriwether Lewis in 1917. That same year, Camp Lewis was part of the constellation of bases preparing American soldiers to fight in WWI. The camp became Fort Lewis and thus part of the Army's permanent assets in 1927. Shortly before the Second World War, the Air Force commandeered an airstrip constructed next to Fort Lewis and named it for Colonel William C. McChord. Today, JBLM is one of the largest military bases anywhere in the world, with a population of 175,000 soldiers and civilians.

Our Little Town

South Prairie is a modern town that doesn't wear its history on its sleeve. A visitor has to go looking for it. The Flett family moved to Steilacoom, where Flett's dairy operated until 1994. Besides the Bisson House, homes and buildings in town are new. Yards are tidy. Colorful signs welcome visitors to the South Prairie Community Center, adjacent to a sparkling fire station. While the timber and coal industries are long gone, construction and related trades continue to employ the largest portion of South Prairie's workforce. Fishing and hiking draw tourists to the area, and the southwest face of Mount Rainier is just 20 miles away. Halfway between, Wilkeson

Coke Oven Park emphasizes the importance of coal in Washington's early industry.

Unlike the transcontinental railroad, the Northern Pacific meant to reach the West without the aid of government loans. Investors were threatening to pull out of the railroad's development when coal discoveries near South Prairie offered them a new financial incentive to stay. While the mines closed for good in the 1970s, visitors can still see Wilkeson Coke Oven Park, though the beehive ovens may reflect vandalism and general neglect.

The Bisson House is the former home of South Prairie's first business owner, who settled on the site of Paul Emery's original donation land claim. The home is the sole building in town linking its founding to its present.

Adjacent to downtown South Prairie, before you cross the creek, a stone monument in Veterans Park calls citizens to remember the town's recent history while focusing attention on the present. Its dedication reads in part, "For your tomorrows, we gave our todays." The RV park across South Prairie Creek is full of visitors. Swing sets and picnic tables await a park full of families. People running errands in town see a stranger with a camera and stop to say hello. "You doing a story on our little town?" one asks. The setting is beautiful. The characters are friendly. The story of South Prairie is still in the making.

The picnic area in Veterans Park provides a restful retreat just outside of town. Veterans Park sits on the bank of South Prairie Creek, which empties into the Carbon River, one of four rivers in Pierce County.

DEDICATED TO
THE MEN & WOMEN OF
SOUTH PRAIRIE WHO SERVED THEIR
COUNTRY IN WAR & PEACE
AND IN REVERENT MEMORY OF
THOSE WHO GAVE THEIR LIVES
"FOR YOUR TOMORROWS,
WE GAVE OUR TODAYS"
Dedicated by the citizens of

25

Population: 299
Founding: 1908

INSETS L to R: The narrow streets of the village are densely lined with trees. • The wealthy enclave started as an artists' colony. • The City of Bellevue administers most of the village's services. • Azaleas burst over the squash courts in wealthy Beaux Arts Village.

TOP: Many of Beaux Arts' few hundred residents live lakeside.

Beaux Arts Village

Little Romes Everywhere

In 1648, the Italian politician Cardinal Mazarin was minister to Louis XIV, then five years old and the king of France. Mazarin founded L'Académie des Beaux-Arts as a school for the study of the classics, namely art and architecture. Louis XIV would later recruit students to decorate the royal apartments at Versailles. In 1863, the school was renamed L'École des Beaux-Arts. Among the renowned artists who trained there during the 1800s were painters Camille Pissarro, Pierre-Auguste Renoir, and Georges Seurat.

The architectural style popularized by the Beaux Arts movement is Greco-Roman, featuring heavy pillars and archways, grand staircases, and balconies and pediments carved in bas-relief. In the mid-19th century, American architects imported the style, incorporating it into the City Beautiful movement and building "little Romes everywhere."

Seattle's first Society of Beaux Arts found a home in the University Building, now the site of the Four Seasons Olympic Hotel. In 1908, three of the society's members, Frank Calvert, Alfred Benfro, and Finn Frolich, started the Western Academy of Beaux Arts. They bought 50 acres of forest on the eastern shore of Lake Washington, intending to establish a village of like-minded artists. Part of the requirements for joining the village were that residents build "creative" homes, though not necessarily massive Greco-Roman ones.

At the time, the only way to access the Village was by ferry, and the site lacked basic services like water and electricity. The village grew slowly, though many new homeowners used their properties for vacation purposes only. The I-90 bridge across Lake Washington improved access, and nearby Bellevue began to grow rapidly. In order to avoid being subsumed by the larger city, Beaux Arts Village incorporated in 1954. The town just barely met the incorporation requirement of 300 citizens.

It never became the arts village its founders envisioned, but Beaux Arts Village later became a symbol of extreme wealth in the last decades of the 20th century. In 1978, a three-bedroom house on a third of an acre cost about $125,000, or about $500,000 in today's dollars, adjusting for inflation. In 2019, the average cost of a home in the Village was nearly $1 million, and 95% of residents own their homes. The entire area of the village is not quite 60 acres, smaller than one-tenth of a square mile.

One County, Two Kings

In 1981, singer Stevie Wonder led a rally asking Congress to make Dr. Martin Luther King, Jr.'s birthday a national holiday, inspiring Seattle radio DJ Eddie Rye to ask the City of Seattle to rename Empire Way after Dr. King. Seattle businesses pushed back, but eventually the street was renamed. Similarly, King County was only named for Dr. King in 1986. Its first namesake was William Rufus King, a US Senator from Alabama who was briefly vice president under Franklin Pierce. A native of North Carolina, King was a slaveholder who established a cotton plantation near Selma, Alabama; with his family, he enslaved as many as 500 people, more than any other family in the state. He died of tuberculosis in 1853—the same year Washington became a territory—after having served only six weeks as vice president. He was buried at his plantation, Chestnut Hill, and later reinterred at Old Live Oak Cemetery in Selma.

A little more than a century later, in 1965, Dr. Martin Luther King, Jr., led a march across the Edmund Pettus Bridge from Selma to the state capital, Montgomery, in defiance of racial injustice and insistence on the right to vote. The Voting Rights Act was passed the same year. The motion to change the namesake of King County makes reference to both William Rufus King's inhumanity as a slaveowner and Martin Luther King's commitment to justice, dignity, and freedom for all people. Motion No. 6461 passed on February 24, 1986.

Bozart's Private Beach Club

In Beaux Arts Village, I spoke with Pete Marshall, who's lived in Beaux Arts Village for 41 years. I met him at Chesterfield Beach Park where he was throwing a stick for Cappy, his golden retriever. Pete says you can pronounce it "Bozarts" or "Bo Arts." He's never known which is correct, but he hears it both ways, and he figures it's "Bozarts"

since it's French. In lieu of a city hall or other administrative buildings, people in Beaux Arts Village meet at each other's houses, including for city council meetings. Most of the houses have large yards made private by a combination of fences and elaborate landscaping.

Quaint signage welcomes visitors to Beaux Arts Village, a wealthy enclave just South of Bellevue, Washington. In lieu of a city hall, the mayor and council members meet in one another's homes.

Chesterfield Beach is public, and most of the beaches here belong to the City of Bellevue, but Beaux Arts Village has its own private beach. After 40 years, Pete says people still see him walking Cappy and say, "You know, this is a private beach."

"I have to bite my tongue," Pete says.

Azaleas burst with color next to the squash courts. Trellising wisteria perfumes the air next to the Enatai School, where the elementary-school kids go. Older students go to schools in Bellevue. Most people who live in the Village are white and highly educated. The neighborhood is gorgeous and wealthy, a privileged enclave tucked among enormous fir trees and landscaped blooms. But is it a town? It has a mayor and elected officials and a school, even if Bellevue provides for most of its services. The city of more than 120,000 people gleams lakeside, just a 30-minute walk from Beaux Arts Village.

Beaux Arts Village sits on Lake Washington, with views of Mount Rainier to the south and Mount Baker to the north. The lakefront in Beaux Arts is almost entirely under private ownership.

26

Population: 1,786
Founding: 1912

INSETS L to R: The name Tolt comes from the river, Tolthue. • The campground has 38 camp-sites and a number of yurts, but watch out for wildlife! • Valley Memorial Park backs up to the Snoqualmie Valley Trail. • A mural on the side of City Hall depicts Tolt's early days.

TOP: A suspension bridge connects downtown Carnation to Tolt-Macdonald Park.

Carnation

Land of Contentment

In 1857, the US Surveyor General published a map of the nascent Washington Territory, marking the recently decided boundary between American and British land. Where freeways run across today's maps like neural networks, the 1857 map is all rugged mountains and coastlines and spidery waterways. The Tolthue River appears for the first time on this map.

In 1858, James Entwistle filed a homestead claim at the confluence of the Tolthue and Snoqualmie Rivers. He'd recently deserted the Army and his post at Fort Steilacoom, 60 miles away. He wasn't alone. Recruitment and desertion were common problems for the military at the time, particularly in the West.

Entwistle farmed hops and opened a trading post on land formerly used as a tribal meeting site and administrative center. The first inhabitants of the area were the Snoqualmie Tribe. The hilly terrain offered the tribe protection from unforeseen attacks. A cemetery may have been located here once, although flooding has destroyed any evidence. The village at the Tolthue held an important

longhouse used as a capitol. The Snoqualmie had long since cleared the flatlands for military training and cultivating a sustainable ecosystem for plants and wildlife by the time Entwistle arrived.

Under Chief Patkanim, the Snoqualmie ceded their land in the Treaty of Point Elliott in 1855. According to the tribe at the time, they numbered 4,000 people and made up one of the largest Indigenous groups in the region. Today, roughly 500 people identify as Snoqualmie Indian.

Hops farming and lumber mills were the valley's first industries, and farmers employed Indigenous people to pick hops. Entwistle prospered until the Panic of 1893, when the hops market fell from $1.25 per pound to just 6¢. By then, the community of Tolt was well on its way. It was named for the Tolt River, the name having evolved in previous years from Tolthue, or "river of swift waters" in Snoqualmie. By the time Tolt incorporated in 1912, Great Northern ran through town and Tolt was on its third schoolhouse.

The same year that Tolt incorporated, its future swung in a new direction. Hops farming seemed permanently over, and lumber was already a declining industry. Eldridge Stuart cleared the land and established a dairy called Carnation. From his original claim of 320 acres, Stuart quickly added 400 more. He led innovations in dairy production and distribution, and Carnation Farms became an international source of breeding stock for dairy cows. In 1917, Tolt changed its name to Carnation, in recognition of the dairy's prominence. Carnation Farms' success led to the Snoqualmie Valley's reputation as "the home of the contented cows."

Remlinger Farms

Many people encounter Carnation today through a visit to Remlinger Farms, a family-run farmstand turned full-fledged tourist attraction. The farm began in 1955 when Eleanor and Floyd Remlinger bought a strawberry farm they'd helped plant. The Remlingers marketed their berries as far as Seattle and opened the farm to anyone who wanted to come pick. Eleanor was born in Tolt in 1916, just before the name was changed to Carnation.

Today, Eleanor and Floyd's son Gary runs the business with his wife, Bonnie. The two have focused on the "u-pick" aspect of the farm. With opportunities to tour the farm and pick your own fruits and vegetables, as well as a market, restaurant, and even a family-fun park, Remlinger Farms draws visitors to experience the beauty of Snoqualmie Valley's farmland. Some 200,000 people visit the farm annually.

Your Big Backyard

Carnation today is a pastoral paradise offering a rural life with modern amenities. On the wide porch at Sandy's Espresso, visitors can recharge from a morning's adventure in Tolt-Mac Park, whether swimming, running, hiking, or just lying in the grass contemplating the beauty of Snoqualmie Valley.

In the 1970s, Boy Scout Chief John MacDonald led more than 20,000 Boy Scouts in an effort to turn the one-time Snoqualmie

winter village site into a campground and park. They built campsites, yurts, and trails, and the Army Reserves built a 500-foot suspension bridge over the Snoqualmie River, making the park easily accessible from downtown Carnation. A dozen miles of trails in the park connect to the trails in Ames Lake Forest.

Carnation is hemmed in by the Snoqualmie and Tolt Rivers, with vast public park lands and well-maintained trails spanning dozens of miles. No wonder they call it "your big backyard."

Across the river on the other side of town, the 27-mile Snoqualmie Valley Trail leads cyclists on a farm tour. Between river and trail lies the town. Just half an hour from the madness of an increasingly densely populated urban life in Bellevue, Kirkland, and Seattle, Carnation feels built for relaxation. Signs around town point to trailheads and welcome visitors to "your big backyard." Hemmed in by parks, rivers, and, in the distance, the Snoqualmie Mountains, Carnation is rural enough that there are warnings of bear sightings on the campground signs but urban enough that the local coffee shop has free Wi-Fi.

Farming still drives the local economy, and in recent years, heavy flooding in the valley has limited u-pick pumpkin patch success in the fall. Carnation recently secured funding to move the existing levee where the Tolt River joins the Snoqualmie in hopes of returning the river to its natural floodplain, improving wildlife habitat in the process. The Tolt River Corridor project will also reduce flood and erosion risk. In town, the Tolt Avenue Project recently began revitalizing a four-block section of the avenue, focusing on improved aesthetics and pedestrian access. "While things are [already] good," City Manager Amy Arrington says, "[the project] will make our charming downtown even stronger."

Boy Scout Council Chief John MacDonald began planning the development of the 574-acre park in Carnation in the early 1970s. A bridge across the Tolt River joins the greater part of Tolt-MacDonald Memorial Park and Campground to downtown Carnation.

27

Population: 198
Founding: 1893

INSETS L to R: Skykomish welcomes visitors to "a Great Northern town." • The model railroad in the center of town emphasizes the movie-set feeling of Skykomish. • Skykomish is in the foothills of Stevens Pass, in the foothills of the Mount Baker-Snoqualmie National Forest. • Environmental remediation efforts in the wake of BNSF's pollution have been disruptive, if restorative, in the town known as "Sky."

TOP: A Burlington Northern train runs through Skykomish on rail built in 1893.

Skykomish

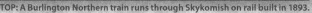

The Great Northern Sky

James Hill was born to a poor family near Ontario, Canada, in 1838. His father died when he was 14, and James had to leave school to earn money. At age 17, he moved to the US. In Minnesota, he was a part of the volunteer corps; he couldn't serve in the Civil War, as he'd lost one eye as a child.

Hill's resourcefulness is the stuff of legend. He worked his way from literal rags to riches, eventually turning a failing railroad into the St. Paul, Minnesota & Manitoba Railway Company. Hill was known as "the empire builder". Still, people doubted his plan to take his railroad all the way to the Pacific, calling it "Hill's folly." In 1889, Hill went for it.

Hill sent John Stevens, who'd engineered the Panama Canal, to explore the eastern face of the Cascades. An associate named Haskell went looking for the headwaters of Nason Creek. When he found them, he carved the words *Stevens Pass* into a tree. Another man on the advance team, John Maloney, saw the potential for a town to support the coming rail. Maloney filed a claim and called it Maloney's Siding. With the completion of the rail in 1893, the town was named Skykomish, meaning

"inland people." The town formerly known as Maloney's Siding may have served as a fair-weather campsite for the Skykomish Tribe, though their permanent villages were farther downstream.

In short order, the population of Skykomish, well, skyrocketed. Building the Cascade Tunnel cut the track distance and energy required to get trains over the pass and employed engineers, miners, and timber workers. By 1899, when the Maloneys platted the town, 150 people called Skykomish home.

The Maloneys built a store, and Frank Wandschneider built a hotel. In 1904, a fire took out most of the town, including the hotel but sparing the store. The next year, D. J. Manning built the Skykomish Hotel and Restaurant, boasting 24-hour dining services and card rooms to entertain the railroad workers. The hotel still stands today. Patrick McEvoy was the engineer on the very first train through town, in 1893. A few years later, he moved to Skykomish and opened a saloon. Today it's called the Whistling Post Tavern. The Cascadia Hotel went up in the early 1920s. Skykomish had reached its apex.

Tunnel Trouble

Great Northern's Cascade Tunnel at Stevens Pass provided a quick solution to a tedious problem. Namely, trains crossing the pass had to traverse eight switchbacks to surmount the 4,000 feet of elevation. Each train required two engines, one to pull and one to push. All told, the traverse required four times as many track miles as the linear distance covered.

While the tunnel solved the switchback problem, it created others. In 1903, a passenger train stalled in the tunnel. Choking on the coal-powered smoke, the train crew lost consciousness before they could solve the problem. Luckily, a fireman on board figured out how to release the brakes, and the train eased out of the tunnel. In 1909, electrification eliminated the pollution issue, but heavy snow in winter led to avalanches and landslides that blocked the tunnel. Nearly 100 people died in an avalanche in 1910. In 1921, Great Northern decided to build a new tunnel.

Four times longer than the original, the new Cascade Tunnel would run 500 feet lower in elevation than the first. Engineers estimated its cost at $1 million. Nearly 2,000 men worked for three years to build the tunnel, and several men died in accidents in the process.

The new tunnel opened on December 28, 1928, three days before the anticipated deadline. While the tunnel came in on schedule, it was vastly over budget. The final cost was $25 million. The original tunnel was abandoned the following year.

Model Town

In 1852, the map of King County spanned from the Cascades to the Pacific east to west, and from Tacoma in the south to Skykomish in the northeast, 95 miles away. The eastern border later moved from the Pacific inland to Puget Sound, but the county is still Washington's 11th largest. Its 39 cities and towns are spread from river valleys to the Cascade foothills, from densely packed Seattle to sleepy Skykomish.

As the founding industries in Skykomish declined, interest in outdoor recreation began taking off. Stevens Pass became a popular skiing destination, bringing weekend visitors to Skykomish, which continued to offer hotels, restaurants, and dance halls.

In Skykomish, the high school, library, downtown businesses, and most homes are visible from the river. A sign welcomes visitors to "A Great Northern Town"—a nod to both the company that built the town and its location in the Cascades.

In the 1990s, efforts began to rectify the environmental damage caused by Great Northern. Skykomish High School students got involved, filming a documentary, *An Oily Sky,* which helped propel an agreement between the state and railroads to cleanup the pollution. The cleanup has been no small undertaking, involving lifting or relocating homes, reinforcing the levy, and excavating contaminated soil. BNSF paid a fine of $5 million and covered the cost of the cleanup, an estimated $100 million.

In 2011, Skykomish built its Town Center Park, featuring a model railroad at one-eighth scale. Just next to the actual BNSF tracks, the model train comes through, sounding its horn, though no one is there to get out of the way. There's a gift shop and a museum, and train rides are free. By September 2014, the park had transformed the center of town, and 350 people came to ride the model train every weekend.

Houses in Skykomish are small. People live on both sides of the railroad tracks, and everyone lives on the river. Tin roofs slough off the snow in winter. Porches sit a mere 6 inches above the grass. A tiny library looks like an old trading post. Light passes through the windows of the Skykomish Hotel. Put together, it feels like a model town, built for the model train set at its center. Still, there are a few cars parked outside the Whistling Post and the Cascade Cafe. Every now and again, a car crosses the double truss bridge over the river into town. The driver always waves.

A tiny model train runs alongside the actual train tracks in Skykomish. Visitors can ride the train for free and learn about the history of the railroad in Skykomish at the museum.

28

Population: 165
Founding: 1848

INSETS L to R: Calm inlets and abundant public access characterize the island's coastline. • The Village Market is in the heart of Lopez Village. • Need a break from biking? Learn island history at the Lopez Historical Museum. • Art imitates life in downtown Lopez Village.

TOP: Cycling is a popular way to experience Lopez Island.

Lopez Village

From Battle to Bachelor Party

The Salish, Lummi, Haida, and many other Native American and First Nations peoples have resided in the islands we now call the San Juans since the end of the last ice age. As European settlement began in the area, these tribes frequently warred with the invading whites and with each other.

Around 1850, Hiram Hutchinson piloted his canoe into a Lopez Island harbor and found a battle just getting underway between the Salish people and the northern Haida. Any foreign party from the north may have been referred to as Haida, though they may not have been part of that group. Hutchinson, only 19 or 20 years old, threw in his lot with the Salish, and after the battle was over, he decided to stay. He married a Salish woman and opened a trading post, clearing land that today is the site of Lopez Village.

Hutchinson traded with Hudson's Bay Company, which at the time administered the San Juan Islands from its position in Victoria on behalf of England. In exchange for wool, mutton, and deer, Hutchinson procured items like flour, sugar, and tobacco. Over the next few years, 11 bachelors

followed in his footsteps. They were Irish sailors, like Billy Barlow, jumping ship, or they were moving through on their way to the Fraser River gold fields. Others, the Island County Historical Society notes, simply came for a better life.

Seven of the 12 first European men to colonize Lopez Island married Salish women, a practice that seems to have been common at the time. The wives became cultural liaisons, and in so doing became keys to the economic success of their husbands. Not all of the men married Salish women, though; some were already married. Preserved letters show their efforts to persuade their wives to join them on the island.

At this point in history, Britain and the United States had issued competing claims to the territory now known as the San Juan Islands. Spain made the initial claims and was the first to name the islands, but gave up that claim in 1818, after the British and the Americans agreed to manage the islands jointly. Despite the agreement, each side felt affronted by the other, the British in terms of their rights in keeping with the work of Hudson's Bay Company, and the Americans in terms of their rights to claim the land under the concept of Manifest Destiny. An 1846 treaty designated the 49th parallel as the line that neither side would cross; unfortunately, the San Juan Islands lay in the path, and both sides claimed ownership of them.

Tensions continued to rise. Washington became a US territory in 1853, claiming the San Juans for the States. The British responded by establishing a farm on San Juan Island. Each side regarded the other as squatters and unlawful trespassers. In 1859, an American farmer shot and killed a pig owned by the British company. The situation escalated quickly, and both countries engaged their militaries to occupy and defend the land. This was the beginning of a long-running standoff known as the Pig War. Twelve years later, in 1871, the British and Americans signed the Treaty of Washington and agreed to let an outside arbitrator decide the fate of the islands. He ruled on the side of the US, and the San Juans became American property once and for all.

By this time, Lopez Island had become agriculturally important. Products included sheep, cattle, grains, produce, and dairy. Farmers worked collaboratively. When the Columbia Basin Reclamation Project brought irrigation to Eastern Washington, demand for the island's agricultural products dropped, and the population followed suit: In 1870, the official census data for all of Lopez Island noted just 70 residents. That number increased to 180 in the next 10 years. The population continued to increase for the next 40 years before it began to decline. In 2010, 2,383 people lived on Lopez Island. Of those, just 165 lived in Lopez Village, where the economy is now largely driven by tourism.

The Gourley Commune

In 1910, a Pentecostal preacher named Thomas Gourley led a commune to Lopez Island after Seattle kicked them out for being too rowdy. The group aimed to live in a way that protected them from mainstream society's corrupt ways. Life on Lopez was difficult for the "Holy Rollers," as locals called them. Gourley promoted pacifism to the extent that he forbade his followers from eating seafood, though it was locally abundant, in order to avoid killing. When WWI began, Gourley advised his followers not to serve in the military, and he was charged with violating the Espionage Act. Many adherents died of typhoid and tuberculosis, possibly because of the commune's marshland location.

In 1974, the Boldt Decision divided fishing resources equally among Native and non-Native populations. Many fishermen protested. Within a few years, Native catches increased, and non-Native fishermen largely moved out of the industry.

Gourley predicted the second coming of Christ late in 1918, and when his prophecy went unfulfilled, his reputation suffered. A few years later, he abandoned the commune, leaving his followers to share the property and rejoin mainstream society.

Lopez Today

The only town on Lopez Island, Lopez Village today is the picture of austere modernity. Phone service came during the same decade that women secured the right to vote, but electrification was still three decades away. In the 1990s, the roads were renamed to make EMS access more effective. Many roads are still marked by the most rustic of signs—a wooden board inscribed here, a colored square stapled to a tree there. Others bear the names that locals saw fit to give them: Mozart Road for the classicist, Dizzy G. Road for the jazz fanaticist.

Lopez is a cyclist's paradise. Wooden bike racks grace every storefront and corner. Rolling hills lead to wildlife sanctuaries, rocky outcrops, and vistas of the Pacific Ocean, lighthouses, and migrating orcas and humpbacks. Among the San Juans, Lopez is the easiest to circumnavigate on a bicycle, and maps available everywhere from aboard the ferry to the local coffee shop clearly mark the best routes and points of interest.

A trip to the Lopez Island History Museum breaks up a day of cycling on Lopez Island. Here, visitors learn that women were key to early economic success in Lopez Village. Irene Weeks, Hiram Hutchinson's sister, became the island's first postmistress. Mary Jane Brown spoke the Chinook trading language and mediated between Native Americans and settlers.

29

Population: 1831
Founding: 1852

INSETS L to R: Coupeville holds
its history close. Most of the
buildings prominently feature
the date of their founding.
• Libbey Beach offers a long
stretch of coastline for walks at
low tide. • Only four blockhouses
remain on the island. • Coupeville feels like a place equally
built for tourists and locals.

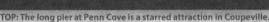

TOP: The long pier at Penn Cove is a starred attraction in Coupeville.

Coupeville

A Paradise of Nature

Natural prairies and marshes characterize Whidbey Island's landscape, the product of glacial lakes
left by a receding Vashon Glacier nearly 17,000
years ago. The island's first inhabitants, the Salish,
maintained the natural prairie environment with
controlled burns that encouraged growth and
provided feeding opportunities for wild game.

Captain George Vancouver's 1792 exploration of the Strait of Juan de Fuca led to the
discovery of Deception Pass and then Whidbey
Island, which Vancouver named for his navigator,
Joseph Whidbey. Prior to the development of Seattle, Coupeville vied for the title of the premier city
in the Puget Sound region.

In 1850, Isaac Ebey was the first permanent
settler to Whidbey Island. Isaac and his wife,
Rebecca, named their 640 acre claim Ebey's
Landing, setting up an adjacent parcel for Isaac's
father, Jacob. In letters to family, Isaac referred to
his claim as "a paradise of nature." Pioneers that
followed homesteaded in the parcels around the
Ebey clan, so that by 1855, pioneers had completely
filled in Ebey's Landing and Penn Cove. Captain

Thomas Coupe, a shipbuilder and merchant and
Coupeville's eponymous settler, claimed 320 acres
of Penn Cove in 1852. Coupe holds the distinction of being the only person to have sailed a
fully rigged sailing ship through Deception Pass.
Washington's territorial government created Island
County in 1853, and Coupeville soon became the
county seat.

Shellfish in Penn Cove provided a staple
of the diet for the Native Americans and are still
commercially valuable today. However, logging
and agriculture drove Coupeville's early economic
success, as did its access to waterways for both
transportation and shipping. Much of the land
around Coupeville is still owned and farmed by
descendants of Coupeville's original families.

In the early 20th century, the island became
an important outpost for national defense. The
population increased with Coupeville's increasing
importance, and the town incorporated in 1910 with
a population of 310. More than double that number
occupied Fort Casey, just a few miles up the road.

The mid-19th century was marked by
occasional violent clashes between the Native

Americans who first lived on the land and the settlers who made their claims. Clashes in Coupeville didn't involve the Salish, with whom the settlers generally had good relationships, but with Native peoples coming from Vancouver Island to the north. The raiding parties often enslaved captives. In 1857, one such party killed Isaac Ebey. By some accounts, the murder was in retaliation for Ebey having killed one of their people.

In the early days of Coupeville's settling, the ratio of men to women was nine to one. Asa Mercer, then 25 years old and president of the University of Washington, traveled back to his native Massachusetts to recruit "educated ladies of good moral standing" to follow him back to Washington State, because "children need teachers, [and] men need wives." These women, known as Mercer Girls, filled many roles in the Puget Sound area. Mercer Girl Flora Engle served as a historian, teacher, and pastor in Coupeville, and she negotiated with farmers and mill men to build a sidewalk to the church.

From the 1880s to the 1920s, Chinese immigrants settled across Admiralty Inlet from Coupeville. Local farmers employed the Chinese as laborers, but other settlers discriminated against them, fearful that the immigrants would take their jobs. The citizens of Whidbey Island targeted them with exclusion acts, hostility, and violence, and the Chinese population on Ebey's Prairie gradually declined. From a population of 200, all that remains of their presence is a single grave in Sunnyside Cemetery, that of tenant farmer Ah Soot. Today, Coupeville recognizes the contributions the Chinese immigrants made to the local economy, and to Coupeville's history in general.

Sunnyside Cemetery

Built atop a rise in the glacial floodplain of Ebey's Landing, Sunnyside Cemetery captures the island's history from pre-Columbian contact through today. It's the final resting place of Susie and Alex Kettle, whose graves lie along the fence line, the only place in the cemetery that accommodated the burial of Native Americans. A blockhouse built as a domestic and defensive structure stands nearby, a reminder of

the Indian Wars. Winfield Ebey was the first to be buried in the cemetery, in 1865. A few years later, his sister sold the land to the county for a single dollar. The cemetery has continued to expand as Whidbey Island's population has grown. In the summer, the Island County Historical Society leads tours of the cemetery. Visitors are welcome year-round.

Racing canoes highlight local Native American seafaring traditions. The annual Penn Cove Water Festival draws thousands of visitors to Coupeville to learn about past and present Native American culture, including canoe racing.

Coupeville Today

Coupeville has preserved its history better than have many small towns. A self-guided walking tour boasts 65 places of interest, including the wharf, a livery and stable, the island's first car dealership, original storefronts, preserved and remodeled 19th-century homes, and blockhouses that served as both homes and protective structures in the years when residents feared attack by Native Americans.

Coupeville also bridges industry and the arts with community events. Penn Cove Shellfish has the largest, oldest mussel farm in the country. Together with the Coupeville Historic Waterfront Association, the company sponsors the annual Penn Cove Musselfest, with farm tours, cooking demonstrations, a mussel-eating contest, and more. The festival has brought tourists and locals together in celebration of the Northwest staple for more than 30 years. Coupeville also hosts an annual Shakespeare Festival; a Water Festival, focused on Native American culture; and numerous art-centric events.

State Route 20, built in 1967, enabled easy access to all of Whidbey Island and the ferry system. Coupeville is also home to the island's hospital. Continued growth led to a need for the preservation of Coupeville's historic importance. The Central Whidbey Island Historic District and Ebey's Landing National Historic Reserve, both established in the 1970s, formed to protect Coupeville's heritage while leaving space for continued population and industrial growth.

Penn Cove is famous for its oysters. At the end of the dock, visitors will find local eateries and shops. According to Penn Cove Shellfish, "Eating an oyster is like kissing a mermaid."

30

Population: 1,035
Founding: 1891

INSETS L to R: The Langely Whale Center offers education about marine mammals. • Prima Bistro is one of several restaurants in Langley. • At the Firehouse Glass Gallery, visitors can try their hand at glassblowing. • Visitors to Langley can walk the promenade along Saratoga Passage.

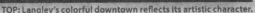

TOP: Langley's colorful downtown reflects its artistic character.

Langley

The Village by the Sea

If the town of Langley were a secret club, the not-so-secret password would be "Anthes." Jacob Anthes, Langley's first European settler, arrived from Germany in 1879 at just 14 years of age, motivated to leave by the threat of compulsory military service. Anthes worked his way from Kansas to San Francisco, heading north to Seattle in 1880, where he met a man who needed someone to work his homestead claim on Whidbey Island. On the island, Anthes cut cordwood and sold it to the Mosquito Fleet, the steamships that transported everything and everyone between Olympia and the Alaskan Panhandle.

Anthes platted the town in 1891 with the help of James Weston Langley, a judge in Seattle and president of the Langley Land and Improvement Company, for whom Anthes named the town. Anthes Avenue, Langley's main street, ran through town to a dock where workers loaded ships with corded wood from the island's dense forests. Steamships carried the wood to the logging camps dotting the island's shores. Within a few years after Anthes platted Langley, economic depression

and a severe storm that damaged the shipping dock threatened the town's survival. A new wharf allowed shipping to resume within a few years. During the gold rush of the late 1890s, Anthes won a contract to supply development efforts north of Seattle. He built a store, a post office, and roads from the shores to the central island, as well as between Langley and nearby Clinton. Anthes' efforts ensured that Langley became a center for transportation and trading.

In the early part of the 20th century, loggers maxed out Whidbey's resources. As a result, transporting goods became expensive, and island farmers lost market share to mainland farmers, whose distribution costs were lower. Eventually, business and residential development replaced much of the farmland. Midcentury, Langley established a port district, with a new focus on a public marina replacing the prior need for a shipping hub.

Artists have long found a haven in Langley. Painters Margaret and Peter Camfferman started the artists colony Brackenwood in the early part of the 20th century. Artist-activists flocked to Langley in the 1960s and '70s, finding kinship with other ecologically minded Whidbey Islanders and joining the existing fight against commercial overdevelopment. The working artists in Langley today represent art from all disciplines, from architecture to theatre, and include the internationally renowned Hedgebrook retreat for women artists.

These days, Langley—the only incorporated city on the southern part of Whidbey Island—is best known as a great place to recreate. Though it's a thoroughly modern town, Langley's history is still visible if you know where to look. The Langley Main Street Association highlights the historic plaques on downtown buildings: "Every older building tells us something about the previous history of the town. When we lose a bit of our history it becomes easier to forget those who came before us."

When Women Ran Langley

In 1910, Washington became the fifth state in the country to allow women to vote, 10 years before the ratification of the 19th Amendment. Washington State was at the forefront of the suffrage effort. Seattle founder Arthur Denny proposed the vote for all women over the age of 18 at Washington's very first legislative session, in 1854.

In 1919, Langley became the focus of national attention when it elected an all-female government in an off-year election. The sitting mayor resigned and two male councilmen followed suit, leading the new mayor, Helen Coe, to replace them with women. Mayor Coe and the city council focused on city improvement, including cleanup and renovation efforts, as well as the construction of sidewalks and a library.

Some observers felt that the women had run the men out of office. A political cartoon commenting on the women's election depicts a woman with the word *truth* above her head shooting arrows at the back of a fleeing man alongside the headline "Running 'em ragged." A small verse accompanying the cartoon reads, "It's quite the rule for gentlemen / To give their seats to ladies fair, / But gosh, It's tough on mayors when / The ladies want the mayor's chair." Councilwoman Margaret McLeod succeeded Mayor Coe in the next administration.

Who Killed Merlin Mariner?

Was it his fiancée, Goldie Digger, or maybe his ex-wife, Rainey Gray? In a unique event that captivates the town and draws tourists as well, the Chamber of Commerce in Langley pulls off an annual Mystery Weekend. A fake newspaper, dozens of clues, and more than 20 actors guide thousands of participants who hope to solve the mystery and take home the grand prize.

A sign on the United Methodist Church in Langley welcomes immigrants and refugees.

Now in its 35th consecutive year, Mystery Weekend is just one of many creative community events in this community known for its artistic expression. Other popular annual events include the Djangofest Northwest Music Festival, billed as a "gypsy jazz festival." Djangophiles from around the world attend this five-day bash. Springtime visitors may catch the Welcome the Whales Festival, held each March to celebrate the return of the gray whales, which often pause at Whidbey Island on their way back to Alaska from Mexico to take advantage of the rich mud-flat feeding grounds.

Imagine a town where people of all ages dress like their favorite sea creatures for the annual whale parade; where public art is everywhere, from sculptures to totem poles to fabulist sidewalk chalk art; where transformed historical buildings house winemakers, coffee roasters, and glassblowers. That's Langley, the Village by the Sea.

Langley has become a haven for all manner of artists, including glassblowers.

31

Population: 1,338
Founding: 1912

INSETS L to R: Nooksack lost its post office in 1992, but it has a great city park. • Old farm equipment decorates a well-maintained yard in Nooksack and highlights the Valley's agricultural lifestyle. • A historic building once used as a funeral home has found new life as Iglesia Hispania, a church serving the Latinx community of Nooksack and Whatcom County, led by Pastor Ivan Montenegro. • Raspberries, blueberries, and black currants are crops grown in Nooksack Valley.

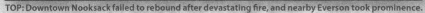

TOP: Downtown Nooksack failed to rebound after devastating fire, and nearby Everson took prominence.

Nooksack

A Valley, a River, a People, a Town

For 12,000 years, the inhabitants of today's Whatcom County were the Lummi, Samish, Semiahmoo, and Nooksack people. The Lummi occupied the westernmost coastal area, and the Semiahmoo and Nooksack lived farther inland, though traditionally groups shared access to the land's diverse resources. One of the Nooksack villages became the town of Nooksack, and today, after more than a century of persistent effort to regain and retain some of their ancestral land, the tribe's headquarters are just down the river in nearby Deming. The river, valley, and town all bear the name Nooksack, whose meaning is somewhat in dispute. The word is often said to mean "mountain men," but the tribe itself states that the name comes from a place, and that it translates to "always bracken fern roots," a reference to close ties between the Nooksack people, their homelands, and their resources.

In the first half of the 19th century, Nooksack took shape. By 1865, 11 city blocks had formed, and the Village of Nooksack was officially platted. Officials Moultrey and Heney of the Nooksack Land Development Company replatted the town in 1890 and renamed it Nooksack City. The newly platted city improved lot standards and claimed more land just before the railroads came through. On the heels of the railroad, a mining boom pushed the population of Nooksack to over 400 residents. Mining continued to thrive, and the lumber, fishery, dairy, and poultry industries followed suit. Fires in the early part of the 20th century repeatedly destroyed much of the city, and Nooksack never recovered the thriving business center it had before the fires. Today, however, Whatcom County is one of the fastest-growing counties in the state, and Nooksack's proximity to Bellingham makes for an easy commute for those who work in the city but want to live in a more rural environment.

In addition to the success of its industrial development, Whatcom County became a hub of educational opportunity in the Northwest as early as the 1890s. The town of Sehome was home to the first regional high school in 1890, and nine years later, the New Whatcom Normal School, known today as Western Washington University, welcomed its first class. Bellingham Technical College, Whatcom Community College, and the Northwest

Indian College added to the county's educational constellation over the next 75 years.

NookChat Keeps the Conversation Going

NookChat is a video series and part of the Washington Rural Heritage project, which documents the early culture and development of Washington State and provides digitized primary resources. The Washington Rural Heritage initiative is helping to pick up where the limits of local libraries and historical societies often leave off due to a lack of funding. NookChat is a series of interviews with longtime Whatcom County residents on topics like early schools, transportation, farming work, and important events. NookChat is an important resource in the preservation of local history and a way to visit the Nooksack Valley and begin to understand what life is like there, even if an in-person visit isn't possible.

The Valley Adapts

Nooksack today appears to be little more than a collection of buildings along State Route 9. As with its past, Nooksack's present is best understood by considering its broader geographic context. Farming is still thriving in Nooksack Valley. Twin Brook Creamery has produced dairy in the valley for five generations, and its products show up in urban centers like Bellingham and Seattle. Demand for locally made products helps keep the valley and county prosperous, but continued prosperity depends in part on whether or not their needs are prioritized politically. Though neither side may have a real sense of what life is like for the other, the line between rural and urban is as thin as milk.

In 2016, Whatcom County grew 2.2%, coming in at 26th place in population growth among metropolitan areas in the country. This growth has affected not only the city of Bellingham, but the entire county, and Nooksack schools are struggling to keep up. The 2016–17 academic year was the largest in terms of student enrollment in area history until the next year, when the numbers increased again. School infrastructure isn't expanding quickly enough to meet the needs of the growing student population. Superintendent Mark Johnson worries that the district will run out of space in 2020 if the community doesn't find a way to meet the district's needs.

Nooksack Valley is a subsection of the larger Skagit Valley. Farmers here raise dairy cattle and grow root vegetables, berries, peas, and other produce.

Despite the rapid pace of growth, Whatcom County in general and Nooksack in particular feel rural. The rural nature of the town is more than a fact—it's a closely held value. Limited access to services and amenities means that communities like Nooksack are less likely to see future economic development, but efforts to preserve existing agricultural cultivation, the steady trickle of tourism to Whatcom County, and the appeal of a rural life lived close to nature may equally likely mean that Nooksack is in no danger. More than a quarter of homes in Nooksack are considered recreational. At the county level, economic development strategies that take Nooksack into account focus on maintaining the rural lifestyle people there hope to keep.

Nooksack and Everson, not 2 miles away, share a school district and a police department. Still, Nooksack retains its identity, and county development plans differentiate the two towns. Recent community development in Nooksack includes new sidewalks and pedestrianized areas, parks, and an improved water system.

So what makes Nooksack different from Everson? It's tempting to define Nooksack in terms of what it lacks in comparison: Everson has restaurants, grocery stores, and a pharmacy, sure. It also has about twice as many people as Nooksack. But what Nooksack lacks in convenience and amenities, it makes up for in a peaceful lifestyle, wide open spaces, and the ever-present view of the North Cascades.

Fires damaged Nooksack's business district in 1906, 1909, 1911, 1913, and 1922. It has never fully recovered, though some businesses have made a small but active comeback.

32

Population: 1,503
Founding: 1891

INSETS L to R: This Sumas home was once the residence of a Methodist minister and later a youth center. Now it houses the museum. • Busy downtown Sumas is a mixture of new and old, bright and dull, nature and commerce. • Gail Kihn brings her journalism background to her current work as Vice President and Treasurer of the Sumas Historical Society and Museum. • The bustle of downtown Sumas quickly gives way to wide open fields and farmland.

TOP: Sumas established its first US Customs office in 1891. The building shown here dates to 1932.

Sumas

Land Without Trees

Just south of the US–Canada border, the Fraser and Nooksack Rivers regularly flood the valley where the town of Sumas lies, preventing much tree growth. In Salish, *Sumas* means "land without trees." The Nooksack people inhabited this grassland prior to the Point Elliot Treaty of 1855, in which they and other Indigenous nations signed away their lands in exchange for fishing and hunting rights. The terms of the treaty required them to relocate to the Lummi Reservation, but they held their ground. Twenty years later, the US government allowed some of them to make small claims on their ancestral land, none of which is held by tribal members today. The Nooksack fought for federal recognition for the next 100 years, finally securing it in 1973.

Robert Johnson became the first non-Native settler of what is now Sumas in the late 1870s, declaring it "the most delightful place I'd ever seen." Dense forest made travel to the area possible only by water at first, but a wagon trail from Bellingham later made travel from the north a bit easier.

Early settlements were simple, consisting mostly of tents that housed settlers and immigrant laborers; many of the latter were Chinese who'd made their way up from California to build the railroads. By 1891, three railroads allowed for travel between Sumas, Vancouver, and Bellingham. With that ease came opium smuggling. Opium was legal at the time, but high tariffs made legal trade expensive. In 1891, Lawrence Flanagan was appointed to catch smugglers at the border. The Sumas border station is the fourth oldest in the nation.

At about the same time the railroads converged in the area, Russ Lambert came to Sumas from Illinois. A lawyer by training, he took the necessary steps to incorporate Sumas and went on to serve variously as mayor, marshal, and judge. Soon, Sumas was a town divided. It had schools and churches as well as saloons and gambling halls, and the community was split between family life and the life built for trappers, loggers, and gold prospectors. During Prohibition, Sumas was the only "wet" town in the region, bringing people from all over.

The Panic of 1893 reduced Sumas's citizens to a subsistence lifestyle, but advances in logging, as well as the discovery of gold, revitalized the community at the turn of the 20th century. The town's population surged when up to 2,000 people came for the gold that Jack Post, Lyman Van Valkenburg, and Russ Lambert had found while prospecting around Mount Baker. After gold and timber ran their course, dairy farming filled the economic void.

John Pen and the Honky Tonk Girl

In the summer of 2019, John Pen of Sumas was 98 years old. More than 60 years earlier, he nurtured a musical legend. After a performance of the Westerners, a country band led by Pen and his brother, at the local Grange, a man approached him and asked if his wife could sing with them. "She has a pretty good voice," the man said. Pen invited her to attend a practice session, and as it turned out, her voice was both pretty and good.

After performing with Pen's group for a few years, she went on to record some of country music's biggest hits, including "Don't Come Home A-Drinkin' (With Lovin' on Your Mind)" and "You Ain't Woman Enough." The 1980 movie based on her 1976 memoir earned Sissy Spacek a Best Actress Oscar. She was inducted into the Country Music Hall of Fame in 1988, published another memoir in 2002, and won a Grammy as recently as 2004.

One of eight children, she grew up in a one-room cabin in Kentucky. When she was 13 years old, she baked a pie for a fundraising auction, only she'd mistakenly loaded it with salt instead of sugar. The highest bidder got to meet the baker. That bidder was Oliver Lynn, better known as "Doolittle" and "Mooney." One month later, he married the baker—you know her as Loretta Lynn.

Digging Up History

With the advent of online commerce, shipping and receiving has become a robust business in Sumas. To avoid international shipping fees, many Canadians have goods sent to Sumas, then drive across the border to pick them up. Out-of-state business is also part of Sumas's economy: Across the railroad tracks is a Foreign Trade Zone, and a Canadian company runs a shingle mill nearby.

With changes in industry have come changes in demographics. Sumas's official website laments that recollections of the town's early years are fading. "It is to be hoped," the site pleads, "that someone, sometime will make an effort to preserve the stories, memories, and photos that exist today for the generations of tomorrow." Enter Gail Kihn.

With the Colors is a yearbook of soldiers from Washington State who served in WWI in 1917, 1918, and 1919. Gail Kihn found a copy of the Whatcom County volume among a box of old papers, one of which contained a handwritten note from Thomas York, an early settler of the area.

Gail grew up in Mission, British Columbia, and made frequent trips to Sumas with her family. After decades in the newspaper business in California, she bought a house in Sumas, sight unseen, when she was ready to retire. She then threw herself into researching and preserving the town's history.

Gail has an encyclopedic knowledge of Sumas, past and present. The building that houses the museum, formerly a parsonage, dates back to 1910. "Metal detectors" turn up treasures such as military badges and give them to the museum, whose volunteers, Gail among them, track down their significance, shine them up, and put them on display.

Gail also exhaustively researches old buildings in town, and in a strange twist of fate, she discovered that she's related to the original owner of the home she lives in. His last name was Nims, an Americanization of Nîmes, the name of the town he came from in France. Mr. Nims came to Washington from New York, which he left around the time of the French and Indian War.

The extent of Gail's research work is amazing; the sheer volume of information she has at her memory's fingertips astonishes. She's vice president and treasurer of the historical society, but her business card should also say "Lead Detective." "Look at this," she says, over and over again, pointing out another piece of Sumas's history. "This is like gold."

A federal building in Sumas known as the Customs House held the offices of customs and immigration from 1932 to 1990. The townspeople saved it from demolition and relocated it just a few blocks from the still-busy border with Canada.

33

Population: 939
Founding: 1883

INSETS L to R: Magnus Anderson's cabin demonstrates how historical preservation efforts draw a through line from past to present. • Riverine industry. • The Courtyard Gallery, formerly home to the Puget Sound Mail Museum and Americana Library. • Skagit River Boutique, formerly home to the Palace Meat Market.

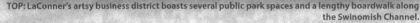

TOP: LaConner's artsy business district boasts several public park spaces and a lengthy boardwalk along the Swinomish Channel.

LaConner

Planted and Grown

In 1867, 15 years after his family founded Seattle, Alonzo Low opened a trading post on the eastern bank of the Swinomish Slough, across from the already established Swinomish Reservation. Low would give up his enterprise, but another early arrival, John Conner, would succeed where Low failed. Conner bought a trading post and post office and renamed the town of Swinomish after his wife, Louisa Anne, combining her initials with their last name to form *LaConner*. To this day, disagreement exists over whether the town's name should be one word or two. In 1869, Conner purchased the deed for the entire town for the sum of $500.

Other notable early settlers include John Hayes, from whom Conner purchased the trading post, and A. G. Tillinghast, who started a mail-order seed supply store. Tillinghast, originally from Pennsylvania, started by experimenting with cabbage seeds, purchasing them from the East Coast and packaging and selling them in Washington. Soon, he had contracts to sell seeds to local farmers. In 1896, Tillinghast produced his first seed catalog under the company's name, Puget

Sound Seed Garden. Eventually renamed the Tillinghast Seed Company, the business continued to produce catalogs until 2003.

The Swinomish Slough flooded regularly, and around the time of LaConner's founding, settlers began diking and damming the land. Settlers worked their own land claims, first clearing and then building dikes to prevent flooding. They worked when the tide was low, reclaiming land from the marsh, leaving channels that they could navigate at high tide. With the dikes in place against the tides, farmers began planting. Like Holland, where many early settlers to the area came from, the Skagit Valley became a major flower bulb growing location of international importance. Other major crops in the area include oats, barley, hay, and potatoes. Tulip production continues to be an important part of the area's agricultural output, as well as its tourist economy. Since the 1980s, pilgrimages to celebrate the valley's beautiful blooms have brought tourist dollars and heavy traffic to LaConner every spring.

Fishing and timber were passingly important to the area, but unlike other nearby towns and towns across the state, the railroad never took hold in LaConner, limiting its economic development. Mount Vernon, which welcomed the railroad, eventually claimed the county seat, and LaConner's population began to decline in size. An influx of artists in the 1960s and '70s contributed to local culture and earned LaConner a reputation as an eclectic hippie town. Today, LaConner's economy is largely tourism-based.

The importance of the Swinomish culture is highly visible from downtown LaConner. The Swinomish Reservation, created by the Point Elliott Treaty of 1855, lies just across the man-made channel, its public event space prominent along the bank. Like other Native American nations, the Swinomish were decimated in the years after first contact with European settlers. Today, the Swinomish Indian Tribal Community is a federally recognized sovereign nation.

One Pioneer's Story

One of the first Scandinavian settlers of LaConner was Magnus Anderson, a Norwegian carpenter who worked on a ship that made frequent trips to the Americas in the days before the Panama Canal. One one voyage, Anderson decided to leave his job and bushwhack through the Panamanian isthmus, and he made it to the West Coast, where he caught another ship headed for San Francisco. There, he took another job as a carpenter, this time on a US transport ship during the Civil War. Anderson became a citizen and voted to reelect Lincoln. After the war, he heard about a mill in the Skagit River Valley and headed north. In 1869, he built a cabin on the north fork of the Skagit River. He went on to build many cabins for his neighbors, and eventually he built the successful Fir Hotel. His original cabin is on display in downtown LaConner, just below City Hall.

Big Life in a Small Town

LaConner has one foot comfortably in the past and the other in the present, as headlines like this, from the *LaConner Weekly News,* show: MESMAN FARMERS COOPERATE ACROSS GENERATIONS and ART COMES ALIVE NOV. 9TH WEEKEND. Walking through the residential area just off downtown, visitors see beautifully preserved Civil War–era homes alongside more-modern construction. Faded signage on businesses like the Skagit River Boutique and the Courtyard Gallery remind shoppers of the Palace Meat Market and the Puget Sound Mail Museum, which originally occupied these buildings. Four museums draw a through line from LaConner's history to the modern Skagit Valley arts scene. A tour of the town may include as many as 160 sites of historic importance, or it can be a pub crawl. From its pleasant public parks and charming downtown business district to its visible preservation of history, LaConner feels like a town that takes pride in itself.

The Swinomish Reservation is directly across the channel from LaConner's boardwalk. In telling the story of its founding, LaConner highlights the importance of the Swinomish.

In the last 20 years, the population of LaConner has grown by 20%. The cost of living here is low, and the opportunity for community is high.

Magnus Anderson, a Norwegian immigrant and carpenter, built a cabin in 1869 on the north fork of the Skagit River. In 1952, the Daughters of Pioneers of Washington moved the cabin to downtown LaConner.

34

Population: 468
Founding: 1909

INSETS L to R: The Skagit River winds through the valley between Lyman and the mountains. • Lyman's city government lives in the historic Birdsie D. Minkler House, built in 1891. • Turning into Lyman, visitors are greeted first by "the horniest tavern in the northwest." • Lyman's business district occupies two blocks on Main Street.

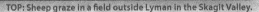

TOP: Sheep graze in a field outside Lyman in the Skagit Valley.

Lyman

Klement, Cooper, and Minkler

A massive logjam on the Upper Skagit made settling prohibitively difficult in much of the valley, and Congress refused to front the estimated $100,000 to solve the problem. James Cochrane, one of the original settlers of Lyman, helped form a company to clear the logjam in 1876. Clearing the logjam meant the river was navigable, reducing the cost of transporting goods back and forth and enabling settlement in the northern part of the valley. Despite the difficulty navigating the river, at the time, nearly 2,000 Skagit Native Americans lived in what is now Lyman. As with many tribes, the smallpox epidemic of the 1920s decimated the Skagit people.

With the logjam cleared, the next step to making the Lyman area habitable was clearing the forest. Logging and timber were Lyman's first industries, and as industry thrived, newcomers arrived. Among the new settlers was Otto Klement, who owned a trading post that functioned as a town center, as well as a post office, after Congress established a mail route including Lyman in 1881. That same year, Scots-Irish immigrants Henry Cooper and his cousin Henry Leggett cut a road through the woods. Prior to the road, the Skagit River had been the only way to transport everything from merchandise to news. Three years later, County Surveyor George Savage platted the town of Lyman, named for the town's first postmaster, Lorenzo P. Lyman. In 1890, the Great Northern Railroad laid tracks through Lyman, and the town began to orient around the rail rather than the river.

Three settlers define Lyman's history: Otto Klement, Henry Cooper, and Birdsey Minkler. Minkler's first important contribution to the area was building the first sawmill on the bank of nearby Mill Creek, in 1878. Minkler grew wealthy and influential as a mill owner and eventually got involved in politics.

Minkler and his family moved to Lyman a few years before the railroad. In 1881, he built a large home known today as the Minkler Mansion, which serves as both a place of historic importance and as Lyman town hall. The eight Minkler children planned to renovate the mansion and repurpose it as a hospital in the early 1910s, but didn't. Maude, the eldest of the Minkler children, lived in the mansion with her husband until she died in 1954.

In 1889, Minkler represented Skagit County in the first-ever Washington State Assembly. In 1906, he became a state senator and went on to earn election to a second term. Upon his death at age 61, an unknown newspaper contained an obituary noting the following:

> The name of Birdsey D. Minkler will ever be associated with those of the sturdy characters who, with unfaltering courage and determination battled with nature in her swamp and forest strongholds, bringing order out of chaos, making fertile the waste places. To such as he the Northwest will ever pay tribute.

From his influence on the local economy and his expansive family to his participation in national politics, Birdsey Minkler left a lasting legacy in Lyman.

History's Mysteries

The Minkler family history in Lyman contains a few notable mysteries. In the 1855 Point Elliott Treaty, 81 Indigenous leaders surrendered their land in exchange for protected reservations and the retention of Native sovereignty. The chief of the Upper Skagit people did not sign the treaty, and the Upper Skagit protested the subsequent seizure of their land. Tensions rose, but war did not break out. The best records available don't tell a perfectly clear story, but they indicate that part of the disputed land fell on what Minkler claimed as his property. Ultimately, the Native Americans mostly relocated to undisputed areas.

The most mysterious Minkler family story centers on the death of Birdsey and Hannah's third child, Garfield Arthur Minkler. Born at the beginning of his father's success, Garfield was the first Minkler to attend university in the early years of the University of Washington, where he played football. After his academic career, he moved back to Lyman and was elected mayor. Five months later, he died by gunshot. Rumors of Garfield's feeling inadequate in comparison to his brother John, paired with an

annulled marriage, support the theory that Garfield killed himself. However, rumors persist that one of Garfield's brothers or a disgruntled union member may have killed him, or even that he died in a fire at the mill. His death shocked the town of Lyman, and as suicide seemed unbelievable, rumors of murder took root.

The Lyman Tavern, prominently located near the entrance from Highway 20, advertises itself as "the horniest tavern in the Northwest." You'll have to visit Lyman if you want to be in on the joke!

Lyman Is Just Right

Lyman is a well-kept town of tidy yards lining a wide front street. Banners affixed to light posts announce the annual car show. The town has a stable population that has seen slow but steady growth since its founding. Most people work in construction or manufacturing. With proximity not only to the natural beauty of Skagit Valley but also amenities like nearby colleges, hospitals, and a passenger railway, Lyman offers an affordable life in an idyllic location that's not too far from modernity to be isolated and not close enough to a city to be urban.

As with other towns in the Skagit Valley, Lyman faces flood conditions that occasionally reach the level of emergency. Rising waters erode the bank at the end of Main and Second Streets, displacing families and putting pressure on local government to find a solution. Lyman residents hope to preserve land that has in some cases been a family asset going back to the early days of the town's existence.

Since 2000, Lyman has hosted an annual car and craft show, drawing residents and car enthusiasts from around the region. The event features local art, a community breakfast, raffles, and classes.

35

TOP: Hamilton's cheerful town sign and well-kept park contrast with some of the buildings in town.

Population: 309
Founding: 1877

INSETS L to R: Nature takes back old farm implements, lending a pastoral quality to Hamilton. • The Hamilton Cafe and Store, one of Hamilton's only business-es, is the center of town life. • Hamilton's main intersection. • Of the few buildings in down-town Hamilton, many seem to be in disuse.

Hamilton

A Logjam for the History Books

It's not always easy to see a town's history. Ham-ilton is one such town: Skagit County historians and folklorists have spent a decade tracking down information about its founder, William Hamil-ton, in a search that has taken them all over the country. According to their research, the earliest attempts at settlement in what would eventually become Hamilton were by miners hoping to repeat the success of the Fraser River gold rush, followed by railroad prospectors. Both groups found that a tremendous logjam on the upper Skagit made travel in the area too difficult to consider settling. A group of three prospectors named Everett, Graham, and Stevens made it around that logjam and, aided by Native Americans, found deposits of coal ore. Civil War veteran James Conner, brother of LaConner founder John, soon joined. Conner developed the first coal mine in the area and shipped its product to San Francisco, despite the extreme difficulty required to navigate around the logjam in present-day Mount Vernon. The first shipments began in the spring of 1875. A few years later, the settlers cleared the logjam. More settlers came, from as far

away Iowa, Bavaria, and Quebec. In 1876, William Hamilton arrived with a wife and children, bring-ing a family to what had been a bachelor town. 1877 was a big year. Settlers cleared the logjam, and on the Fourth of July, Hamilton named the town for himself, going on to build several houses, a hotel, a post office, and a store.

Stories of early settlers to Hamilton reveal that then, as today, Hamilton was a place to live but not necessarily a place to work. Companies promoting work in Coal and Iron Mountains just across the river drew laborers with the promise of lucrative employment. Miners and loggers set up camp in what would become Hamilton but tended to work farther up or down the river.

So Tarnal Many Slippers

Less is known about Hamilton's namesake than its other early settlers. The Slipper brothers left behind a much more detailed legacy. Today's town hall, open to the public for one hour per day, is in the three-story home on Maple Street known as the Slipper Mansion. A high school trouble-maker and one of nine siblings, John Slipper left his home in eastern England just after graduating. In striking out for America, he left behind three centuries of family history in the area. Three of the Slipper boys would emigrate and work their way across American farmlands, eventually landing in Hamilton, where John soon created the Eagle Shingle Company, which would in turn be the genesis of more than two dozen local businesses that John owned with his brother, Fred. Massive flooding a few years later prompted the Slippers to move their business back from the river's edge. At the same time, they started a hardware store, which quickly became successful, cementing the Slipper brothers as important members of the community. Soon, the brothers married sisters, Lola and Gertrude Sprinkle, and they began to grow their families. The *Hamilton Herald* reported on the Slipper family in 1909, noting, "There are now so tarnal many Slippers in town that it will be difficult to segregate them when such partition is necessary. There are three Mesdames Slippers, four Messrs. Slippers, three Miss Slippers, and one Master Slippers and one naturally hesitates to say how many more there will be." The Slipper family invested in logging, mining, and manufacturing, in addition to their retail businesses, and they got involved in banking and local politics. A fire in 1925 ripped through the town, destroying 19 buildings, and Hamilton struggled to rebuild. The grocery store chain Piggly Wiggly had recently opened in nearby Sedro, and the introduction of the automobile meant that people were free to make purchases outside their town. Though the Slipper family decided not to rebuild their businesses, their legacy lives on in Hamilton—which somehow wasn't renamed Slippertown.

In the Flood Zone

A visit to Hamilton today begs the question: What makes a town a town? Though the number of people living in Hamilton has fluctuated over the years, the current population is 25% below the level it was in 1900, shortly after the town's founding. It's a town that contains many stop signs, but it doesn't seem to need them. A smattering of homes cluster along short roads leading quickly to dead ends. The main intersection is home to a small bar and a smaller combination store and deli. For most of their needs, including work, many residents have to travel to nearby Sedro-Woolley or other towns.

Like many towns known for coal and iron, Hamilton has been referred to as the "Pittsburgh of the West." Towns claiming this title include nearby Coal Creek and Concrete, as well as Kirkland, Washington, and Pueblo, Colorado. (Often, this title indicates a town that didn't live up to its initial promise of economic success.)

Unemployment in Hamilton is higher than the statewide average. Still, many residents of Hamilton stay. Some of them have historical roots here, and others appreciate the affordable housing. In addition, Hamilton is beautiful, tucked between the shadow of the North Cascades and the Skagit River. The river, though, is part of the problem.

Hamilton is smack in the middle of the Skagit River floodplain, and for the last 30 years, the residents have been considering moving the town outside of it. In the meantime, regular flooding has forced many families out. Barring federal support, it isn't likely that the residents of Hamilton will come up with the needed funding to move their town. In the meantime, they remain committed to Hamilton, and to each other.

With just a few dozen more people living in Hamilton now than at the time of its founding, Hamilton is in danger of becoming a ghost town. At least one source notes Hamilton as "semi-ghost."

WELCOME	
Hamilton Cafe & Store	Boots Bar & Grill
Museum	Centennial Resources LLC
A Bend In The River RV Park	
Norm's RV Park	Janicki Industries
Dills Creek, Inc.	Post Office

36

Population: 729
Founding: 1909

INSETS L to R: The breezeway of Concrete High School spans the road to the school. At the time of its construction, the school held the title of "finest in the state." • A mural over the old police station and fire department building depicts the town in its environment, nestled in the foothills of the North Cascades. • The quiet streets of Concrete. • The Baker River Dam, constructed in 1925 from Concrete concrete, created Lake Shannon.

TOP: If someone in Concrete says they're going to "the store," they're likely headed to Cascade Supply.

Concrete

Company Town

In the late 1800s, Amasa Everett, one of the original three prospectors to find coal ore in Hamilton, sold his coal stake and settled a short distance away, near the mouth of the Skagit River. A decade later, he discovered his ranch contained a great deal of limestone. Everett's samples convinced financiers of the likelihood of success in the area, and they formed the Washington Portland Cement Company in 1892 on the Baker River. Six years later, the Superior Portland Cement Company opened on the opposite bank. Either side of the river seemed its own company town, and in fact, residents used two names: Baker City, for the west side of town, representing Magnus Miller's original platting, and Concrete City east of the river, where the community centered around the Washington Portland Cement Company. In 1909, shortly after Superior Portland Cement got underway, the towns voted to merge and adopt the name of Concrete. In every way, Concrete is a company town. The town sprang up around the company, and the company's name represented its product: concrete. Ten years after the merger, Superior bought out their competitors

and dismantled Washington Portland. A rail trestle allowed for the transport of clay and limestone over the Baker River. The Baker River dam, completed in 1925, created Lake Shannon, which inundated the trestle. After that, the company constructed a tram that transported material above the town. They installed nets to protect the homes below from falling rocks.

Despite the town's name, wooden buildings made up most of Concrete until 1921, when fires destroyed much of the town. Subsequent buildings made use of the town's eponymous material resource, and many of those early concrete buildings are still there today. The National Register of Historic Places includes several structures in Concrete, such as the 200-foot Henry Thomson Bridge, completed in 1918 and spanning the Baker River, at one point the longest single-span concrete bridge in the world. Concrete High School, opened for the first time in 1952, took the prize that year for "finest high school in the state." The school is architecturally interesting in that it lies on both sides of a road, the two halves joined by a breezeway that visitors drive beneath. The school, as well as the town, became well-known after the publication of *This Boy's Life* in 1989, a memoir recounting author Tobias Wolff's upbringing in Concrete. A 1993 movie based on the book starred Leonardo DiCaprio and Robert DeNiro as Tobias Wolff and his stepfather, respectively. Visitors to Concrete today will first notice the old concrete silos painted for the movie in towering red letters that say WELCOME TO CONCRETE. Lone Star Industries, the final owner of the cement plant, closed it down in 1967.

Mount Baker–Snoqualmie National Forest

The foothills of the North Cascade Mountains rise just beyond town, and Concrete and surrounding towns are popular jumping-off points for hiking in Mount Baker–Snoqualmie National Forest. Sauk Mountain offers 5,500 feet of elevation gain for ambitious hikers, while nearby Rockport and Rasar State Parks have many easy and wheelchair-accessible trails.

A little farther east on Highway 20, an arduous 18-mile hike leads to Desolation Peak, where Jack Kerouac lived in the fire lookout he wrote about in the 1958 novel, *Dharma Bums*. Known as much for lush old-growth forests as alpine lakes and meadows, the North Cascades in the Concrete area are on many a traveler's must-do hiking list.

More than Meets the Eye

Concrete today is similar to other small towns in the area. As with other towns, changes in the industrial economy have affected it negatively. It's the type of place where a store might be referred to as *the* store. It's the type of place where, as one resident told me, a kid might like to come home to visit and even stay awhile, but only when the weather's nice. The town is quiet, and most businesses are closed, permanently, it seems, but a new bakery on the west side of town shows that commerce in Concrete isn't strictly past tense. A children's garden is an explosion of color on the hill behind Silo Park.

The Concrete Historical Museum is a tiny building tucked behind the main thoroughfare. It's closed for much of the year, though the community holds meetings there. Though it occupies a small space, the museum does a tremendous amount to preserve the history of the town of Concrete.

The Concrete Heritage Museum has preserved yearbooks, photography, and newspapers, ensuring the posterity of headlines like this, from February 4, 1913: "Let Mr. Stickley Explain About the Main Street 'Improvements': Conscientious Socialist Warns Comrades to Beware of the Man Who Wrecked Local Organization for Personal Gain."

There, visitors can learn about life in a timber town before concrete production when industry centered around logging. The museum's website offers a downloadable walking tour of town, as well as yearbooks and articles from the *Concrete Herald* going back as far as the early 1900s. As well, signs placed around town explain the history and importance of local buildings and monuments. Visitors who take a quick look around Concrete will appreciate the beautiful setting and the novelty of the welcome sign. Those who take the time to take the walking tour will learn that there's a lot more to this small town than initially meets the eye.

On Halloween in 1938, Orson Welles broadcast the now-infamous radio play *War of the Worlds*. Unfortunately, the town of Concrete lost power mid-broadcast, and many residents really did believe that Martians were invading.

37

Population: 1,406
Founding: 1945

INSETS L to R: The gym at the Darrington Community Center. • 428 students attend school from grades pre-K through 12, and all of them are Loggers! • It's tough to keep a bookstore and coffee shop going in a small town. • Darrington lies at the foothills of the Mt. Baker-Snoqualmie National Forest, a key resource for recreation in the region.

TOP: Logging and milling are still a meaningful part of the Darrington economy.

Darrington

From Logging to Loggerheads

Darrington's location on a plain below Mount Baker–Snoqualmie Wilderness was originally a gathering place for the Skagit Indians, and the Sauk-Suiattle had a village nearby. In the late 1880s, James Bedal homesteaded on the plain. He married a Sauk-Suiattle woman named Susan Wa-wet-kin and started the first logging business in the area. Though that first business would fail, by any account, the heyday of Darrington lasted a long time.

Unlike other small towns in Washington, whose history of logging derives directly from the development of the railroad, Darrington's logging industry has always been home-grown. Before timber, miners pursued mineral wealth in the area. According to Dan Rankin, who's served as mayor since 2010, there's a local saying: "We were looking for gold. We found the gold was in the timber."

In the 1970s, an industry of entrepreneurial loggers was in full swing. Mayor Rankin remembers as many as 30 companies with between 2 and 50 employees each. These small operations referred to themselves as "gypo" loggers, working independently to deliver timber from surrounding

old growth forest to the mills. In 1974, Washington State adopted the Forest Practices Act (FPA), which regulates timber growth and harvesting. The FPA, in combination with subsequent environmental protection legislation, led to Washington having some of the strictest forest practices rules in the country. Today, Rankin says, independent logging companies still operate in the Darrington area, but their numbers have dropped by as much as 90%.

The 1994 Northwest Forest Plan was particularly influential in changing the logging industry in Darrington; it helped resolve a land-management conflict that pitted local loggers against wildlife advocates committed to protecting the northern spotted owl. Residents variously remember the time between the height of logging and the Northwest Forest Plan as the years of "the owl wars" and "the timber wars." Mayor Rankin describes the conflict as a bitter one: "People left. They went into the urban and suburban core and found different ways to make a living." Though bitterly divided, both the owl-habitat preservationists and the loggers identify as environmentalists. "The foresters of yesteryear saw ourselves as environmentalists because we lived here every day," Rankin says. "A working forest and preservation run in tandem."

Darrington's future, like its past, remains tied to the forest, though the terms have changed. Today's forest management practices seek a balance between creating economic opportunity through continued logging with a focus on the bio-diversity and health of the forest. Visitors to Darrington might enjoy a short hike on the Old Growth Reserve Loop. The trees there are between 150 and 600 years old, transporting visitors to a time long before the owl or timber wars, before logging, before Darrington even had a name.

Home of the Loggers

The Darrington Community Center is truly the center of this community. It's the place where the town comes together for everything from basketball games to weddings and funerals. Mayor Rankin says that when someone dies, "the funeral ladies" get together and provide all the food so that the grieving family doesn't have to worry about it. Once a year, the women host a Happy Day feast, providing dinner just to celebrate and share community.

Courtside in the Center's gymnasium, Mayor Rankin explains that the building came together through volunteer labor, from architectural drawings to the tongue-and-groove floorboards. Local loggers harvested, planed, and prepared the timber. In 1954, the center opened its doors. High above the basketball hoops near the vaulted ceiling, light streams through the windows. Through the southern window, Whitehorse Mountain is visible from center court, as it is from any other point in town.

A Changed (and Changing) Economy

Looking at a topographical map of Darrington, it's easy to imagine it returned to its pre-contact state, as though nature might take it back. The Boulder, Stillaguamish, Sauk, Suiattle, and White Chuck river drainages flow around the town. Mountains rise in every direction. Zoom in, and see street signs; zoom out, and wonder that civilization ever manages to establish itself in such a far-flung place.

Despite, or perhaps because of, its distance from a larger community, Darrington is home to a number of businesses, including a sizable grocery store, recreation outfitters, healthcare, banking, and graphic design. For some, owning a business in Darrington is a labor of love that can't last forever.

Whitehorse Mountain stands watch over the south end of Darrington. According to local mythology, Whitehorse stands between her husband, Three Fingers, and his mistress, Mount Higgins.

The owner of Mountain Loop Books and Coffee has been in business for eight years and has decided to sell. He's hoping to sell the place as is, but if no buyer appears, he'll empty the place and close the doors. "I'd like to have a coffee shop to go to," he says. Without his business, there won't be one.

Though local businesses struggle, The Darrington Collaborative strives to provide opportunities for economic growth. The Collaborative, a partnership between federal and local stakeholders representing legislators, educators, conservationists, and the timber industry, aims to maximize community involvement in forest management. Their mission is to provide forestry and business education for young people while creating jobs, increasing harvest, and safeguarding the health of waterways.

Darrington High School's annual graduation is the "happiest and saddest day of the year," Mayor Rankin says. The town watches its youth leave, knowing they likely won't return, although Mayor Rankin did. Born in Darrington, he left for 20 years but didn't go far. By now, he's been back for as long as he was away. In 1919, Rankin's grandfather came to Darrington to open a butcher shop. In 2019, the Rankin family celebrated 100 years in Darrington. Dan Rankin has been mayor since 2008, having returned to reinvest in his home community, and he's optimistic that with the right opportunities, others will too. Like a forest in a period of regrowth, Darrington is a beautiful and hopeful place.

Though the industry has declined greatly since its heyday, logging and milling are still a meaningful part of the Darrington economy.

38

TOP: Dorothy and Lee Pickett's former home now serves as the Pickett Historical Museum.

Population: 160
Founding: 1907

INSETS L to R: Doolittle Pioneer Park boasts an original saw used to quarry Index's granite. • Index lies at the foothills of the Cascades, cut through by the Skykomish River. • Bush House, currently under renovation, is one of Index's early hotels, dating from 1893. • Another view of the historical museum.

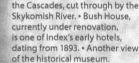

Index

Four Industries Become One

When local historian Louise Lindgren walks up the steps at the Washington State Capitol building in Olympia, she knows she's looking at granite from Index. Granite quarrying has long been a part of Index's history, but industry in the tiny town didn't begin with quarrying. As was the case in many other towns, it was the railroad that brought the first workers to Index. Logging followed the railroad as an industry in its own right, but initial logging was to clear the right-of-way for the Northern Pacific Railroad. Then came quarrying, mining, and a mill, and finally tourism.

Index has resident and nationally known photographer Lee Pickett to thank for the photographic record he left of the town, and of most of Washington State. After Pickett died, his wife, Dorothy, gave much of his collection to the University of Washington, where it remains protected in the Suzzallo Library. Of late, the Index Historical Society has begun buying the photographs back from UW, one archival piece at a time. The Picketts' home is now the Historical Society's museum and is equal parts labor of love and scholarship. Louise Lindgren describes taking care of her friend, Dorothy Pickett, after she had a stroke in the early 1990s. Though the Picketts' house is now the local museum, some of the house remains as it was. Lindgren pointed out the stove where Dorothy would make tea for the two of them and the table near the window where they'd sit and chat. "She could look out the window from her kitchen table and make sure everything in her town was okay," says Lindgren of her friend.

The Picketts were an important family in Index, but Persis and Amos Gunn hold the blue ribbon for first family. The Gunns, who moved to Index from Kansas, owned a mine in the area and platted the town of Index in 1893, already imagining a community based on natural resource development and recreation. In 1891, the town got a post office, and so it needed a name. Persis Gunn chose Index for the mountain, which she said looked like an index finger, leading to the popular myth that Index's first family named the mountain, when in fact the mountain's name appears on maps that precede the Gunns' arrival in town.

Before the mines, the quarry, and the railroad, the Skykomish people inhabited the area now called Index. The Point Elliott Treaty of 1855 dissolved distinctions, from a federal perspective, between several Native American nations, lumping them all under the Tulalip reservation. None of the seven villages that once existed in the Skykomish river basin remain today, and very few photos exist of the Skykomish people.

Industry in Index went from boom in 1905 to decline by 1940, and the construction of Highway 2 made Index an easily bypassed destination. Today, it's a hot spot for outdoor recreation.

Saving Heybrook Ridge

In 2006, Buse Timber announced plans to harvest Heybrook Ridge, overlooking Index, for the first time since 1975. With images of the formerly clear-cut land in mind, the people of Index launched an effort to raise $1.3 million to buy the land from the company. Thanks to a few years' hard work, a local bequest, an international effort, and a matching conservation grant, the Friends of Heybrook Ridge secured 130 acres of the land—35 more than Buse had planned to clearcut—for Snohomish County Parks. Though media sought to cover the story in terms of David versus Goliath, Louise Lindgren cites Buse Timber as a key player in a cooperative effort to find a solution that met the community's needs, as well as those of the company. Today, Heybrook Ridge is available as a resource for natural and historical interpretation and recreation.

Washington's Yosemite

What makes Index tick? As visitors can find out by doing a scavenger hunt at the Pickett Historical Museum, the answers include key concepts like recreation and responsibility, as well as pragmatic concerns such as the post office and maintaining an educational system. Index is a town run nearly entirely on volunteer labor. Even the mayor earns a small stipend, but not enough to be called a salary. When floods or fires happen, or when a building or a piece of land needs saving, all hands are on deck, as they are every day, to keep the town alive.

As early as 1905, Index had a reputation as a recreational paradise for hunters, fishermen, and climbers alike. Organizations like the Seattle-based Mountaineers and the Access Fund have prioritized stewardship of Index as a regional resource for recreation. A few local businesses provide professionally guided rafting and kayaking trips on the Skykomish River, and rock climbers regularly visit the Index Town Wall, site of a former quarry, as well as the boulders of nearby Goldbar.

The Pickett Historical Museum is the former home of Dorothy Pickett, wife of Lee Pickett, who documented Washington State through photography. His works are now housed at the University of Washington in Seattle.

Though significant change might seem unlikely or distant for this tiny community, renovation is underway now of one of Index's original five hotels, the Bush House, seen in photos as early as 1893. The new Bush House will offer hotel rooms, a restaurant, and space for special events, as well as the promise of local economic opportunity, in terms of both jobs and revenue for the town. Some fear that this kind of change will bring greater development and rising real estate prices, and generally be the ruin of the collaborative community Index has always been. Since its founding, the population of Index hasn't moved much in either direction, and people here like it that way. Louise Lindgren says the long winters and rain discourage most. "If people can stay for more than two years, they're keepers," she says. As for Louise? She came in 1976 and never looked back. Index is as much her town as anyone's. She's supposes she won't be around to see the changes that feel inevitable, and she's glad for it. "I'll never leave," she says. "They're going to have to float me down the river."

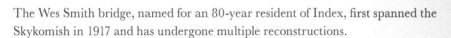

The Wes Smith bridge, named for an 80-year resident of Index, first spanned the Skykomish in 1917 and has undergone multiple reconstructions.

39

Population: 712
Founding: 1892

INSETS L to R: Taniya Roberts painted this mural of Sacagawea looking over the Columbia. Lewis and Clark are silhouetted in the bottom-right corner. • Established in 1912, the Bingen Congregational Church became the Gorge Heritage Museum in 1984. • Viewed from above, Bingen's industrial zone appears to take up nearly as much area as the town. • The land in Bingen cedes quickly to the basalt foot-hills of the Columbia Gorge.

TOP: Bingen sits just down the hill from the larger community of White Salmon.

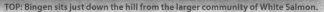

Bingen

What Lies Beyond

It must be true that there are only so many kinds of landscapes in the world. Still, it seems terrifically lucky to think of leaving one's home country in the late 1800s and arriving in an entirely new country, only to find that the landscape seems to replicate the one left behind. Such is the situation in which Theodor Suksdorf found himself in 1892.

Bingen, Washington, sits on a curve of the Columbia River just across from Hood River, Oregon. Drive up the hill to White Salmon, or east toward Stevenson, and Mount Hood comes into view, but from the flats of Bingen, the mountain is hidden. Suksdorf's home city of Bingen am Rhine, Germany, occupied a strikingly similar landscape, with forested land sweeping down toward habitable flats that meet the wide Rhine River, hills rising across the water. As Suksdorf settled into this new Bingen, the Jewett family, settlers from Wisconsin, moved in just up the hill. Though details are uncertain, it seems the Jewetts and the Suksdorfs did not get along. The post office became central to their feuding.

At the time, the job of postmaster was an important one. Postmasters were exempt from military service. They had to post a bond to secure the post, and they had to agree to work on the roads. The President appointed postmasters to larger towns. Most postmasters performed the duty as a second job.

The post office had been established in Bingen Landing, *née* Warner's Landing, in 1868. Theodore Suksdorf was the postmaster. In 1880, Jacob Hunker started a store up the hill and took over the job of postmaster, moving the location of the office to his store and thereby establishing the town of White Salmon. To this day, the railroad stops at Bingen–White Salmon, as neither town would concede to the other.

Klickitat County, nearly 1,900 square miles, takes its name from the Klickitat people. The Klickitat were a nomadic group whose territorial home ranged from the North Cascades south to the Rogue River Basin and all the way to the coast. Malaria outbreaks in the early 19th century devastated area Indigenous populations, and the

Klicktat may have settled in what were previously Chinookan village sites. After participating in the strife between the US and Yakama and Cowlitz peoples, the Klicktat integrated with those tribes and were signatories on the treaty that led to the Yakama Reservation. By some estimates, in 1970, Washington State was home to only a few dozen Klickitat people. The word *Klickitat* may mean "beyond" in Chinookan, a reference to the people who lived beyond the Cascades.

She Who Watches

As Klickitat County's economy moved from sheep ranching to timber and agricultural products, development included bridging and, twice, damming the Columbia River. Construction of the Dalles Dam created Celilo Lake, inundating a fishing and trading site important to Indigenous populations, who had inhabited the area for more than 10,000 years. Inundating the area required exhuming and relocating Native cemeteries, petroglyphs, and pictographs, as well as the entire village of Wakemap. William Clark, of Lewis and Clark fame, described Wakemap as "a great emporium . . . where all the neighboring nations assemble."

One petroglyph preserved from inundation is a depiction of Tsagaglalal, or She Who Watches. According to the myth, Tsagaglalal was a regional chief who lived in the rocks above the villages. The trickster Coyote turned her into a rock, telling her that the world would not allow women to be chiefs much longer. In rock form, Tsagaglalal watches over her people forever.

Bingen Is in Business

Bingen's early economic development depended on the timber industry, which began to ramp up in the area around the turn of the 19th century, and fruit orchards, which predated the timber industry in the area by three decades. To this day, both trades remain a productive part of Bingen's economy.

Despite a severely curtailed timber industry in the state, SDS Lumber, based in Bingen, is a major employer. The company started in 1946, when "there was a sawmill behind every stump." Now in its eighth decade of operation, SDS continues to generate nearly $60 million in annual revenue and provides jobs to 250 employees in Bingen.

Farmers began developing Klickitat County agriculture by planting wheat, oats, and barley, but soon, apples, pears, and cherries became highly remunerative crops. Still today, orchard-based products make up nearly 25% of the county's farm products, not counting the county's recent foray into winemaking.

The towns of Bingen and White Salmon, separated by just a few miles, seem together to make one community, despite the feuds of their past. Bingen has a theatre and the Gorge History Museum; White Salmon has one of Klickitat County's two libraries.

Underwood Fruit Company in Bingen employs 300 people, working with 55 growers on 90 orchards between Mount Adams and Mount Hood. The company suffered a setback in 2017, when a fire destroyed its pear-packing line, but the company was able to salvage its apple-packing operation.

Visitors to Bingen and White Salmon may not be able to distinguish between the two towns, which feel interconnected. They will notice, however, the many opportunities to participate in nature. The Columbia River watershed and the hills of the gorge offer endless opportunities for hiking, fishing, and windsurfing. A $2 fare gets you across the Hood River Bridge and into Oregon, and Portland is a mere 60 miles away. Then again, why leave? It's "a place to live and work," as banners flying from light poles advise.

The view looking southwest from a hill between Bingen and White Salmon shows a glimpse of the town of Bingen and the wide Columbia River as it heads through the gorge toward The Dalles.

40

Population: 1,302
Founding: 1942

INSETS L to R: Businesses line up along the four blocks that surround a park in downtown Tieton. • Tieton's town square is also its City Park. • Tieton's high elevation creates a microclimate suitable for late-ripening fruit. • Fruit packing and storage is an important part of Tieton's economy.

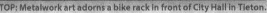

TOP: Metalwork art adorns a bike rack in front of City Hall in Tieton.

Tieton

You Have Arrived

Prior to white settlement, the area known today as Tieton was a rest stop for the Taitnapam people who had seasonal settlements along the Tieton River, a tributary of the Naches River. The conflicts known as the Indian Wars following the treaties of 1855 drove the Taitnapam people out of their home lands, and many enrolled with the Yakama Nation. Indigenous people in the Yakima valley lost 6 million acres of their ancestral homeland. By 1902, the United States Post Office had established an office on the hill above Naches River and named it Tieton.

Tieton is well-known for its lush orchards and its economy is based on fruit production, but early agricultural development was difficult. Until the Reclamation Act brought irrigation to the area in the 1910s, only dryland farming was possible in Tieton, which receives just nine inches of rainfall annually. With irrigation, the Northern Pacific Railroad's promises of a land of prosperity came to fruition.

In the early years, the community worked exceedingly hard with very little yield. Philande Kelley claimed a homestead in 1880. That winter, he froze to death attempting to rescue his horses

from a blizzard. History recognizes the hardworking women of Tieton too. Margaret and Wesley Crews had a homestead in Tieton. When Wesley left for work in nearby Naches, Margaret took care of their three children and all the farm required. Margaret went on to start the first Sunday school in Tieton, as well as the first women's club in central Washington, the Tieton Mothers' Club.

In 1908, Tieton built its first school, and by 1944 the school district had consolidated. Post-irrigation, a wave of Finnish immigrants brought the tradition of saunas to the community. The agricultural economy flowered, and trains began carrying apples and pears out of Tieton. Soon, several companies produced, transported, and warehoused Tieton's products. By the 1940s, Tieton's farmers earned north of $500 per acre, and the union became the first in the nation to repay the government for the expensive water reclamation project.

Visitors can learn much about Tieton's history from the Tieton History Project, a series of tile mosaics affixed to buildings. The mosaics detail the history of downtown as told through interviews with local residents. Tieton's development slowed in the second half of the 20th century, as automobile travel became widely accessible and box stores moved into the much larger city of nearby Yakima. At the same time, Tieton experienced another population boom. In the 1980s, Latino immigrants began moving to Tieton. Their participation in the local community and economy helped keep Tieton alive. Visitors to Tieton today will find the town's history lettered on the glittering town walls, rivaled only by the apple- and pear-colored shine of its present.

Endless Possibilities in Tieton

In the 1980s, Elidia and Juan Delgado became the first Mexican family to buy a home in Tieton. All five of their children grew up to become teachers in the local school district. Today, more than 70% of Tieton's residents identify as Hispanic or Latinx, many of whom are second- and third-generation Mexican American. Latinx families don't just work farms in the area; they own farms in the area. They travel to Olympia, the state capital, to advocate for policy that accounts for the needs and interests of the agricultural industry.

Food safety is a hot topic in agricultural production now. *Good Fruit Grower,* a publication covering fruit production in Washington State, recently highlighted the story of Erika Espinoza, a Safe Quality Food expert who began working on the line repacking apples when she was 15 years old. After earning a business degree, she now works in human resources for Domex Superfresh Growers. When asked what she'd say to a young person in the industry today, she said, "The possibilities are endless in this industry."

Tiny but Mighty

Tieton is a small town uniquely positioned to make a big comeback. It sits atop a vast valley of interconnected communities in a county of 250,000 people. Yakima, a city of 100,000, is just 20 miles away. Both residential and commercial real estate are affordable in Tieton, and the town is set in a beautiful landscape. These are some of the reasons Ed

Marquand and Mike Longyear of Seattle founded Mighty Tieton, a business incubator for artists.

Ed and Mike were out on a bike ride one day when Ed got a flat tire. He pulled up next to an abandoned fruit warehouse to fix it and noticed that the building was both for sale and unlocked. Stepping inside, he saw the kind of space any artist would love to have. The two transformed the warehouse into living and working spaces.

The Tieton River, a tributary of the Naches River, flows through the lush landscape. Orchards climb toward Tieton, giving way to the gentle rise of furrowed hills.

Today, the Mighty Tieton houses a metalwork studio, printmaking shop, and sound studio. Marquand set up the printmaking shop and bindery in the town square, near a gallery space, and established a nonprofit, Tieton Arts and Humanities. The organization sponsors art projects like LitFUSE, a poetry workshop; Art in the Park, offering free art classes for kids; and the Tieton Mosaic Project, a public-art initiative that received a grant from the National Endowment for the Arts. Another organization, Friends in Tieton, is fundraising for a new soccer field and basketball court and working to promote local sports in the area.

Cyclists should check out Tour de Tieton, a midsummer bike ride with 25-mile and 50-mile scenic routes, plus locally made beer and cider at the finish and proceeds going to support Tieton Arts and Humanities. Later in the summer, the Highland Community Days festival is a weekend of parades, live music, family fun, and community togetherness. Día de Muertos (Day of the Dead) provides a space for everyone to celebrate life and remember the deceased, including a community *ofrenda* (altar) to which everyone is welcome to contribute.

At first, Tieton may seem like a sleepy town with little going on. If you sit in the park in the middle of the town square and let your eyes adjust, you may start to notice that there's something special about this place.

The tallest things in Tieton are the fruit boxes. Though commerce has waxed and waned in the region, an infusion of new residents and a focus on the arts are revitalizing this beautiful town.

41

Population: 710
Founding: 1908

INSETS L to R: Downtown Naches offers locally owned shops and restaurants like this cafe, Nier the Nook. • Historic Naches Trail is paved where it runs near the town of Naches. • Thompson's Farm is open for u-pick during harvest season. • This historic service depot has been transformed into a welcome sign.

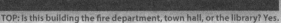

TOP: Is this building the fire department, town hall, or the library? Yes.

Naches

A Steep Descent to Turbulent Waters

In 1860, Major John Thorp drove 250 head of cattle to the Yakima Valley. Margaret and Fielding Thorp followed the next year with their nine children, and the Thorps became the first non-Native non-missionaries to settle in the valley.

By the time the Thorps arrived, a lot had happened in the nascent territory. Territorial governor Isaac Stevens pressured more than a dozen tribes into the Yakima Treaty in 1855. Immediately thereafter, he began to renege on parts of the deal, prompting tribal leader Chief Kamiakin's withdrawal from the deal and inciting the Yakima Indian Wars.

By the time the Thorps arrived, they found a land with "rye grass as high as a man's shoulders on horseback." The Indian uprising fully quashed, early European American settlers declared the place a "cattleman's paradise." The Northern Pacific Railroad laid tracks in 1884, and the city of Yakima sprang up around it. The county steadily grew, spreading into the lush valleys and up the hills. Naches was established in 1908 and incorporated in 1921.

Seven years before Thorp arrived in the Yakima Valley, a train of 30 wagons made the first successful journey over Naches Pass through the Cascade Mountains. Led by Virinda and James Longmire and many families of English and Scottish descent, they traveled by steamboat from Indiana to Missouri. There, they purchased oxen and wagons and began the long push west. Six months later, they reached the Yakima Valley. The wagon train followed the course of the Naches River, crossing it dozens of times. At the summit of Naches Pass, the would-be settlers ran out of road. They had no other option but to lower their wagons down the steep descent by rope, one at a time. From there, the group followed a long-established Indian trail. Many families pushed on toward the Pacific, but others stayed behind in what is today known as Naches.

The settlers planted orchards and raised dairy and other cattle. Life in Naches began to take shape. By 1908, the community built the Eureka School, which for a time was also a meeting place and outpost for the Presbyterian Mission. The Northern Pacific Railroad came through Naches in 1905, and a commuter train known as

Sagebrush Annie shuttled people from Naches to Yakima twice per day. Service on Sagebrush Annie continued until 1960, by which time individual auto travel was accessible and the train decrepit. Between fruit production and the resource-rich nearby forests, and with transportation firmly established in a growing county, the town of Naches has seen steady growth since its founding. Though its name is said to mean "turbulent waters," the town of Naches is on solid ground.

Washington's Newest Winemakers

The Naches Heights AVA, established in 2011, encompasses a wine grape–growing region of more than 13,000 acres. Winemakers here produce Bordeaux, Rhône, and Italian varietals, as well as some Portuguese ones. When the area received appellation status, fewer than 40 acres were under cultivation. In order to gain such status, winemakers must demonstrate a distinction in their product compared with other Washington wines. Viticulturists have still only cultivated a tiny fraction of the appellation. The soil within the area's geographic boundaries is clay-heavy, windblown loess.

A million years ago, lava flows covered the area of the Naches Heights plateau, which sits above the level reached by the Missoula Flood waters that raged across the landscape at the end of the last ice age. AVAs that reflect flood conditions have alluvial, as opposed to windblown soil. All of the winemakers in this region employ a combination of biodynamic, organic, and salmon-safe methodologies. Seven vineyards are currently producing wine in the Naches Heights AVA.

At the Intersection of Orchard and Forest

Naches is a small town in the much larger community of the county. An award-winning school district serves students from a wide geographic area. The town itself seems planted in the middle of an orchard, but unlike its nearest neighbor, Tieton, Naches doesn't display agriculture on every downtown street corner. The town sprawls. The downtown core quickly cedes to farmland. Crops carpet rising hills.

State Route 12 follows the river into town. The road was built to withstand a 200-year event in the flood-prone basin. Downtown greets visitors with a nod to the past. The Art Deco service station known as Johnson's Service Station blinks a neon welcome, courtesy of local artist Richard Elliott. In recent years, local high school students have taken charge of renovating and preserving the building. Near the service station, visitors will find the historic Naches Train Depot, built in 1906. The Depot is now a community center. Outside, a small park offers a paved walking path and picnic shelter. Van's Bar and Grill occupies one of the oldest structures in town, with a back bar that came from the East Coast and dates to 1885.

The Town Hall and Library building in downtown Naches once housed the fire and police departments. Before that, it was a territorial jail. In the library, an old cell is now the restroom.

One of the most charming buildings in Naches is the library, a small redbrick building that once housed the town hall and fire station; even earlier, it was a tiny regional jail. It's hard to believe this cheerful building was once a prison—unless you use the restroom facilities, which occupy an old cell.

These sights and more are part of a tour longtime Naches resident Doug MacNeil started offering in 2017 on behalf of the local chapter of the Lions Club. MacNeil's family history in town dates to before the town's platting. As is often typical of lifelong residents of small towns, MacNeil has filled many important roles in the community, from high school basketball coach to council member and mayor. Leading historical tours is the latest form of MacNeil's service to the town.

On a sunny Tuesday afternoon, the library is bustling. People are friendly and eager to share how they feel about their town. "Naches is a nice place to live," they say. With great schools, access to year-round recreation (including White Pass ski resort), and the opportunity to live a rural life in convenient proximity to a mid-size city, it's easy to see why.

The town of Naches tucks into hills carpeted with orchards and vineyards. Naches Heights became the 12th American Viticultural Area in Washington in 2011.

ENTERING
Naches

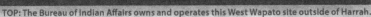

42

TOP: The Bureau of Indian Affairs owns and operates this West Wapato site outside of Harrah.

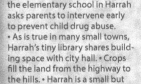

Population: 642
Founding: 1946

INSETS L to R: Signage outside the elementary school in Harrah asks parents to intervene early to prevent child drug abuse. • As is true in many small towns, Harrah's tiny library shares building space with city hall. • Crops fill the land from the highway to the hills. • Harrah is a small but busy town.

Harrah

The Land: Inhabited, Owned, Cultivated

Long before hops and vineyards organized the land into neat squares of marketable products, the Yakama people inhabited a vast swath of the Columbia Plateau. They kept to the valley villages in winter and harvested from mountain slope to river from spring to fall. Under threat of war by the US government, 13 tribal leaders signed a treaty ceding more than 12 million acres of land. The US promised to extend a two-year period of time during which the tribes could move to their newly allocated land, consolidated under the Yakama Nation. But just 12 days after making that promise, the territorial governor, Isaac Stevens, reneged, declaring all of the ceded land available for white settlement. Chief Kamiakin led an effort to oppose Stevens, and a multiyear war followed.

More than 6,000 people belong to the Yakama Nation today. The nation changed the spelling of its name from *Yakima* to *Yakama* in the 1990s to more accurately reflect the original pronunciation. Today, the Yakama control the largest amount of land compared with any other federally recognized nations in the state—more than 1.3 million acres.

Thirty years after the Yakima Treaty, in 1884, Julius T. Harrah was born in São Paulo, Brazil. His mother was the daughter of a British ambassador, and his father was a railway engineer whose own father was a prominent Philadelphia businessman. Harrah studied in London, Paris, and Heidelberg before emigrating to the United States at the turn of the 20th century. In 1909, he visited Seattle, where the Alaska Yukon Pacific Exposition was touting development in the Northwest. Harrah decided to stay in the region and began buying everything from orchards to hotels in the Yakima Valley. He developed more than 200 acres of land and invested hundreds of thousands of dollars in the region.

As Harrah and other towns in the county developed into agricultural hubs, they began to overuse the water supply of the Yakima River. The United States Reclamation Act of 1902 allowed for the construction of dams and irrigation projects, under the condition that the users who benefit from the reclamation repay the government for the infrastructure. The Yakima Project of 1910 is the largest of these efforts. In 1869, farmers planted the first wine grapes in the area. Hops followed shortly after, in 1872, and commercial fruit orchards came five years later. The valley has flourished as a regional agricultural center ever since.

A Brief History of Work

Wine, hops, and commercial fruit production in the Yakima Valley date back to shortly after the end of the Civil War. Immigrant and migrant labor have been integral to this economic flourishing from the start. Native families found work harvesting hops in the valley during the Great Depression. Japanese families began farming the valley in the 1940s before they were interned under FDR's Executive Order 9066. The Bracero Program brought Mexicans and Mexican Americans to fill the labor shortfall during WWII, and the program continued for nearly two decades.

Over the next 30 years, changes in immigration policy led to Latinx immigrants, mostly from Mexico, surpassing in number the Mexican American, or Chicano, population. In the 1980s and '90s, Latinx farm workers pushed for better working conditions. César Chávez visited the Yakima Valley in 1986 to lend his support to their cause. The Yakima Valley Farm Workers Clinic began offering healthcare and other services to laborers in the early 1970s. More recently, a federal guest worker program brought Thai laborers into the Yakima Valley.

The story of work in the valley is one of frequent demographic change driven by shifting global politics. In this region of globally significant agricultural production, working and living conditions for migrants and immigrants remain front and center.

Working Town

The town of Harrah lies entirely within the Yakama Nation Reservation. Its population is diverse, however, with nearly 65% of census respondents reporting Hispanic or Latinx heritage, nearly 20% Native American, and 15% white alone. Between 2016 and 2017, Harrah's population increased by about 2%. The poverty rate in Harrah is slightly higher than that in Washington State overall.

For more than four decades, Barbara Harrer has served as the mayor of Harrah. Now in her mid-eighties, Harrer first took the position in 1977, by which time she'd already been involved in town governance for 10 years. Harrer and her late husband, John, moved to Harrah from Montana in 1966. In her time as mayor, she's helped get modern water and sewer systems in place, winning an award for her efforts to improve infrastructure. Harrer also helps organize the annual Harrah Festival, which for more than 70 years has brought the community together to celebrate its diverse cultural heritage.

The Indian Irrigation Project is part of the federal Columbia Basin Reclamation Project. Across the country, reclamation for irrigation on Native-held land supports 25,000 water users and 780,000 acres of land.

Looking ahead, Harrer hopes to see farmworker housing built soon and to develop a community watch program in response to recent property crimes. Former public works director Gary Decker says Harrer is "just a terrific mayor— she puts the city before anything else." In a 2018 interview with the *Yakima Herald,* Harrer was humble about her accomplishments. "It's no big deal," she says. "It's just serving the community."

Harrah feels alive. In the fields surrounding the town, a man-made forest of hops climbs tall trellises; orchards, clover, and potatoes fill in the understory. The wind whips up field dust and water from the irrigation canals, and the air smells fresh, vegetal, fecund. In town, everything is in motion. Children run around the play field at the elementary school across from a house with a sign saying LARRY AND NANCY LIVE HERE. Men exit the Farmhouse Cafe carrying coffee and lunch, holding the door for patrons on their way in. Women walk between the salon and the grocery store next door. Cars pull up to the store, drive away. On the edge of town, people working in the fields wear masks or bandannas against the blowing grit. The railroad, the churches, and the fire station stand at the ready.

What makes a town a town? The answer is different from place to place. Harrah is a place where people live and work.

Hops grow in the field just beyond the Lower Valley Indian Baptist Church in Harrah. Trellised hop vines can grow up to 25 vertical feet, dying back after the harvest each year.

43

Population: 947
Founding: 1886

INSETS L to R: New and old mural-style paintings and advertisements proliferate over Roslyn's town walls. • Local artist Dan O'Conner painted the Roslyn Cafe's mural. • Basecamp Books and Bites stock local-interest and outdoor-focused books as well as new titles for all ages. • The Roslyn Museum tells the story of a richly diverse town, from coal mining to baseball teams to the town's early business successes.

TOP: The Roslyn Downtown Association focuses equally on preservation and economic development.

Roslyn

Coming Out at the Seams

Before settlers came, the Upper Yakama peoples made their homes near what is today Lake Cle Elum, in the valleys on the eastern slopes of the Cascade Mountains. Roslyn lies in the high ground, platted on a site that seemingly went unused until prospectors found something sure to maximize the profits of the railroad they'd been sent to scout for: coal.

Within three months of the discovery, a small crew was mining coal in Roslyn. In a hurry to create a transportation system for the commodity, the railroad threw up a spur line to the rail already established in Cle Elum. Fast on the heels of that development came hundreds of miners. Within 20 years, Roslyn was a town of more than 3,000 people, including immigrants from around the world, infusing the town with a rich ethnic diversity unique in the state.

The vice president of the Northern Pacific Coal Company, a subsidiary of the railway, was a man named Logan Bullitt. The local paper reported that Bullitt named the town Roslyn after a

woman he fancied. Logan Bullitt ran the crew and Northern Pacific owned the town, including a mill they built, as well as every last local business. Like so many small towns, Roslyn caught fire soon after its establishment, and in rebuilding, the company chose a more durable material to work with—brick.

Within two years of the town's founding, Roslyn's workers went on strike for better pay and improved working conditions. The company responded by bringing in 50 African American miners to break the strike and 40 armed guards to protect them. According to record, territorial governor Eugene Semple feared a militia was forming. Semple ordered the guards to leave. With the pace of mining continually increasing, the company and workers settled the dispute, and many Black miners stayed in Roslyn, further diversifying the town's population. Very much unlike today, when the percentage of Roslyn residents of African American ethnicity is slim to none, at the turn of the 20th century they made up 20% of the population. A full 40% of the town's citizens at that time were of foreign heritage.

Mining disasters and diseases plagued Roslyn toward the end of the 1800s, but coal production kept ramping up. Oil replaced coal as civilization's preferred fuel source, and Roslyn's boom finally began bending toward bust. The last coal companies closed in 1963, but the sooty fingerprints of Roslyn's seminal industry remain.

A Miner's Tale

Halfway back into Roslyn's small and fascinating museum, preserved in plastic, an aging yellow clipping from an unidentified newspaper leads with the headline GIRL WORKS 11 MONTHS AS LOADER IN MINE HERE. Neither coworkers nor supervisors recognized that Tony Bailey was really a young woman named Gloria Bailey until she went into the wrong restroom—the women's. Compelled to confess, she explained that she needed to earn money to care for her sick mother; plus, she wanted to open a restaurant someday. State law prohibited women and girls from miners' work, and Tony/Gloria lost her job. Still, the article notes, "She was a darn good worker . . . admired for her fortitude and stick-to-it-iveness." When discovered, Tony/Gloria revealed it wasn't the first time she had worked as a man. What would Tony/Gloria say about the experience? We'll never know. If it's any consolation, the clipping notes, "That girl has gone to Wenatchee to pick cherries. . . . But before going, she received her vacation pay as a full-fledged miner!"

Roslyn's Charm

While some tiny towns feel lifted out of time and placed into a future in which they may not belong, Roslyn feels on the verge of boom. The increasing cost of city life in nearby Seattle may be driving people to Roslyn and other Kittitas Valley communities. Though over a mountain pass from the city, Roslyn is close enough to Seattle that it's possible to commute to work from there. Another draw is the recently developed Suncadia community, a luxurious retreat with a golf course and spa on 6,000 acres of forest just outside of Roslyn.

Opinions may be mixed about the impact of these changes to the community of Roslyn. Scott Templin, director of the Roslyn Historical Society Museum, has been here for decades, but others in town still sometimes remind him he's "not third-generation." Still, the mood in town is upbeat and bustling, as a sleepy mountain paradise town goes.

Roslyn's historic cemetery complex holds the remains of 5,000 residents, including immigrants from many cultural traditions. The complex is composed of 26 cemeteries divided by ethnicity as well as civic organization. These cemeteries tell the story of Roslyn's diverse history as a coal-mining town.

Roslyn's Downtown Association dedicates itself to a twofold mission of preserving the past and creating future opportunities. Historic buildings hold new businesses, and one feels a through line between faded billboards on old brick walls and newer murals so bright they may have been painted yesterday. Strolling through town, visitors might stop for lunch at the Roslyn Cafe, or pop into Basecamp Books and Bites for an espresso they can sip on the patio at Roslyn Yard, the site of concerts, readings, picnics, and farmers' markets. Nearby, The Brick is the oldest continuously operating tavern in Washington State. Fans of the 1990s TV show *Northern Exposure* can pick up a walking map at the visitor center and get their bearings. Just beyond The Brick, the trailhead of Coal Mines Trail offers nature and history lovers alike the chance to stroll down the original branch line built to haul Roslyn's first coal to Cle Elum.

A few rolling hills out of downtown, Roslyn's historic cemetery is unlike any other. Here, on 15 acres of land, are the segregated remains of the members of various ethnic groups and civic organizations. Among the 25 cemeteries, visitors will find areas specifically for Foresters, Redmen, Moose, and Eagles; Lithuanians, Poles, and Slovaks; the Old Knights of Pythias, and the cemetery of The Old City, where Roslyn's first residents reside. Since 1886, Roslyn's diverse residents have maintained their cultures all the way to their final resting places beneath the ponderosa pines.

The volunteer-based Roslyn Downtown Association focuses on preserving historic buildings while providing revitalization and opportunities for economic development.

44

Population: 1,872
Founding: 1884

INSETS L to R: Local business Glondo's Sausage Company uses an advertising style from days gone by to market their product to today's consumers • The view from the Coal Mines Trail • The Coal Mines Trail became a publicly accessible walkway in 1994. • The home of Cle Elum's first banker is now a museum and art gallery.

TOP: Downtown Cle Elum displays preserved signs from its railroad town past.

Cle Elum

Place of Swift Water

By 1904, writers already described Cle Elum in terms of its remarkable growth and its relationship to the other Kittitas Valley towns. First and foremost, they described its beauty: "It lies on the northern bank of the river at the base of the foothills . . . The valley winds between high, timbered hills . . . and a ragged, pine-clad flank of the main range . . . snow-crested during most of the year."

Thomas Gamble, originally from Pennsylvania, first encountered this landscape in 1883. While at the land office in Yakima, Gamble ran into his old friend from Pennsylvania, Walter Reed. Gamble told Reed about the land he'd located, where "the hazel brush grew dense," and "massive pines and firs in dark thickets reared skyward their stately heads." Reed threw his lot in with Gamble, and the two decided to develop the land together. The following year, prospectors discovered coal in the foothills near what is today Roslyn. When Gamble and Reed struck out together, the nearest settlers were a few days away, ranchers in the lower parts of the valley to the east. With the discovery of coal,

new neighbors came pouring in. One new neighbor came steaming through: the Northern Pacific.

The same year that the Northern Pacific reached the eastern slopes of the Cascades, area mines began producing the very coal the railroad needed to continue its progress. Laborers began clearing access for the railroad to the mountains by Stampede Pass, and "an unusual number of home-steaders and speculators reached the settlement and commenced acquiring possessions of the surrounding country." Reed platted the town and called it Cle Elum, after the Kittitas word, *Tle-e-elum*, meaning "swift water." By 1888, Cle Elum had a railroad spur bringing coal out of Roslyn. Walter Reed's wife thought Cle Elum might become the Pittsburgh of the West. Good fortune seemed guaranteed, until it didn't. As quickly as Cle Elum boomed, a labor strike in Roslyn and the departure of the railroad threatened the developing town's ongoing prosperity. A forest fire destroyed it a few years later, and that might have spelled the end for Cle Elum, but the discovery of coal on Gamble's property gave the town mineral wealth in its own right.

As with Roslyn to the west, immigrants came from around the world to work the mines in Cle Elum. The population soared to nearly 3,000 residents at its first census in 1910. When the highway system brought the possibility of auto travel over Snoqualmie Pass, Cle Elum became a town to stop in on the way from Spokane to Seattle. Less than a generation after the forest fire, some trash beside the movie theater caught fire; more than half the town would be homeless by the time firefighters extinguished the blaze. As it had before, Cle Elum rebuilt. It would go on to survive the decline of the coal and timber industries, finally relying economically on its inexhaustible resource: the natural beauty that coal mining, logging, and fire have not erased.

Walking Through History

Though the city is changed and changing, Cle Elum retains strong ties to its history and offers many ways for visitors to experience it. The Coal Mines Trail leads from Cle Elum to Ronald, following an easy 5-mile route that used to be the branch line used by Northern Pacific to transport coal from the Roslyn mines. The visitor center in town provides a map with 20 marked points of interest. The National Register of Historic Places lists no fewer than 20 buildings in Cle Elum. For those seeking to engage with the past or experience nature in the present, in Cle Elum, there are trails beyond trails.

Recreation Hot Spot

Cle Elum is a small town with a complex identity. It's close enough to Ellensburg that teachers and students can commute daily. For some, Cle Elum is close enough to Tacoma and Seattle to make the cross-mountain commute to those cities. The town has been a haven for outdoors enthusiasts since long before the Seattle Parks Department applied for a permit to create a ski resort at nearby Snoqualmie Pass. Recently, the planned community and resort called Suncadia has cemented Cle Elum as a resort town in the regional imagination, to the dismay of some longtime residents.

The Coal Mines Trail follows the Northern Pacific Railroad line from Cle Elum to Roslyn and Ronald. The railroad transported coal along this route from 1886 to 1986. In 1994, it became a public trail.

In 1995, the Plum Creek Timber Company approached TrendWest, a resort development company, with an offer of a large parcel of land just outside of Cle Elum. Not everyone in town was happy with the move. RIDGE, a conservation group based in Roslyn, had concerns about the negative environmental impact of a resort on wildlife habitat and sued TrendWest repeatedly before finally settling in 2011. Other Cle Elum residents opposed the resort on the grounds that it threatened their way of life. They argued that the land, once used for logging, should stay that way. In the end, despite opposition and running vastly over its proposed budget, Suncadia opened in 2005, adding a lodge and spa in 2008.

The Carpenter House Museum, built in 1914, is the former home of the Carpenter family. Frank Carpenter was Cle Elum's first banker and former mayor. The house also hosts rotating exhibits by the High Country Artists.

45

Population: 560
Founding: 1911

INSETS L to R: Much of the Milwaukee Road's former rail yard is now open for exploration as Iron Horse State Park. • The South Cle Elum station operated for 70 years. • The eastern slopes of the Cascade Mountains are visible from anywhere in South Cle Elum. • This trail is variously called the Iron Horse Trail, the John Wayne Pioneer Trail, and the Palouse to Cascades State Park Trail.

TOP: The arrival of the Chicago, Milwaukee, and St. Paul Railroad created South Cle Elum.

South Cle Elum

The Milwaukee Road

In the 1880s, railroad surveyors heard about the coal deposits in Roslyn, and within a year the Northern Pacific Railroad was running through Ellensburg. A few years later, they'd tunneled through Stampede Pass, and the Kittitas Valley had a rail connection to Puget Sound. Northern Pacific established a depot in Cle Elum, on the north side of the Cle Elum River. The discovery of gold in the Swauk Creek area increased migration to the valley generally, and Ellensburg was stumping to be the state capital. Even as mining explosions and labor wars complicated the burgeoning developments, another railroad sought to establish itself.

The Chicago, Milwaukee & St. Paul Railroad, often referred to as the Milwaukee Road, arrived in Kittitas County in 1909, platting the town of Kittitas in advance and bringing with them new residents and businesses. With the Milwaukee looking to chase Northern Pacific across the mountains, Samuel Packwood, a Civil War veteran and former Kittitas County commissioner and sheriff, platted South Cle Elum on the south side of the river. Cle Elum incorporated in 1911, three years after

the Milwaukee Road set up a depot, roundhouse, workers' housing, and maintenance facilities. The Milwaukee blasted six tunnels through Kittitas, including the 12,000-foot tunnel at Snoqualmie Pass, and laid more than 100 miles of track.

The Milwaukee developed more quickly than other railroads had, taking advantage of newly mechanized equipment like steam shovels. South Cle Elum populated gradually, though some note that it never stood a chance of matching Cle Elum's success. By 1920, the year of its first census, South Cle Elum had about a quarter of the population of Cle Elum, with whom it shared a water supply and school system.

The Milwaukee was fully electric by 1918 and continued operating until 1980. At one time, it had a majority of the business running east from the port of Seattle, and it carried passengers from Chicago to Seattle in 45 hours. Meanwhile, in 1915, the long-planned Sunset Highway opened to automobile traffic across Snoqualmie Pass. Governor Ernest Lister said the moment was more important than the railroad's arrival in Seattle decades prior. His words quickly proved true. Federal funds for a road system increased. By the 1930s, travelers took the road instead of the Milwaukee to go skiing at the summit of Snoqualmie. In the 1970s, railroad mergers presented insurmountable competition to the Milwaukee, and the line closed for good in 1980. Today, the old Milwaukee Road is accessible on foot, bicycle, and horseback as part of the Palouse to Cascade Trail, also known as the Iron Horse Trail and the John Wayne Pioneer Trail.

Missionaries in the Valley

The presence of missionaries in the Pacific Northwest in the mid-19th century stems from this apocryphal story. Reportedly, the Nez Perce, on encountering Lewis and Clark, showed interest in learning about the men's religion. In response, Christian groups began sending missionaries west. In 1852, Catholic priests Louis d'Herbomez and Charles Pandosy started the St. Joseph mission near Ahtanum Creek in the Yakima Valley. The mission shared a location with Yakama Chief Kamiakin's seasonal camp. Kamiakin worked with the priests to establish the mission and use the land for agriculture. He allowed the priests to baptize his children, which spurred other Yakama people to follow. The priests exchanged language with the Yakama as well. A few years later, their relationship soured as white settlers, miners, and the Northern Pacific Railroad began exerting increasing pressure on the Yakama land and on their lives. Soldiers stationed at Fort Vancouver came to the area and assumed the Catholics were helping the Yakama. The soldiers burned the mission and the nearby Holy Cross mission. By 1858, the priests representing the order of the Oblates of Mary Immaculate had left, some through Kittitas Valley and over the Cascades to Puget Sound.

The history of white religious incursion on Indigenous cultures is infinitely complex. One small facet of the story is that in the mid-19th century Pacific Northwest, missionaries frequently mediated between Native peoples and the US government. Both the church and government wanted to—and did—drastically change Indigenous lives. Sometimes, when the government failed, the church succeeded.

The Palouse to Cascade Trail starts in the Seattle area near the popular hiking spot Rattlesnake Ledge, taking explorers up and over Snoqualmie Pass and all the way to the Columbia River in eastern Washington.

South-Going Zaxes?

In *The Zax*, by Dr. Seuss, two groups of very similar people do their best to remain separate. One day, a North-Going Zax crosses paths with a South-Going Zax, and neither will move out of the other's way. This doesn't quite describe the relationship between South Cle Elum and its sister city across the river, but they haven't always agreed.

The two towns have considered combining a number of times, but voters in South Cle Elum have always chosen to remain independent. The towns share some services, such as policing, sewer, and water, but South Cle Elum has "[its] own mayor, city council, and zip code," as Iron Horse Bed and Breakfast owner Mary Pittis notes. Mayor Jim DeVere reinforced the division between the towns' identities, saying "It's different generations, different solutions . . . It just happened to shake out that way."

South Cle Elum keeps on keeping on. The Milwaukee depot sat empty for decades until a volunteer organization formed to restore it. In 1999, the state bought the land and buildings, as well as the railbed, which it transformed into Iron Horse State Park. The Cascade Rail Foundation pitched in on the restoration, and today, the depot holds a museum and a restaurant.

In the Seuss classic, the South-Going Zax had a rule: never budge! In the end, the world grew around the Zax. "The world grew. In a couple of years, the new highway came through." One supposes the Zax are still there, toe-to-toe on the prairie of Prax.

Iron Horse State Park falls along a section of the 220-mile Palouse to Cascade Trail (aka the John Wayne Pioneer Trail). The park features the restored Milwaukee Road Depot and an interpretive area where visitors can learn about the history of the electrified rail.

46

Population: 1,791
Founding: 1908

INSETS L to R: Old farm implements on display at the Olmstead Farm. • Cloud shadows on Uptanum Ridge. • A defunct railway building sits at a Kittitas entrance to the 224-mile John Wayne Trail. • 19th-Century pioneer family the Olmsteads farmed beef and dairy. After three generations of farming, the family donated the land to Washington State Parks in 1968.

TOP: Thrall and Dodge, the self-described oldest-operating commercial winery in Kittitas Valley has a tasting room in town.

Kittitas

Land of Plenty

Between the Central Cascades and the Columbia River lies the Kittitas Valley, a windswept landscape of ranches and farms. Hawks watch the field from fence posts and treetops, red-winged blackbirds and Steller's jays sing their mechanical songs, and great blue herons cut graceful figures in the marshes along the banks of the Yakima River. Kittitas County is home to several small towns and census-designated places, including the eponymous city of Kittitas.

The Kittitas people, or the Upper Yakama, were the first to inhabit the area. Though distinct from other Yakama people, the Upper Yakama were lumped together with the Lower Yakama in the Yakima Treaty of 1855. These Upper Yakama people were known as the *Psch-wan-wap-pams,* or "stony-ground people." The valley provided them with camas roots and berries, and it served as hunting and fishing grounds as well.

Fur trader Alexander Ross is the first non-Indigenous person recorded to have visited the valley, in 1814. Ross arrived hoping to acquire horses while working for the Northwest Fur Company. Ross seems not to have been well liked among his superiors, one of whom noted that Ross sent back reports that were "so full of bombast and marvelous nonsense that it is impossible to get any information that may be depended upon from him." By Ross's own account, he stumbled upon an annual gathering of area Indigenous groups, which Ross described as a "mammoth campsite," writing, "We could see the beginning but not the end! It was a grand and imposing sight in the wilderness." Andrew Jackson Splawn echoed Ross's sentiment in 1861, when he came upon the valley and thought it "the loveliest spot I had ever seen . . . it was truly a land of plenty." Splawn arrived after the end of the Yakama Wars, which resulted from Governor Stevens breaking the treaty terms that allowed the Yakama two years to leave their homelands. Instead, Stevens had invited settlers to begin moving in a mere 12 days later.

An abundance of bunchgrass made the valley a perfect place to graze cattle, and the settlers came, remaking the landscape to support beef and agricultural industries. Kittitas was the last city to be platted, after Ellensburg, Cle Elum, Roslyn, Easton, and Thorp. At the turn of the century, the county brought irrigation to the lower valley, allowing farmers to develop orchards. Subsequent efforts to irrigate further led to federal projects. In order to pay for them, the government asked settlers to move to the area and turn the sagebrush-covered land into salable agriculture. Today, Kittitas primarily exports timothy hay used for livestock feed.

Just as They Left It

Samuel Olmstead was an early settler to Kittitas Valley. After his military service, he and his family moved to a farm between what are today the towns of Ellensburg and Kittitas. The Olmsteads built a cabin from cottonwood, and later, a large farmhouse. Their daughter Clara married in the cabin, and after her father's death, Clara took over with her husband, George Smith, and their family. Three generations of the family raised beef and cattle on the land. In 1968, 20 years after their parents' deaths, the granddaughters of Sara and Samuel Olmstead donated the land to Washington State Parks, asking that the house be left as it was. Through the park, visitors can imagine life as it would have been, from early farm implements to the home's interior. The park is also a good place to learn about the local ecosystem.

Things Change, Things Stay the Same

Ellensburg became the primary city of Kittitas County, and the boundary between the cities is narrowing. New subdivisions are bridging the space between Ellensburg and Kittitas, perhaps encouraging Kittitas away from its farm-based identity. The Thrall and Dodge Winery has a tasting room in downtown Kittitas, serving Columbia Valley wines. Thrall and Dodge is the first winery in Kittitas Valley, but the Kittitas Valley Vintners Association now includes several more winemakers. Just down the street, Bailey's Bibliomania set up shop in Kittitas after several years in Ellensburg, giving Kittitas its very own bookstore.

Whereas Ellensburg is solidly a college town, with more than half of its population made up of students attending Central Washington University, Kittitas prides itself on its rural identity and the tightly knit community that implies. As well, Kittitas is proud of its history. The Chicago, Milwaukee and St. Paul Railroad built a station in Kittitas just in time to transport Washingtonians east of the Cascades to Seattle for the Alaska Yukon Pacific Exposition of 1909. The railroad depot, in disuse for decades, sits now on the Palouse to Cascades trail system converted from the old railbed. The trail runs right through Kittitas.

The barn at Olmstead Place State Park bears two brightly colored "barn quilts," a fairly recent invention, started by an Ohio woman in 2001 who sought to honor her mother's quilt work by painting a pattern on her barn. Kittitas County now has 100 barn quilts installed and offers a trail map to guide visitors.

Though Kittitas is a small town, it is growing. Renewable energy is bringing new economic opportunities to the county, and businesses like Thrall and Dodge are, in their own words, "giving people a reason to stay." Still, a note from the mayor belies the town's rural underpinnings. "Here's what you'll find if you hang out at the local gas station, restaurant, or business," it says—singular. The answer, though, is plural. The people of Kittitas are hardworking, generous, and tenacious, the mayor promises. "We are the real Kittitas!"

Chicago may be the Windy City, but the Kittitas Valley could probably give it a run for its money. With winds frequently up to 40 miles per hour, it's no wonder that the area is perfect for the wind farms cropping up on all sides.

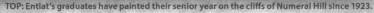

47

Population: 1,112
Founding: 1896, 1914, 1961

INSETS L to R: The Rocky Reach Dam inundated most of Entiat's second town. • Albert "Shorty" Long's family preserves Entiat's history in the house where the family patriarch made his home. • "Chilcosahaskt," a sculpture by Entiat artist Smoker Marchand, greets the morning sun in Entiat Park. • The landscape around Entiat is a blend of lush orchard and high desert, of softly rising hills and river-cut canyon.

TOP: Entiat's graduates have painted their senior year on the cliffs of Numeral Hill since 1923.

Entiat

A Town in Three Acts

Entiat's history is a three-act play starring the First Town (incorporated in 1896), Second Town (incorporated in 1914), and Third Town (incorporated in 1961).

Before white settlement, the first non-Native people in Chelan County were Chinese gold prospectors. They established a settlement at the mouth of the Chelan River within a decade of the treaty signings that consolidated and relocated as many as a dozen local Indigenous nations to the Colville Reservation. The Chinese abandoned the village soon thereafter, following deadly conflict, and European settlers followed closely in their absence.

The Columbia River Chinook Indian Tribe settled the Entiat area in the 1800s, naming the area *Enteatqua*, or "rapid water." Chief Chilcosahaskt built his camp at the confluence of the Columbia and Enteat Rivers, where he kept cattle and horses. His settlement became a trading post, and in 1896, he sold the land to settlers who would establish it as Entiat.

J. C. Ely was the first settler to build in Entiat, where he farmed and established a store and a hotel.

He was soon joined by settlers named Erickson, Farris, Hedding, King, Knapp, Sanders, and Wolf. A sawmill went up and then a dam, which provided electricity to the area. Construction of two more mills meant a stable base of employment for residents. Before long, they built the Harris School, Entiat's first. Union High School followed. The settlers erected telephone wires up a dozen miles of the valley, planted orchards, built churches, and started a newspaper, *The Entiat Times*. By the end of the first decade of the 20th century, Entiat was self-sufficient and flourishing.

A fire in 1913 destroyed nearly all of Entiat, sparing only six original buildings and a sawmill. Entiat's citizens found a silver lining, though, in the arrival of the Great Northern Railroad the following year, relocating their town site to be nearer to the rail. The second town soon contained hardware, drug, and general stores, and a bank. As with the first town, the second town of Entiat boomed. The railroad carried fruit out of town, increasing Entiat's economic viability, and the town made improvements to their water system and schools. In 1921, another fire destroyed the buildings that had escaped the first fire. Entiat rebuilt again, but after the fire came the flood. This time, however, Entiat saw it coming.

The Rocky Reach Dam, constructed in 1961, created Lake Entiat and brought its waters to the second town's doorsteps. In advance of the dam's construction, the Chelan Public Utilities District worked with the town to relocate once more. The PUD paid homeowners for their land before razing or relocating their homes. Many residents used the money to buy new land in the new town site, but not everyone did. Debate over values and the location of the new business district divided the community. Only a few buildings were moved from the second town, including the Community Church and the IOOF Hall. The only home from the second town left standing today belonged to Albert "Shorty" Long, whose children have transformed it into the Entiat Museum, which they lovingly maintain.

Shorty's Place

Albert Long moved to Entiat in 1925 when he was 10 years old. After high school, he married Mavis Bonwell and worked as a logger, mail carrier, and fireman. He raised sheep, cattle, and six children, and he was an avid collector. According to his descendants, Albert Long, nicknamed "Shorty," was interested in anything and everything, especially if it related to the history of Entiat. His book, *Under the Guard of Old Tyee,* offers a thorough account of Entiat Valley's settling and early days. Published five years before Long died at the age of 90, the book represents the work of his life, as does his former home, through which his children have maintained the legacy of their father and their entire town.

Third Town

Entiat's town website notes that despite its periods of complete economic and structural disruption, it "will continue to thrive due to the heart and stamina of its residents."

Entiat is a designated Heritage Community, founded before Washington gained statehood, and since 2001, it has been designated as a Tree City USA by the Arbor Day Foundation. It has also been a non-charter-code city since 1980, meaning that despite its small size, most matters are controlled locally rather than at the county level.

Albert "Shorty" Long's family, Judy Tudor, Joanne and Wayne Long, and Peggy Whitmore, preserve Entiat's history in the house where the family patriarch made his home.

Today, more than 50 years after the opening of Rocky Reach Dam, the City of Entiat is going strong. Plans are in the works to develop 18 acres of undeveloped shoreline, which the city has controlled since 2011. Construction of Fire Station Park, Entiat's newest, began in 2019 and will include baseball and soccer fields and a walking path. Entiat City Park, which sprawls over 40 acres of Columbia River waterfront, is popular with campers and boaters during the summer months. In the future, the City of Entiat hopes to hold music festivals in the park.

Wenatchee Valley College, the Wenatchee Valley Technical Skills Center, and the Entiat School District make up the local educational ecosystem. Numeral Hill rises above Downtown Entiat, visible from the windows of the Entiat School, where about 400 students learn in grades pre-K–12. Each year since 1923, the graduating class has painted its year on the hillside.

With Wenatchee National Forest, Mission Ridge, and Stevens Pass in its backyard, Entiat is a launching pad for outdoor recreation. Increasingly, Chelan County is a tourist destination, especially as wine production has taken root, earning Lake Chelan designation as the 11th American Viticultural Area in Washington State. From its mill town beginnings, Entiat has survived well over a century of economic boom and bust, not to mention the repeated injury of fire. Entiat's been put to the test. It may be the smallest incorporated town in Chelan County, but it's here to stay.

Chilcosahaskt, a sculpture by Entiat artist Smoker Marchand, greets the morning sun in Entiat Park. The Entiat Indian Tribe is one of 12 Indigenous groups who were relocated to the Colville Reservation after the Oregon Treaty of 1846.

48

TOP: Winthrop's planners took pains to get the details of this Old West town right.

Population: 394
Founding: 1901

INSETS L to R: A barn just outside of Winthrop demonstrates the scale of the Methow Valley. • Although Winthrop intentionally evokes the Old West, city planners wanted to make sure the town wouldn't be just for tourists. • Lodging options for visitors to Winthrop range from campsites to B&Bs. • The Barnyard Cinema might be the most modern building in Winthrop.

Winthrop

The Man Who Named the Mountains

In 1894, Guy Waring enclosed some photographs from Winthrop with a letter to his friend Isabella Gardner, who lived in Boston, Waring's hometown. The photos show a sepia-toned Methow Valley in the earliest days of its settlement. The subjects are "my neighboring ranchers" and the landscape. A hand-drawn map included with the letter shows the layout of the Methow Valley, including the road to Twisp and Silver, named creeks flowing into the Methow River, and the Cascade Divide. Waring includes the elevation of some of the peaks and notes the Isabella Range, now called Isabella Ridge, and Mount Gardner, which he named for his friend. Waring writes that the photos afford "an unsatisfactory view" of the mountains. "It gives almost no idea of their clear-cut beauty; or their height, and startling abruptness."

Two years before, at the age of 32, Waring had arrived with his family in the Methow Valley for the second time. They'd tried settling there in 1885 but found the community of miners unappealing and returned east, only to try again a few years later. In 1892, Waring opened a trading post.

Before Waring's post, the few miners and ranchers in the area had to make a four-day journey to Coulee City and back for supplies. Within a decade, the Methow Trading Company purchased and platted the Winthrop town site.

By all accounts, Waring was a maker of grand plans. From his trading post to his apple orchard, his schemes lost the money East Coast financiers had lent him. The population didn't boom the way Waring had told his backers it would, and the railroad he was so certain of never came. After a few years of drought, Waring gave up on his last venture—the orchard—and moved his family back to Massachusetts.

Though Waring wasn't the first settler in Winthrop, his contributions were key to its development. Winthrop's earliest white settlers were Tom and Jim Robinson, brothers and trappers, followed by Louisa and James Sullivan, who opened Winthrop's first hotel. Until the state legislature funded a road built by convict labor, settlers followed Indian trails and risked dangerous river crossings to reach the area.

Winthrop made slow progress as a mining, logging, and agricultural town until 1897, when

President Grover Cleveland placed the entire valley under protected status, allowing residents to stay but limiting future development. After much protest by the settlers who'd established a life there, Cleveland exempted the area of the valley floor from the Washington Forest Reserve, but the area around Winthrop is still today protected land.

The Okanogan Complex Fire

On August 14, 2015, lightning struck Okanogan County, igniting the worst wildfire in Washington State history. The Carlton Complex fire had set the record just a year earlier, and in the same area. Nearly 2,000 firefighters from 33 states deployed in response, and several firefighters local to the Methow Valley died fighting to save it. On the same night, the Chelan Complex fire began. By early September, both fires were 50% contained. The year 2015 was the warmest ever recorded in Washington history, and according to the state Department of Natural Resources, the hot weather, paired with years of drought and decreasing snowpack, led to "the worst wildfire season in human memory." That year, 1 million acres went up in smoke.

The Winthrop Project

If President Cleveland's move to protect the forest around Winthrop first stalled the town's early progress, nature was the bigger culprit. Flooding in 1948 followed a 20-year drought, and a deep freeze in 1968 destroyed the remaining agriculture. Winthrop needed a catalyst for survival, and soon. Tourism was the answer.

Residents Kathryn and Otto Wagner proposed that Winthrop restyle itself as an Old West town in much the way Leavenworth had found new life—and a new economy—as a Bavarian village. They called it The Winthrop Project. Led by Kay Wagner, the community coalesced around the idea. They hired Leavenworth's architect, Robert Jorgenson, whose research ensured that the retooled Winthrop would be an accurate representation of life in the West during the first decades of white settlement. At roughly the same time, construction began on

the North Cascades Highway. Completed in 1972, the highway provides a corridor from Seattle and Puget Sound all the way across the Mount Baker–Snoqualmie Wilderness of the North Cascades mountain range to the Methow Valley. The road closes annually in winter, and Washington residents on both sides of the Cascades unite in anticipation of its reopening.

In redesigning Winthrop, project planners wanted the town to draw tourists—but they didn't want Winthrop to be just a tourist destination.

Some compare Winthrop with Jackson Hole, Wyoming, before that town became a playground for the rich. Visitors can explore the Shafer Museum, a multibuilding complex that includes Guy Waring's home, aka The Castle, and stay in the Guy Waring Guesthouse, built in 1895. Those wanting greater luxury or space to spread out will find it at Sun Mountain Lodge, which bills itself as a destination for everyone from hikers who want to relax in style after a day in the mountains to those looking for a uniquely beautiful wedding venue. Local craftsmen contributed the wood and metal-work, including the lodge's 3,500-bottle wine cellar.

Easily accessible from the lodge, the 200-kilometer Methow Trails system draws visitors for Nordic skiing and fat-tire biking in winter and mountain biking, hiking, and trail running in the summer. The annual 49er Days celebrate Winthrop's past and present. The party begins with a weeklong horsepacking excursion and culminates in a parade and other events held over Mother's Day weekend, which also generally coincides with the annual reopening of the North Cascades Highway. Another way to put it is that every year, Winthrop remembers how it came to be and celebrates the reopening of the road that brought the town back to life.

The Barnyard Cinema, one of Winthrop's newest locally owned businesses, is one of the few buildings to deviate from the Old West styling that has dominated the town since the 1970s.

49

Population: 919
Founding: 1909

INSETS L to R: Downtown businesses are bright and welcoming. • The wall of an old barn serves as a bulletin board for local events. • The old ranger station campus now hosts a community of businesses and artists. • Artistic architectural elements make Twisp unique among towns of its size.

TOP: Twisp's Native Plant Garden teaches visitors about local habitat and cultural use of area plants.

Twisp

Heart of the Methow Valley

In the 1880s, mining boomed in the Methow Valley. By the turn of the century, three major mines in the Twisp Mining District would produce gold, silver, and copper. Decades later, the same mines shipped zinc to support the war effort, to the tune of $1 million in mineral resources. In the years between, the town of Twisp formed and thrived.

Henry Glover platted Gloversville in 1897, and by the next year, when he became postmaster, everyone already called the town Twisp. No one seems to know where the name comes from, but there's speculation that it means "wasp" or "yellow jacket" in an Indigenous language.

Before the mining boom, Twisp lay within the bounds of the Colville Reservation, created in 1872. Twenty years later, by which time the value of the mineral deposits was well known, the US government reduced the size of the reservation again by half. A large swath of the Methow Valley was thus newly opened to white settlement.

A town of wooden homes sprang up, supported by miners and ranchers. In 1903, James Holcomb moved up from Ellensburg and opened

the first creamery in the area. Local dairy farmers sold their milk to the creamery, and from Twisp and Winthrop distributed butter as far as Seattle. With a local economy and a population of a few hundred citizens, Twisp had become a leading town in the greater Okanogan County area. In 1904, 75 school-aged children were attending the Twisp school. Five years later, the town incorporated, and by 1911, it had electricity and even a movie theater.

The Methow Indians lived close by. Having inhabited the land for 10,000 years, they did not want to move to the Colville Reservation en masse. Many continued to utilize their traditional campsites at the confluence of the Twisp and Columbia Rivers, and they traded and interacted with the settlers. Much of their history has been lost due the decimation of their people by disease brought by settlers, as well as their incorporation into other groups. Researchers have found as many as 18 sites believed to be former Methow pit houses in the valley.

Present agricultural products from the Twisp area include alfalfa and emmer, but in its early years, farming was mostly subsistence-based. A drought hit the region in 1913 and continued until the end of the following decade. In between, a fire destroyed much of the wooden town in 1924. In the wake of the fire, the timber industry sprang up, and by the early 1940s, the Wilbur sawmill was a significant employer. Twisp continued to be at the mercy of nature, however, and the 1948 Columbia River flood caused $4 million in damage to the town.

In 1972, the opening of the North Cascades Highway changed the town forever. The new route running east–west across the northern part of the state brought Twisp to the attention of a new and diverse group of people. Today, the town is home to artists, musicians, and organic grocers, as well as families with longstanding mining claims and memories of the logging industry's early days.

Poison in the Well

On April 19, 1925, the front page of the *Methow Valley Journal* led with a photo of 80 local men dressed in robes and hoods—they had met at a fraternal hall in Twisp to celebrate becoming the 37th chartered order of the Ku Klux Klan. The *Journal* described the Klan as "one of the largest and most flourishing organizations in the Methow Valley," dedicated to "duty," "aid," and "fraternal assistance" in service of God and the "Brotherhood of Men." Some Okanogan County residents welcomed the "America first" messaging, but a few years earlier, the *Oroville Weekly Gazette* published an article opposing the Klan, declaring: "Such a movement is damnable in its purpose and if permitted to go unchecked will poison the well springs of liberty, freedom and self-governance in this country."

Washington became a territory in 1853 and prohibited slavery. Women received the right to vote here a full decade before the 19th Amendment granted it nationwide. But despite its history of progressive politics, the state harbored pockets of bigotry. The Klan in Washington focused its hatred on Japanese immigrants, whose numbers had grown in the years leading up to WWI, as well as Catholics, Jewish people, and African Americans. The Klan's appearance in Okanogan County coincided with its decline in the rest of the state, but even today its influence in the state is not entirely gone: the Southern Poverty Law Center noted two active Klan groups in Washington in 2017.

Though tiny—its downtown corridor comprises just a few streets—Twisp offers something for just about everyone. Several storefronts in cheery colors brighten downtown, including that of Cinnamon Twisp Bakery.

Fall in Love with Twisp

The first impression Twisp makes is industrial—trucks and equipment of all kinds stand parked in a massive dirt lot—but for those who venture into the self-proclaimed "Heart of the Methow Valley," beautiful surprises await. Just after the turn toward town stands TwispWorks, a business incubator housed in a former ranger station. In 2008, the town decided to purchase the site in an effort to bring opportunities for economic revitalization to the Methow Valley. An anonymous donor contributed $1 million toward the effort.

Today, TwispWorks is home to everything from the *Methow Valley News* to artists working in multiple media. The Methow Valley Interpretive Center partners with TwispWorks to provide opportunities to engage with the Indigenous cultures that lived in the Methow Valley prior to colonization. Also on-site is the largest native-plant garden in Central or Eastern Washington.

Just a short walk from TwispWorks, downtown Twisp's business facades are brightly colored and its shops inviting. Cinnamon Twisp, a bakery, is next door to Glover Market, an organic grocery with a deli and a downstairs wine shop. In front of the post office, a phone booth has been repurposed as a library. Just off the center of downtown, the front wall of an old barn is barely visible beneath dozens of posters advertising music performances, art shows, and community events.

Twisp is sure to delight tourists, but it's not strictly a tourist town. Maybe that's because once you visit, you'll want to stay.

Situated on the 6.4-acre campus of the former Twisp Ranger Station, the Methow Valley Interpretive Center features exhibits that educate visitors about the natural and Native American history of the area.

50

Population: 667
Founding: 1885

INSETS L to R: Winemaking and fruit trees are growth industries in Pateros. • The museum inside city hall preserves photos of early days in Pateros. • Lake Pateros resulted from the construction of the Wells Dam. • Before the dam, sternwheelers were dragged up the rapids a mile away by a winch connected near this dock.

TOP: The Pateros City Hall also houses a museum.

Pateros

Ives Landing

The Methow Indians belong to the Confederated Tribes of the Colville Reservation, though according to that organization, little is known about them today. Their homeland fell within the short-lived Moses-Columbia Reservation, created in 1879, at which time the Methow population had declined from an estimated 800 people a century before to around 300. The town of Pateros lies at the southeastern corner of the land used by the Methow, at the confluence of the Methow and Columbia Rivers. In 1886, when Rena and Lee Ives arrived at what is now Pateros, they found a community of Methow Indians living across the river, as well as a few dozen Chinese miners.

The miners had built a 5-mile ditch to divert water from the Methow for sluicing gold out of the Columbia River sandbars. Like the Methow, little is known about the Chinese placer miners here and elsewhere in the region. The Columbia River dams erased much of the physical evidence, and the Chinese Exclusion and Geary Acts likely contributed to the lack of documentation about the lives of the miners. Even before the Chinese abandoned the

ditch, settlers in Pateros—including the Ives family, who had a large garden across the river—began using it to irrigate their orchards.

Ives established a trading post and hotel and named the site Ives Landing. He traded furs with the Methow, traveling by wagon to Spokane twice annually to ship them. In his second year of operation, Ives sold $24,000 worth of furs. In 1888, the land was opened for homestead claims, and the town began to grow. Knight Parker bought a homestead next to the Ives and built a second irrigation ditch. Eventually, Parker purchased the Ives's hotel. In 1895, Ives Landing received a post office under the name Nera, an anagram of Rena, Ives's wife; the next year, however, the town changed its name back to Ives. In 1899, Charles Nosler purchased the Ives homestead and renamed it Pateros, after a Filipino town near Manila that he had visited during the Spanish-American War.

The first orchards produced peaches and cherries, but apples became the dominant agricultural product. Before the railroad's arrival in 1914, farmers had to hold their harvests through the winter, until spring thaw allowed boats to navigate upriver.

Harsh winters meant lost crops, prompting farmers to build warehouses to store the apples over the winter. Pateros grew, one road at a time, until about 1950. In 1962, the town relocated to avoid inundation by the Wells Dam, built 8 miles downriver.

Roadside Poetry

In the mid-1990s, forest rangers Sheela McLean and Curtis Edwards wanted the many tourists to the Methow River Valley to take away something special from their visit, so they contacted poet William Stafford and commissioned him to write a series of poems. Alongside art and interpretive plaques, the poems were installed along 50 miles of the Methow River. The first poem is in Pateros:

Time for Serenity, Anyone?

I like to live in the sound of water,
in the feel of mountain air. A sharp
reminder hits me: this world is still alive,
it stretches out there shivering toward its own
creation, and I'm part of it. Even my breathing
enters into this elaborate give-and-take,
this bowing to sun and moon, day or night,
winter, summer, storm, still—this tranquil
chaos that seems to be going somewhere.
This wilderness with a great peacefulness in it.
This motionless turmoil, this everything dance.

—by William Stafford, *reprinted with permission of the estate of William Stafford*

After the Fire

The Pateros Museum, opened in 2011, tells the story of the most significant event in Pateros since the Wells Dam. In 2014, the Carlton Complex fire raged through Pateros, cutting down orchards and melting the town's electrical system. Pateros lost more than 150 homes in the month it took 1,600 firefighters, many of whom were volunteers, to extinguish the blaze. When the smoke cleared, 20% of the buildings in Pateros were gone. Years later, the town is still rebuilding.

At the end of the 19th century, wooden towns caught fire across Washington. Rebuilding efforts focused on materials, and towns began using brick, sandstone, and concrete. Modern rebuilding efforts also take climate change into account. After the 2014 fire, the Carlton Complex Long-Term Recovery Group formed to aid rebuilding efforts across the county. Subsequently renamed the Okanogan Long-Term Recovery Group, the organization has rebuilt 39 homes in the first five years since the fire.

Route 97 winds down from the eastern slopes of the Cascade Mountains into the Columbia River Basin. Pateros sits at the confluence of the Columbia and Methow Rivers.

Immediately after the fire, Pateros councilman George Brady contacted Team Rubicon, a nonprofit organization of military veterans focused on helping towns recover from natural disasters. Marine veterans Jake Wood and William McNulty had formed Team Rubicon in 2010 after the earthquake in Haiti; the organization now has more than 16,000 members. Team Rubicon spent three weeks in Pateros, removing debris and managing volunteer labor and donations. The Pateros Museum preserves the town's memory of what happened during the disaster and documents the recovery. During the last few years, Pateros has upgraded its water system, better preparing the town for another fire.

The fire-scarred hills bear witness to the recent past, but today Pateros is thriving. Lush orchards fill the valley from the cliffs to the water's edge. With the Lake Chelan wineries and the trails of the Methow Valley nearby, Pateros welcomes visitors year-round.

In the early days of Pateros, families worked together to harvest, sort, and pack their apples. In 1913, Okanogan County had 1 million fruit trees.

51

Population: 210
Founding: 1887

INSETS L to R: In the Scotch Creek Basin outside Conconully, metamorphic rock on the west meets limestone on the basin's eastern walls. • Conconully has one grocery store and a few restaurants and taverns. • A modern tin roof peeks out behind the Red Rock Saloon's Old West facade. • A restored wagon and coach stand outside Conconully's tiny post office.

TOP: Conconully is thought to translate as "the beautiful land of the bunchgrass flats."

Conconully

Silver City

A 1904 history of Conconully notes the meaning of its name as "evil spirit," and that the "Natives" believed the lake nearby to be the home of a "huge and ferocious monster that was the author of a host of ills." White settlers testified to having seen the monster "rear its hideous head above the placid waters . . . and shake a long, heavy, sea-green mane in a threatening manner." A dozen years later, another source records *Conconully* as "a corruption of the Indian word meaning *cloudy*" and suggests that a tribe living along the river referred to themselves as the *koneonl'p*. According to the Okanogan County Historical Society, *Conconully* derives from an Indian word meaning "the beautiful land of the bunchgrass flats," though they don't specify from which nation or language.

In its earliest days, Conconully was a mining town, one of several in the area. Before 1886, the site of Conconully fell within the short-lived Moses-Columbia Reservation. As soon as the government made the site available, miners rushed in to stake claims on known lead and silver deposits. A group of prospectors organized the Salmon River

mining district near Conconully Lake and established a mining camp known as Salmon City. Other mines and camps nearby soon followed, including the Poorman, First Thought, Second Thought, and Fourth of July Mines. Perhaps the most significant was the Ruby Hill Mine, which became the city of Ruby, home to as many as 1,500 citizens.

Silver mining was a fair-weather endeavor. When winter came, the miners put up cabins and hunkered down. In the spring of 1888, a rush of miners brought the population to 500 and new businesses opened, including the *Okanogan Outlook*, the camp's own newspaper.

Over the next few years, the town continued to grow, gaining two sawmills and a hotel, among other businesses. Then, in 1892, a fire nearly destroyed the entire town. On the heels of rebuilding, a flood wiped out the town a second time, in 1894. The Panic of 1893 was the proverbial third strike.

The Sherman Silver Purchase Act of 1890 led to an explosion in silver production. The act mandated that the government purchase a monthly quota of silver, to be exchanged for gold at a ratio of 16:1, gold to silver. As silver production increased, the market price dropped, and the US Treasury's gold supply declined. Suddenly, miners weren't making money. Then, in 1893, the Philadelphia and Reading Railroad went bankrupt. At home and abroad, investors cashed in their securities for treasury gold. Soon, the treasury's gold supply fell below the $100 million required threshold. Small-town residents rushed the banks. This was well before the FDIC, so many depositors lost everything.

Once the Okanogan County seat, Ruby was abandoned immediately. Travelers passing through in 1898 noted just three remaining citizens. The next year, one noted, "The buildings were still intact but there was not a single inhabitant." By then, Conconully was the county seat. While Ruby never recovered, mining resumed near Conconully in 1901, but the revival was brief. The town of Okanogan took the county seat in 1914.

As one historian notes, "the boomier the town, the further it had to fall." Conconully's economy, dependent on silver, had fallen hard. The town settled into itself, a few hundred people on the "sunny side" of the Cascades.

Frontier Photographer

Among the miners and homesteaders, an unusual immigrant arrived in Conconully in 1903. By his own narrative, Sakae "Frank" Matsura had sailed from Japan to Alaska in 1901, working his way to Conconully, where he took a job as a handyman at the Elliot Hotel. In his spare time, Matsura took photos, developing his prints in the hotel's laundry sinks. Soon, newspapers commissioned Matsura to take photos. In 1908, Matsura was able to quit his job at the hotel and open his own studio in Okanogan County. Matsura photographed frontier life, from the hotels and saloons to the railways and telephone lines. He documented the dams that forever altered the landscape. And, he documented the people: Families paid Matsura to create their portraits, and Matsura photographed Native American communities as well. The Okanogan Historical Society and Washington State University maintain archives of Matsura's work, numbering more than 2,500 photos, many of which made significant contributions to the diverse story of life in the emerging towns of Okanogan County at the end of the 19th century.

Scotch Creek Basin, outside of Conconully, was a popular homestead site in the late 1800s and part of an ancient trail system between Okanogan County and the Sinlahekin Valley on the way to Canada.

Weird, Wild Washington

While the town of Ruby flamed out, Conconully kept a low fire burning. These days, the town is known as the home of one of Washington's stranger winter events: the annual Outhouse Races. Participants must construct a privy of wood or metal, mounted on two skis. The outhouse must have a roof, a toilet seat, and TP on a roll, and it may not include a motor or steering device of any kind. Since 1983, teams of three have participated in the races, which consist of two pushers and one sitter skidding down a 100-yard stretch of iced-over Main Street. In the bucket races, the pushers wear five-gallon buckets over their heads, navigating only by the voice of the sitter. More than 2,000 people attend the races annually.

In warmer weather, Conconully State Park, accessible on foot from anywhere downtown, offers rustic cabins in an 81-acre park on the shore of the Conconully reservoir. The Angel Pass Trail and Ray Trail are easy hikes in nearby Okanogan-Wenatchee National Forest. For more ideas, check in at the Sit 'N Bull or Ross and Mary's Red Rock Saloon, or just stroll through town responding to the greetings offered by people who notice your unfamiliar car. If ever there was a place where everyone knows your name, Conconully is it.

Conconully is a few blocks situated on a quarter-mile square, tucked between mountains and lakes. Ross and Mary's Red Rock Saloon is one of the few businesses in town.

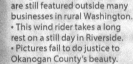

52

Population: 280
Founding: 1902

INSETS L to R: Okanogan County Fire District #7 has 16 volunteer firefighters. • Wooden Indians are still featured outside many businesses in rural Washington. • This wind rider takes a long rest on a still day in Riverside. • Pictures fail to do justice to Okanogan County's beauty.

TOP: Like many historic buildings, Riverside's grocery store has a sordid past.

Riverside

The Good Old Sternwheeler Days

In its tiny city park, the town of Riverside collapses its history onto a single sign that describes the place as, "the head of navigation on the Okanogan River during steamboat days until 1914 when the railroad came." Riverside, just a handful of miles north of Omak, lies at the mouth of Johnson Creek, where it meets the Okanogan River. Before Great Northern's arrival in Okanogan County, Wenatchee was the end of the line. Beyond that, pioneers, supplies, and the mail alike traveled upriver by steamboat.

The *City of Ellensburg* was the only steamboat in the county until 1893. From 1888, the Ellensburg traveled north from Pasco to the Okanogan Valley. Inclement weather conditions often delayed the boats in winter months, but in the spring, when the river ran high, if the boats could make it north of Brewster, near Pateros, they had a good chance of making it to Riverside and maybe even all the way to Oroville.

The Okanogan County sternwheelers were much smaller than their counterparts elsewhere in the country, and shipwrights built them to navigate the specific conditions on the Columbia and Okanogan watersheds. Crews connected winches to bolts drilled into the bedrock and lifted the sternwheelers up and over the rapids at Entiat and Pateros.

Riverside sought to capitalize on this commerce. James Forde platted the town in 1902, first calling it Republic Landing, as though the mining camp of Republic, 60 miles east, were accessible via Riverside, presumably by going north on the Okanogan River until Tonasket and then following a series of creeks to the east. Indeed, Riverside thrived as a supply center, and it had one of only two bridges across the Okanogan River. The year James Forde platted Riverside, $1.25 million worth of goods moved through town.

By 1913, Riverside was flush, with multiple stores, two hotels, and businesses of all kinds. The next year, Great Northern completed its line from Wenatchee to Oroville. The sternwheelers went out of business as quickly as the railroads would later, when the interstate highway system came along.

In 1916, two fires devastated Riverside. The town's water system was under repair at the time, so firefighting efforts were limited to what a bucket brigade could accomplish. The two fires razed entire blocks, burning more than a dozen buildings, including the C. E. Blackwell and Company store. In the years that followed, Okanogan and Omak continued to burgeon while Riverside dwindled. By 1956, Riverside had lost its high school. Two decades later, Omak annexed Riverside's elementary school as well. These days, Riverside counts itself as a bedroom community for Omak.

The World-Famous Suicide Race

In 1933, Leo Moomaw and Tim Bernard, two Okanogan County cattlemen, started the Omak Stampede. Close to a century later, the Stampede has evolved into a four-day weekend of "western entertainment," the centerpiece of which is the so-called Suicide Race.

The race started in 1935. Looking for a way to add excitement to the usual rodeo fare, local businessman Claire Pentz suggested that the Stampede mimic the event he'd heard about across the Colville Reservation; the story went that in Kellar, across the reservation, riders raced through a dry riverbed.

Pentz got his race. Riders reined in their horses until the starting gun fired, and, in one fierce, senseless mass, horses and riders dove off a 50-foot cliff into the Okanogan River, swam the river, and raced up the opposite bank and into the rodeo arena.

These days, there's $40,000 in prize money on the line, and the cliff is 210 feet high, with a 60-degree slope. The Omak Stampede is one of the most popular annual events in the region, drawing up to 8,000 fans in daily attendance. Most of the competitors in the Suicide Race are Indigenous.

Suicide is in the name for a good reason: since 1983, more than 20 horses have died during the competition. Multiple animal-welfare organizations have protested the race, even filing lawsuits in an attempt to stop it. Riders, however, say the race is an accurate representation of the kinds of terrain they navigate on horseback every day.

The Sun Sets in the West

A visit to Riverside begins with the view from above. From Highway 97, the valley slopes dramatically toward the river's edge, the Okanogan Highlands rising in the distance. Imagine a smaller-scale version of those famous shots of Yosemite Valley featuring Half Dome and El Capitan lording over the lush valley floor. From these dramatic heights, the road winds into a humble, peaceful town of low-slung buildings and Old West architecture.

Bleached caribou skulls bristle with antlers over the storage area kept safe behind an electric fence at Dave's Gun & Pawn. Across the street, Our Riverside Grocery is more welcoming. Rosemary bursts from the ground-level planters out front, nearly meeting the trellising greenery hanging from the overhanging roof. Locals say the place was a saloon in Okanogan County's frontier days.

Looking down into Riverside feels like gazing at Washington's own Yosemite Valley. A smattering of homes line the creek through the cultivated valley floor, while the arched backs of the Okanogan Highlands draw the eye toward the horizon.

Here and there, a bit of whimsy brightens up the town. In front of the grocery store, an enormous metal rooster crows in shades of rust. Next to the town hall, a miniature cyclist rides when the wind turns his wheels. Someone's dressed the fire hydrant in a striped purple T-shirt. The sign at Detro's, the biggest establishment in town, promises, "Behind these walls is a big 'honker' of a Western store!" Once upon a time, Riverside was a big honker of a Western *town*. Nowadays, however, the streets are quiet. Under the low bridge on Tunk Valley Road, the Okanogan River flows as slow and silver as the clouds overhead.

Our Riverside Grocery, one of the only businesses in town, used to be a saloon. Legend has it that Frank Watkins shot up the saloon when the barkeep didn't have the ingredients for the drink Frank wanted.

53

Population: 1,032
Founding: 1888

INSETS L to R: Lakeside resorts in the county are popular with vacationing families and fishermen. • Historical markers at the outskirts of town invite visitors to imagine 19th century travel and trade. • Towns in Okanogan County back up to rough rock walls. • Murals in Founders Day Park honor Chief Tonasket and the town's prominent settlers.

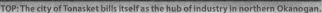

TOP: The city of Tonasket bills itself as the hub of industry in northern Okanogan.

Tonasket

Follow the River of Gold

In April 1916, the Omak Commercial Club, predecessor to the Chamber of Commerce, announced in the *Omak Chronicle* that the Colville Reservation was soon to be opened for homesteading. "One of the most wonderful chances for the incoming settlers on the Colville Indian Reservation," the paper notes, "will be the privilege that is granted the Indians to lease their fine land holdings on terms and periods of time that will allow the renter to make some big money on a small investment." While homestead claims were newly available, the area had been open for mining claims since 1898, but miners had been using the area long before that.

The Fraser River gold rush began in 1858, drawing as many as 30,000 Americans and prompting Canada to create a new colony, British Columbia. The Cariboo rush followed closely behind. From the first strikes in 1860, miners recovered between $40 and $300 worth of gold every day. In today's dollars, that's as much as $10,000 daily. By the end of the next year, the Cariboo fields had produced nearly $2.6 million.

American miners followed the so-called Cariboo Trail beside the Okanogan River into the gold fields. Cattle ranchers drove massive herds up the same route to sell fresh beef to the miners. Before the miners came, the route was well established by Native Americans.

A few decades after the Cariboo rush, in 1888, W. W. Parry established several businesses near what is today the town of Tonasket, including a hotel, a trading post, and eventually, a ferry. In 1895, Parry secured a post office for the town, naming it Tonasket after an Indian chief who had left the area 10 years earlier, having sold his land to Hiram Smith.

Prior to his departure, Chief Tonasket had been party to what history remembers as the McLaughlin Massacre. In July 1858, 160 miners led by David McLaughlin left Walla Walla headed for the Fraser River. When the shoreline of the Okanogan River became unnavigable, the party began to climb into the canyon. Members of the Chelan, Okanogan, and Columbia Tribes lay in wait to ambush the miners in resistance to incursions on their land. Six of the miners died in the conflict.

Okanogan was one of the last counties settled in Washington, and Tonasket one of the last towns to develop in Okanogan County. After the gold rush and mining booms subsided, Tonasket settled into a new identity as a regional agricultural center.

Tonasket's Nobel Laureate

Among its notable citizens, Tonasket honors Joshua P. Douglas, who built some of the first roads in the area; Hildegarde E. Lorz Laurie, a nurse anesthetist and surgical assistant; Arthur Lund, one of the men who platted Tonasket; and Walt Clarkson, owner of an early mill and employer to 100 people. One of Tonasket's most famous and honored citizens is Walter Brattain, who helped invent the transistor as a physicist at Bell Telephone Laboratories.

Before Brattain's family bought a flour mill and moved to Tonasket, they lived in China, where Walter Brattain was born. After earning his doctoral degree at the University of Minnesota, Brattain joined Bell Labs in 1929. In 1947, he and his partners, John Bardeen and William Shockley, shared the first transistor with the world. Before the transistor, electronic devices—from televisions to alarm clocks—used vacuum tubes, which are less durable and take up more space than transistors.

While history remembers Brattain as part of the Nobel-winning team in 1956, Tonasket's memory of Brattain is more specific. He rode to and from elementary school on horseback, five miles each way. When times were hard, he dropped out of school to help his family. He made his hometown proud.

Of Mountain Lions and Modern Conveniences

Tonasket today is the kind of wild, modern town where most of the news is about the local high school sports teams and an occasional mountain lion wanders into town. The Tonasket Ranger District covers more than 400,000 acres off Okanogan County, backing up to the Pasayten Wilderness and the Methow Valley Ranger District. This biodiverse district includes shrub–steppe grasslands as well as subalpine and alpine forests. Just east of Tonasket are as many as 40 peaks between 3,000 and 7,000 feet in elevation; just west, the North Cascades offer even more challenging terrain. Opportunities for hiking and backpacking abound in the mountains and along the Okanogan River, the 115-mile tributary of the Columbia that runs through downtown Tonasket.

Downtown Tonasket retains the feel of an old mining town, though unlike Winthrop to the southeast, Tonasket hasn't shaped its identity around foregrounding its mining past.

In town, Tonasket has every modern convenience, although just barely. When a business closes in Tonasket, it's not a sure thing that another will come along to take its place. With Oroville just 15 miles north and Omak just a little more than that to the south, Tonasket is close enough to other communities that folks can make the drive for necessities. Still, local businesses are thriving in Tonasket. When longtime pharmacy Roy's closed in 2018, drugstore owners in Oroville noticed an uptick in customers and decided to open a location in Tonasket. Still, Omak has Walmart, The Home Depot, and Costco. Time will tell whether Tonasket can retain its local businesses with national and international giants within an easy drive.

Among the features that make Tonasket unique, the US Armed Forces Legacy project stands out. Located on a half acre of land at the edge of town, the Legacy project honors both living and deceased veterans of foreign conflicts from all branches of the military. About 4% of Tonasket's citizens are veterans. Nationwide, the Veterans Administration estimates that fewer than 0.5% of Americans are active-duty members of the military, and that active duty and veterans together make up just over 7% of the population. In Tonasket, more than 450 plaques honor the servicemen and women of the American armed forces.

Murals in a park downtown pay tribute to Tonasket's cultural and industrial history. One wall memorializes individual pioneers with portraits and stories.

54

Population: 1,686
Founding: 1892

INSETS L to R: Mining ceded to agriculture as Oroville developed. • Great Northern built the line from Wenatchee to Oroville in 1914. • Rail access was a game changer in the pioneering days of northeastern Washington. • Oroville, town of gold, lives up to its name in the afternoon light.

TOP: Oroville lies along the Cariboo Trail where the Similkameen and Okanogan rivers meet.

Oroville

Okanogan Smith and Chief Moses

Okanogan County, a swath of land larger than the state of Connecticut, lies between the eastern slopes of the North Cascades and the western edge of Colville National Forest. The Columbia River Basin spreads to the south. Towns in the county sit beside rivers flowing out of British Columbia. In 1942, a historian wrote, "The Okanogan country has not changed greatly in 50 years." Oroville lies on the southern tip of Lake Osoyoos, the lake divided by the US–Canada border. Hiram F. Smith, the first white settler, arrived in the early 1850s.

Smith learned the newspaper business in New York. In his early 20s, he migrated to Washington by way of California and took a job carrying mail to Washington from the Hudson's Bay Company in British Columbia. His route took him through the Okanogan Valley, where he took a squatter's claim, eventually buying nearly 1,000 acres from Chief Tonasket.

On the job, Smith carried more than the mail. One by one, he wrapped 1,200 apple trees in blankets and brought them across the border from British Columbia. His transplanted trees became an orchard covering 24 acres beside the lake, and with that orchard, Smith became the founder of the apple industry in Washington.

The Okanogan Tribe, among others, declined to sign a treaty and retained sovereignty of their homelands until 1872, when President Ulysses S. Grant created the Colville Indian Reservation. The executive order brought the forebears of today's Okanogan onto the reservation, though protesting miners eventually succeeded in getting the reservation reduced so that miners and settlers could make legal claims to the land.

When the order went through, Smith's land fell within the territory slated for the Columbia-Sincayuse, led by Chief Moses, from whom Moses Lake and Moses Coulee take their names. Smith joined the miners and other ranchers in protesting the move. Meanwhile, Moses invited other tribes to join him on his reservation. The Spokane Tribe decided to wait for a reservation of their own, and other groups didn't want to move north at all. As a compromise, the Department of the Interior offered to provide Moses and his affiliates with infrastructure and supplies including mills and livestock, as well as a cash annuity, if he would cede the newly created reservation and move onto the Colville Reservation instead.

In the years between his first orchard and his opposition to the Moses reservation, Smith established a trading post, specializing in providing dried fruit. In the 1860s, his post was the only commerce for 100 miles. He served first in the territorial and later the state legislature. Additionally, he became involved with mining, inventing the "rock bottom" sluice box. In 1861, at the age of 32, he married the 14-year-old daughter of Chief Manuel of the Colville-Okanogan Tribe. He left her for a Seattle woman in 1892 and died the next year of pneumonia.

Irrigation came to the Okanogan River in 1905, one of the Bureau of Reclamation's first projects, and Great Northern arrived in 1914, with two daily passenger trains between Oroville and Wenatchee. The population boom began. For new settlers, the trip took a fraction of what it had when Smith made the journey 50 years earlier.

Weathering the Years

During the winter of 1908–09, a deep freeze set into Okanogan County. All of the county's apples froze except Smith's. Everyone else had to rebuild their orchards from scratch. Through the years, Smith's trees have gained a reputation for being both hardy and remarkably productive. A single Winesap tree yielded 112 boxes of apples in 1948. That tree and several others yield in the realm of 100 boxes annually. Smith's trees became a grafting source for orchardists as far away as Australia.

Gold Town

Gold strikes along the Fraser River brought miners up the Cariboo Trail to Oro, established in 1892 just this side of the border. When the town needed a post office, they added *-ville* to the name to avoid confusion with the town of Oso. Though agriculture dominates Oroville's economy, there are still nearly 1,700 mines in and around Oroville, including 38 active ones.

Oroville continues to grow steadily, and Lake Osoyoos is becoming a popular tourist destination on both the American and Canadian sides of the border. Outdoorsy visitors to Oroville will find an abundance of hiking opportunities. The Similkameen Trail follows an old railbed created to haul ore from the mines. The trail crosses the Similkameen River gorge nearly 100 feet above the river, offering views of the Enloe Dam. The Whistler Canyon Trail is a part of the Pacific Northwest Trail, which when completed will lead from Glacier National Park to the Pacific Ocean. The trail runs through downtown Oroville and climbs into the North Cascades.

While the timber industry in many parts of the state focused on supporting the railroad, in Oroville, it supported the orchards. The Zosel Lumber Company's main product was pine apple boxes.

Over the last decade, Canadian demand for recreational housing has driven a development boom in Oroville. Resorts like Veranda Beach have put up entire villages of beach cottages, 80% of which are Canadian-owned. In response, Oroville has expressed concern about the rising cost of property and an annual influx of tourists like Osoyoos, British Columbia, experiences across the border, where summer tourism brings exponential, if seasonal, population growth. Others express hope that new business opportunities will follow. The Canadian side of the valley has more than 50 wineries, and Washington's Okanogan County is starting to catch on. Perhaps the newest gold in town will grow on vines.

The Borderlands Historical Society maintains the Depot Museum in downtown Oroville. Stop by the museum and visitor center to learn about the history of town and get directions to the local trailheads.

55

Population: 212
Founding: 1913

INSETS L to R: The Chief Joseph Rest Area describes the 1877 flight of the Wallowa band of Nez Perce. • The Colville Tribal Federal Corporation in Nespelem employs over 800 workers. • Some structures in residential Nespelem are abandoned and in disrepair. • Chief Joseph died in 1904 and was buried at the Nez Perce cemetery in Nespelem.

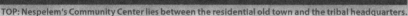

TOP: Nespelem's Community Center lies between the residential old town and the tribal headquarters.

Nespelem

Our Land, Your Land

In 1872, the Grant administration created the Colville Reservation on land traditionally occupied by several groups of Indigenous people, including the San Poil and Nespelem, whose first known encounter with non-Native people was meeting David Thompson in 1811. Both groups spoke Interior Salishan dialects and shared cultural practices, leading government officials to mistakenly count them as a single group, an error that would stand until the early 20th century. By then, while neither group had signed a treaty, the San Poil had continued a subsistence lifestyle organized around hunting, fishing, and gathering, while the Nespelem had adopted agriculture. As few as 45 Nespelem were living in 1910.

Though the San Poil and Nespelem people retained access to their homelands in an era when the government relieved many other tribes of theirs, they had to deal with increasing disruption to their way of life. In 1898, the US government declared the southern half of the Colville Reservation open for mineral exploration. By one account, 1,500 whites awaited the signal from across the Columbia River. When the ruling came, the miners and settlers stampeded, rushing into the territory and establishing claims. At the time, the land was only open for mining, not for homesteading. Many of the settlers established mining claims only to hold their place on the land, anticipating that homesteading would be legalized in the area soon. Some did mine, however, hauling ore to the railroad in Almira, dozens of miles away, or to the Nespelem River, where steamboats took the ore downriver to Bridgeport to meet the rail there, ending up finally in Tacoma's smelters. Ten years later, many of the miners left, following the Klondike Rush north. By then, Nespelem had become a town.

In 1913, the community finally platted the town. By then, the Jesuits and Methodists had established missions. Nespelem had a post office, hotel, butcher shop, livery, and two stores. As part of its treaty terms with the Colville Confederated Tribes, the US government was mandated to provide services on the Reservation. These included medical services and an agricultural consultant, a farmer tasked with teaching Indigenous people how to cultivate crops. A female counterpart traveled by horse and buggy to teach women how to run a household and care for children as the settlers did. The town incorporated in 1934 as construction of the Grand Coulee Dam brought a second wave of economic opportunity.

Chief Joseph's Resting Place

The Nez Perce led by Chief Joseph lived near the Wallowa Mountains, well southeast of the Colville Reservation. In 1877, resisting forcible relocation, Chief Joseph led several hundred Nez Perce, many of whom were women and children, in a months-long flight, pursued by 2,000 US cavalrymen. He surrendered just 30 miles shy of the Canadian border, with the words, "I am tired. My heart is sick and sad. From where the sun now stands, I will fight no more forever." After exiling the Nez Perce for eight years in Oklahoma, the government offered to send Nez Perce converts to Christianity to the Lapwai Reservation in Idaho. Those unwilling to accept, including Chief Joseph, went to the Colville and Umatilla Reservations.

The San Poil, under Chief Skolaskin, who claimed to be a prophet and held enormous power over the tribe, opposed Chief Joseph's band of Nez Perce joining the Colville Reservation. Others, like Chief Moses, opposed Skolaskin and welcomed the Nez Perce. Making his case, Skolasin asked, "Then why should the white race, whom we have always befriended when they were few and we were many, now that they are strong and numerous, take our land from us and give it to our enemies?"

The US military arrested Chief Skolaskin, imprisoning him at Alcatraz, and released him three years later. Chief Joseph never saw his homeland again. He is buried in Nespelem. The Chief Joseph Rest Area sits at the entrance to Nespelem off Route 155. Signage about the Nez Perce Conflict and an iron sculpture in front of the restrooms tell Chief Joseph's story.

Eagles, Fly!

Today, nearly all of Nespelem's residents are Native American. The Nespelem school educates about 140 students in kindergarten through eighth grade. The school lies between downtown Nespelem and the tribal headquarters, figuratively as well as literally.

The Nespelem Community Center, built in 1973, is a gathering place used for weddings, funerals, graduations, potlucks, pow-wows, and other community events.

In town, Nespelem seems to be falling apart. The roofs of long untended homes fall in, and shingle siding peels off the exteriors of others. One abandoned home has boarded windows but is missing a front door. Next to the town hall, a brightly colored jungle gym stands in a patch of gravel, empty seesaws and a picnic table completing the picture of a park. The senior center needs a paint job, but the fire hall and post office are in good shape, demonstrating that bureaucratic funding still finds its way to Nespelem.

In stark contrast, the tribal headquarters occupies a gleaming multistory campus of glass and steel set in the midst of a massive mowed lawn. Along the walkways leading to the building, visitors can stop at the Skolaskin Church, saved from inundation during the construction of the Grand Coulee Dam. Part of Skolaskin's power came from his prediction of an earthquake in 1872. Behind the church stands a black marble monument "in honor of the Colville Indians who honorably served their country and homeland in times of war and peace." Two flags fly high above the etched names, the American flag, and the flag of the Confederated Tribes of the Colville Reservation.

The school is a bit closer to town, on the crest of a hill that descends toward the tribal headquarters. Attendance is an issue at Nespelem, and the school looks in need of repair, but exciting things are happening here. In 2019, a robotics team from Nespelem competed in the first annual GeekWire Robotics Cup in Seattle. Not long ago, the school changed its mascot. Long known as the Savages, today Nespelem is home of the Eagles.

Fire and emergency services in Nespelem are provided by a combination of the Colville Confederated Tribes, the USDA, and the Town of Nespelem. The fire hall is the most modern building in town.

56

Population: 238
Founding: 1933

INSETS L to R: The six-mile Downriver Trail runs through Elmer City beside the Columbia River. • Elmer City homes are built against naturally terraced cliffs. • The nearby Grand Coulee Dam, pg. 118 • The vegetation in Elmer City changes drastically descending from the high-desert scrub into the river valley.

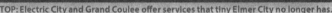

TOP: Electric City and Grand Coulee offer services that tiny Elmer City no longer has.

Elmer City

Standing in for America

Construction of the Grand Coulee Dam inspired not one but three company towns. Grand Coulee Dam (1933), Grand Coulee (1935), and Electric City (1950) were "New Deal Towns," created as worker housing for the dam project. The first of these towns was Mason City, which was eventually annexed by Grand Coulee Dam. Nearby Elmer City was always supposed to be something different.

In 1918, Rufus Woods, who published *The Wenatchee World* newspaper, started stumping for a man-made dam to replicate conditions at the end of the last ice age, when an ice dam over the Columbia forced water into Grand Coulee. The goal was irrigation of the Columbia Plateau. The Bureau of Reclamation had already poured a river of money into the pursuit but thus far had failed. Lobbyists for the plan couched their messaging in the promise of hydroelectric power. As one noted, "The revenue from the sale of electric energy alone would surely pay all the upkeep, interest on the investment." In 1929, the Corps of Engineers studied the potential for hydroelectric projects on the Columbia. They delivered their report in support of a dam in the

same year that Franklin D. Roosevelt won the presidency. In the wake of the Great Depression, Roosevelt's New Deal policies included construction of the dam, for irrigation and recreation, as well as to generate power.

The dam project was underway, but, as one historian noted, "There was virtually nothing at Grand Coulee but the river, jackrabbits, and rattlesnakes." Three companies shared the contract for the first iteration of the dam, but before they could begin building, their workers needed places to live.

These towns were meant to be little more than housing, but, scholars note, they "soon took on more political and substantial responsibilities." The government hoped the towns would demonstrate the government's ability to pull the country through the recession and restore people's faith in both governmental programming and in the country's economic potential.

Elmer City's first name was Elmerton, after the homesteader and first postmaster, Elmer Seaton. Nearby Whatcom County had an Elberton, so to avoid confusion at the post office, the community of Elmerton changed its name to Elmer City. When

Elmer City was first platted, the late Elmer Seaton's wife, who'd sold the land, extracted a promise that the town would be a "normal residential community suitable for family life."

In 1934, Elmer City became home to the area's trading post on wheels, nicknamed the "biggest little store by a dam site." (Get it?) Starkey's Real Estate Office opened the next year, and that winter was so cold that the Columbia River froze over. The town expanded gradually over the next 10 years, accompanied by small orchards as irrigation increased. In 1947, Elmer City incorporated. The Elmer City Commercial Club formed the center of civic and social life in town.

A 1953 report by the Bureau of Reclamation notes that Elmer City lacked "serious local government problems. They are sufficiently apart from other settlements that questions of consolidation do not arise, and for the foreseeable future they should be able to finance and maintain themselves." Around this time, Elmer City hit its peak in terms of population, topping out at nearly 600 residents.

A City on Fire

Since the early days of Elmer City, the threat of fire has plagued the town. A volunteer fire department started in 1937. In the next decade, the town formed a new fire district and bought a modern fire truck. Better construction methods led to decreased risk. In recent years, wildfires have repeatedly struck Elmer City, prompting repeated evacuations and resulting in significant losses.

In 2018, a fire destroyed four mobile homes, despite responses from agencies including Elmer City, the Colville Confederated Tribes, the US Bureau of Indian Affairs, the Mount Tolman Fire Center, and others. Artist Ric Gendron, a member of the Umatilla and Colville Tribes, lost his home and studio in the fire. His murals adorn the exterior of the Hotel Ruby in Spokane, and his evocative paintings are sold in Spokane's Marmot Art Space.

The next year, a fire scorched nearly 2,000 acres in a single day just north of town. The disaster recovery response to events like this falls

to the Okanogan County Department of Emergency Management, who have their work cut out for them. At nearly 5,300 square miles, Okanogan County is the largest in the state and makes up nearly 10% of Washington.

In Elmer City, the wilderness of the Colville Reservation meets the controlled landscape of the Columbia River dam projects.

Room for Improvements

Modern challenges facing Elmer City include a diminished financial capacity to provide water and sewer services to the community. In 2016, the town of Grand Coulee Dam billed Elmer City to the tune of more than $30,000, though Elmer City disputed the bill. While Elmer City tries to rein in its expenses, it is also considering building its own wastewater treatment plant, freeing itself from dependence on Grand Coulee Dam, with which Elmer City has had an agreement since 1975. Mayor Tillman lists solving the problem as his biggest concern.

A recent improvement in town came in 2018, when the Downriver Trail system expanded to connect Elmer City, improving access for bicycles and pedestrians to the 6-mile trail. Regionally, the Coulee Corridor National Scenic Byway offers unlimited opportunities for recreation. Elmer City falls near the middle of the corridor, which spans from Omak in the northern part of Okanogan County to Franklin County, where the Channeled Scablands meet the Palouse.

One of the more popular non-dam-related tourist attractions nearby is Steamboat Rock State Park. The rock, named for its resemblance to the steamers that once navigated Washington's waterways, is nearly 800 feet high and covers 600 acres. Able hikers can ascend the butte. From the top of the rock, the trail offers sweeping viewpoints of Grand Coulee, all the way to Okanogan-Wenatchee National Forest.

The Tillman family, former owners of the now-boarded-up Trustworthy Hardware store, goes way back in Elmer City. In 2018, Jesse Tillman became the fourth generation of Tillmans to hold the mayoral position.

57

Population: NA
Constructed: 1933–1941

INSETS L to R: Interactive and visual displays explain the physics behind the enormous gravity dam. • The dam, nearly a mile long, created Roosevelt Lake, which spans more than 80,000 acres. • The construction of the dam obliterated Columbia River Salmon runs, the economic mainstay of many Indigenous cultures. • The bust of FDR forever gazes over the defining public works project achieved during his presidency.

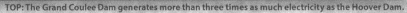

TOP: The Grand Coulee Dam generates more than three times as much electricity as the Hoover Dam.

Grand Coulee Dam

A Great Amount of Good

The first dam in the place where the Grand Coulee Dam sits today was a glacier. The Okanogan lobe of the Cordilleran ice sheet in the Pleistocene epoch, 2.5 million years ago, formed a natural dam across the Columbia River. Lake Columbia, the result of this natural dam, was nearly twice as far above sea level as today's Lake Roosevelt, the reservoir formed by today's Grand Coulee Dam. At the same time, the Cordilleran ice sheet formed a dam across the Clark Fork River near Idaho, resulting in Glacial Lake Missoula. Eventually, the lake burst the walls of its ice dam, cascading with great force across the northwest, cutting canyons through the basalt, including the canyon known as Grand Coulee.

In the 1930s, the US Bureau of Reclamation began construction on a massive gravity dam that would provide agricultural irrigation over hundreds of thousands of acres. Up to that point, farmers had practiced dryland farming, which relies on drought-resistant crops and natural cycles of rainfall. With the onset of WWII, the goal of irrigation became secondary to producing hydroelectric power, and nearly 20 years would pass before pumping operations began in service of irrigation. Work on the dam continued, with the construction of a third power plant in the 1970s.

Today, the dam has a generating capacity of more than 21 billion kilowatt-hours of electricity: enough to power 4.2 million households in 11 states and parts of Canada. It's made of more than 12 million cubic yards of concrete—an amount that could wrap a 4-foot sidewalk around the equator twice or build a highway from Seattle to Miami.

More than 5,000 workers built the dam over eight years (1933–1941). Seventy-seven workers died; Frank A. Banks, the head engineer, watched his hair turn from black to white. On a visit to the site in October 1937, President Franklin D. Roosevelt commented: "Coming back to Grand Coulee after three years, I am made very happy by the wonderful progress that I have seen . . . we are building here something that is going to do a great amount of good for this nation through all the years to come."

River of Remembrance

The reservoir behind the Grand Coulee Dam filled slowly. By 1940, it covered one of two important fishing sites used by Indigenous people for millennia. Within 20 years, the second site went under. Visitors to the Grand Coulee Dam Visitor Center can learn about the impact the inundation had on Indigenous cultures. An exhibit quotes Alex Sherwood of the Spokane Tribe of Indians:

> *Sometimes even now I find a lonely spot where the river still runs wild. I find myself talking to it. I might ask, "River, do you remember how it used to be—the game, the fish, the pure water, the roar of the falls, boats, canoes, fishing platforms? You fed and took care of our people then. For thousands of years we walked your banks and used your waters. . . . Sometimes I stand and shout, 'River, do you remember us?'"*

As floodwaters rose around Kettle Falls, the Confederated Tribes of the Colville Reservation mourned. Over three days, they eulogized the river. Washington state senator Clarence Dill, a proponent of the dam, nevertheless acknowledged the loss it represented to the local Native population in a speech during the ceremony: "The Indians have fished here for thousands of years . . . it is a source of both food and of beauty." Dill advocated for the dam to be a nonprofit enterprise, "so that the Indians of future generations, as well as the white men, will find the change made here a great benefit to the people."

Construction of the dam did not make allowance for salmon to pass, effectively ending the salmon fishery for the 645 river miles above the dam. The dam inundated 400 farms, 10 communities of white settlers, and innumerable sites of importance to Indigenous peoples, including villages, burial grounds, and fishing grounds, and it displaced thousands of people. Between 1930 and 1993, the annual salmon catch on the Columbia fell from 33.9 million pounds to just 1.4 million. Efforts to restore the Columbia River salmon are ongoing and represent the most expensive wildlife habitat restoration project in the history of the United States. To date, those efforts have not been successful. As one member of the Colville noted, "The promises of the government were written in sand and then covered with water, like everything else."

Maintenance and Restoration

At the time of its construction, the dam was hailed as the Eighth Wonder of the World and employed 12,000 people. This was during the Great Depression, when the rate of unemployment nationwide reached 25%. Its initial purpose was to provide irrigation that would lead to the creation of 10,000 new farms. Though the area never experienced quite the boom imagined, today's nearly 2,500 farms earn

The Grand Coulee Dam Visitors Center hosts more than 250,000 people a year. Its exhibits include interactive demonstrations of the physics of the dam, historical artifacts, and displays demonstrating the impact of the dam, for better and worse.

a return many times greater than the dollar amount envisioned at the dam's infancy. In return for the infrastructure, farmers would repay half the cost of the dam's construction in purchased water.

Today, a massive restoration effort is underway to repair cracks and worn bearings discovered in the turbines in 2013. The Bonneville Power Administration (BPA), the federal agency that sells the energy produced by the Grand Coulee Dam and 30 others, has struggled to remain financially viable, raising its rates by as much as 30% in recent years. As a result, some northwestern utility companies are considering sourcing power elsewhere, according to *The Seattle Times*. Over 40 years, $17 billion of the BPA's budget has gone toward salmon and wildlife habitat restoration, yet Columbia River steelhead and salmon remain on the list of endangered species. Meanwhile, in August of 2019, the Colville Tribal Fish and Wildlife department released the first salmon to swim above the Chief Joseph Dam in nearly 80 years. Plans are in the works to release more fish above the Grand Coulee Dam. Representatives of the Confederated Colville Tribes are calling the event a "cultural release," intended to raise awareness around the issues of salmon passage and traditional Indigenous cultural practices. The release is an act of reparative justice.

A bust of Franklin D. Roosevelt gazes across the reservoir that bears his name. Visible in the distance, the BPA's company towns lie nestled in the river valley.

58

Population: 788
Founding: 1885

INSETS L to R: Glaciers cut v-shaped valleys into u-shaped "teacups" like the one surrounding Rock Island. • Steven Thomas Schooler enlisted in the Army the day after his high school graduation and was killed at the age of 19 in the Vietnam War. • The Rock Island Community Church is the only one in town. East Wenatchee, 15 miles away, offers other worship opportunities. • Vancouver-based Columbia Ventures Corporation recently purchased this WWII-era pig iron production facility.

TOP: Rock Island pays tribute to its history as a company town.

Rock Island

Like a Rock

J. E. Keane, a mining engineer who'd made his fortune on a California gold mine, arrived in Rock Island in 1885. Two years later, he brought his family up by covered wagon. More than 100 years later, Keane's granddaughter Lucy filled in the details of her family's story for the Initiative for Rural Innovation and Stewardship's program called Gathering Our Voice. "Grandpa Keane brought the first Aberdeen Angus cattle here from Missouri," she says. "During the devastating winter of 1889, Lucy's grandfather snowshoed all the way to Waterville, dozens of miles away, to buy flour to feed his cattle. He lost his entire herd that year, as did so many area farmers."

Keane established a small town site and secured a post office, which he called Hammond, just upriver from the Rock Island Rapids. The town center diverted to its current location shortly thereafter, when James Hill brought the Great Northern through Douglas County.

To complete its route to the Pacific, Great Northern needed to bridge the Columbia River. The steel, cantilevered truss bridge at Rock Island

became the second bridge to do so and is the oldest remaining. Hill contracted Edgemoor Bridge Works in Delaware to design and build the bridge, which spans the river for 416.5 feet. The bridge meant jobs, and more jobs meant more businesses. It was a temporary burst of good fortune.

By 1904, historians were already talking about Rock Island in the past tense. The bridge's completion in 1893 "marked the downfall [of Rock Island] . . . the laborers who had been employed at this point moved away and the business houses were discontinued." Decades later, another large construction project would repeat the boom–bust cycle, revitalizing the town. All they had to do was hang on.

Just before the Great Depression began, the company that owned Puget Sound Power and Light applied for a license to put a dam across the Columbia at Rock Island. In 1930, work began. The same year, Rock Island incorporated, with 421 residents. For decades, the dam provided intermittent bursts of job opportunities as workers built the dam and two powerhouses. As had happened before, with the bulk of the project completed, in

1932, workers went elsewhere. A WWII-era iron plant purchased by the Hanna Mining Company in 1974 got Rock Island's economic hopes up again, but the plant sold in 1988 and after operating in bankruptcy for three years, closed for good. Its waterside infrastructure still stands, like the dam and the bridge, a reminder of Rock Island's single-pointed success stories. Despite these significant setbacks, Rock Island is hanging in there, with nearly twice the population it had at incorporation.

Memories Under Water

The Rock Island dam was the first to span the Columbia. Today, there are more than 18 dams on the main stem of the Columbia and its main tributary, the Snake River. Eight of the dams allow for fish passage; however, the dams have undeniably destroyed the Columbia River salmon runs beyond repair. The federal government operates 10 of the dams. It has ignored repeated calls by Indigenous Nations to remove the dams, which supply power to the region. In an article for *Columbia: The Magazine of Northwest History*, William Layman writes that "Memory of the unregulated Columbia flows like the river itself, segment to segment, reservoir to reservoir, each section of river having its own constituency of elders who knew its untamed waters—the rapids, currents, back eddies, and falls—now vanished from our view." The Rock Island Rapids were last seen in 1931.

A New Era?

With no large-scale projects on the near horizon, Rock Island has become a bedroom community for the larger nearby cities of East Wenatchee and Wenatchee. Still, Rock Island hopes to capitalize on tourism to the area. The city recently zoned a new commercial–industrial district on the site of the old silicon plant and invested $3.2 million in a new sewage system. Previous industrial pollution at the site may complicate plans for development, but the state ranked the contamination on the low end of the scale. In 2011, the town expanded the

Rock Island golf course from 9 to 18 holes. Golfers can play a full round for $30.

In addition to these improvements, Mayor Randy Agnew thinks Rock Island may be well-positioned to become a future center of technology. "Ag[riculture] is still important, but we're transitioning," he said. Data centers like Seattle-based Sabey like the valley for its access to hydroelectric power and weather conditions that allow for natural cooling. Agnew sees these companies as potential anchors for a new flush of economic development. It would be a change for Rock Island, but then, things are always changing.

Orchards and vineyards line the golf course below basaltic cliffs in Rock Island. Deep channels and glacial erratics left by the last ice age bring geologic time into the present.

Before the war, Lucy Keane remembers, "Rock Island had three gas stations, two grocery stores, [and] three cafés." Now everything's just a little smaller. "Times have changed so much." Rock Island's town website features Lucy's lengthy poem, "Rock Island Era," on its home page. Strangely, the poem is attributed to "author unknown," though Lucy Keane is the granddaughter of the town's founder. The poem walks the reader through Rock Island's entire history, from glacial erratics at the end of the last ice age to the current community development plan. Its last two lines read, "And what James Keane inspired in 1885 / Rock Island is keeping that vision alive."

Rock Island's welcome sign reminds visitors of the town's importance. The Rock Island dam was the first of many on the Columbia. The US operates 11 dams on the main stem of the Columbia, but the entire river system holds more than 400 dams.

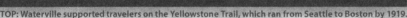

59

TOP: Waterville supported travelers on the Yellowstone Trail, which ran from Seattle to Boston by 1919.

Population: 1,138
Founding: 1886

INSETS L to R: Theatrical productions and movie screenings alike take place at The Nifty. • A bright white spire draws a striking contrast to red brick on the Douglas County courthouse. • The Waterville Hotel features high ceilings, clawfoot tubs, and a wide front porch for socializing. • The courthouse was listed on the National Register of Historic Places in 1975.

Waterville

Their Pretty Little City

In 1883, J. W. Adams, a town promoter from Kansas, saw a scrubby plateau in north-central Washington and envisioned a new county. When the Washington Territorial Legislature created Lincoln County, Adams argued for a second county. About 100 people lived in the nascent Douglas County at the time, but Adams had plans. He platted a town, called it Okanogan City, and started promoting it.

Okanogan City was the only settlement in the county, so it took the title of county seat. Settlers came and staked claims, but when they found there was no water, they left. Adams dug in, literally. Convinced that the land held accessible water, Adams drilled multiple wells, looking and failing to find water. When a 285-foot dig came up dry, Adams finally quit.

Meanwhile, a day's journey of about 7 miles away, Stephen Boise established a squatter's claim where he built a log cabin and barn and dug a well. The next year, he had cultivated 10 acres. A. T. Greene bought Boise's claim that year, 1884, and decided to build a town. Unlike Adams' Okanogan City, the wells in Greene's new town provided.

Greene and a surveyor named Snow platted the town in 1886. In a clever promotional act, they named the new town for the resource Douglas County's first attempt lacked: Waterville. The next year, Waterville became the county seat. Never having gotten on its feet, Okanogan City vanished almost as soon as it began.

In the early days, settlers didn't think the soil on the Waterville plateau was suitable for farming. They specialized instead in ranching cattle and sheep. While ranchers fought with each other over grazing rights, wheat farmers began staking their own claims. The plateau is 2,500 feet above sea level, with average January temperatures between 15 and 30 degrees Fahrenheit. In 1889, a deep freeze on the plateau caused most of the cattle to starve. After that, many ranchers turned to wheat farming.

Close on the heels of that terrible winter, the Panic of 1893 cut wheat prices to 30¢ per bushel, down from 82¢ at the beginning of that year. In a letter describing the hardships homesteaders faced, farmer Ole Oleson Ruud wrote, "Times are so hard and money so scarce here in this good wheat country . . . that property can hardly be sold for money."

In the face of seemingly inevitable economic decline, Waterville pushed back, hard. The newspaper, the *Big Bend Empire,* launched a campaign to brand Waterville as the region's economic engine. Financial records showed the town in debt, and the railroad had decided to run to Mansfield, bypassing Waterville, but Waterville built its own spur line, connecting a 5-mile track to Great Northern's line through the county. They staged the Douglas County Industrial Exposition, bringing thousands of visitors to the town, and followed up the next year with a "massive convention."

By 1897, the town's efforts had paid off. The price of wheat was up, and Waterville made historic profits. A new road in 1916 replaced the treacherous stage line through Corbaley Canyon, and soon the Sunset Highway ended Waterville's isolation. *The Tacoma Globe* described the people of Waterville in 1889 as "hustling, bustling, go-ahead fellows . . . Nothing is too good for their pretty little city and they all pitch in for the common purpose of beautifying and benefiting the town."

Douglass, Douglass, and Douglas

In letters to his cousin, Stephen Douglass, the US congressman from Illinois, spelled his surname with a double *s.* Then, in one letter, he dropped an *s* without explanation and never spelled it with two again. Douglass, who was pro-slavery, had been wooing the daughter of a prominent slaveowner while a US Representative in the late 1840s; his biographer posits that Douglass changed the spelling of his name to avoid association with abolitionist Frederick Douglass, whose autobiography had recently been published. In 1883, the Washington Territorial Legislature created Douglas County, naming it for the Democratic politician, who chaired the US Commission on Territories during his Senate tenure. Douglas fought for the Compromise of 1850 and argued that slavery was a question of public policy best handled at the state level. Abraham Lincoln, the namesake of Lincoln County, defeated Douglas for the presidency. The 13th Amendment, ratified on December 6, 1865,

abolished slavery in the United States. Twenty years earlier, Frederick Douglass had written, "Thus is slavery the enemy of both the slave and the slaveholder."

The Deepest Well Is Community

Waterville today is still a pretty little city. Highway 2 makes a wide turn into town, past the park, museum, and historic hotel and into a small downtown with a sweet theatre, The Nifty, and a few small businesses. Apple and wheat farming and cattle ranching still drive the local economy, employing a third of the county's workers.

Between the Waterville Hotel (1903) and the Douglas County Museum, a historical marker notes the town as a point of interest on the Yellowstone Trail, the first coast-to-coast auto route across the northern US.

Waterville is the highest-situated incorporated city in the state. Nearby Badger Mountain is popular for winter sports, and geocaching and hiking bring people to the coulees in warmer months. A number of annual celebrations bring visitors to Waterville, including the North Central Washington Fair and Rodeo.

The fair traces its roots to the 1899 Douglas County Industrial Exposition. After a record potato crop in 1913, the fair became known as the Waterville Potato Carnival, rebranded the North Central Washington Fair in the 1940s. "The fair is a celebration of all things home cooked, farm grown and handmade," Waterville resident Diane Petersen told the *Wenatchee World.* "It is a space to meet up with old friends and honor the connection between land, people and animals—to show pride in our youth and in our way of life." Waterville has fought hard for that way of life, through natural and economic disaster and physical isolation. Descendants of those pioneering families are still here. Times were indeed tough when Ole Ruud faced foreclosure in the wake of the Panic of 1893; yet, more than a century later, the Ruud family still has the farm.

The Douglas County Courthouse, built in 1905, replaced an 1889 building destroyed by fire. Architect Newton Gauntt designed the new building with a central tower and spire, adding visual interest to an otherwise traditional design.

60

Population: 320
Founding: 1889

INSETS L to R: Oil Can Larry's is an example of a multiple-use station, one of several types of gas stations preserved around the country. • Mansfield may be the only Washington town of its size with a hometown theatre troupe. • Farmers on the Columbia Plateau specialize in dryland farming, which doesn't rely on irrigation. • The community purchased the museum building in 1998 and completely renovated it by 2010.

TOP: With flag-lined streets between a park and a school district, Mansfield is quintessential Americana.

Mansfield

The Town at the End of the Line

In the early 1880s, settlers in Douglas County to the west of the Grand Coulee essentially lived on the edge of the frontier. An informal census from the time counts fewer than 80 people. A 1904 history notes that when the governor authorized the new county, in 1883, Okanogan was the only town, "platted for the express purpose of having a place to designate as the county seat . . . There was not a store, post office, saloon, or blacksmith shop, a railway train or a stage line in the whole territory to be subsequently known as Douglas County, a territory as large as the state of Connecticut." Everything was about to change.

James Hill's Great Northern railroad was charging across the Waterville Plateau. The original route would have skirted Mansfield, but in 1908, an engineer named Whitcomb advocated extending the tracks to the fledgling town, then called the Yeager Precinct. The Yeager family settled in the area in 1888. Henry Yeager, a German whose father had served in Napoleon's military, farmed near Foster Creek in Douglas County and then moved to his son Albert's homestead near

present-day Mansfield. Albert Yeager was a road supervisor who raised cattle and farmed. When Great Northern's tracks came through, settlers in the Yeager Precinct relocated a short distance to be closer to it. R. E. Darling named the new settlement after his hometown in Ohio: Mansfield. Perhaps the landscape reminded Darling of his home city, which celebrated its 100th anniversary that year.

This new Mansfield was the terminus of the rail spur, a town in the middle of a wheat field. A 1910 map shows Great Northern's tracks cutting north through the center of the county like a steel river, at times mimicking the shape of the Columbia. While it marked the end of the line, Mansfield was anything but a dead end. Within a few years, the population exceeded 2,000 people, though records differ. Wheat exports totaled nearly half a million bushels annually. A single fire in 2014 caused $200,000 worth of damage, or more than $5 million in today's dollars, setting back early economic success. Another fire followed closely on its heels. Subsequent ordinances required builders to use fireproof materials.

Record wheat production led to high hopes for Mansfield, but drought in the 1920s followed by the Depression permanently dashed those hopes. The railroad scaled back its activity in the town, and in the 1980s, left for good.

Hometown Pride

In 1999, Mansfield resident Linda Bayless got a phone call saying they were tearing down the old school. If she wanted to salvage any of the wood, she needed to get there quickly. "We rounded up kids and everybody." This is how the community of Mansfield saves its history for its future—one piece at a time. The museum started in 1998 when the community secured a building. By 2010, the community had replaced the floor, ceiling, furnace, bathroom, and windows. The next year, the board started a program to collect area family records.

The Listening Post Network (gatheringourvoice.org/listening-post), an audio archive started by the Initiative for Rural Innovation and Stewardship, holds the oral histories of North Central Washington. One of the questions Linda Bayless answers is, "What are you proudest of?" Bayless recounts the community effort to create the Mansfield Museum. "I'm proud of the people," she says.

Drive to It, Not Through It

In 1884, the county's first wheat crop was an experiment whose success would drive the region's economy beyond any foreseeable horizon. Douglas County is still one of the state's highest-performing wheat producers. Mansfield's economy remains dependent on agriculture, as does its identity, and supporting agriculture is a key tenant of ongoing county planning. But farming isn't the only thing going on in this town.

For the better part of three decades, the Mansfield Theatricals have been writing and performing community theatre productions. Founders Diana and Jim Mickelson, teachers at the Mansfield School, wanted a theatre experience that they didn't have to commute for, one that would provide local opportunities for community theatre. Their first performances in Mansfield sold out; soon after, the Mansfield Theatricals had their own home in a repurposed building across from the museum, right in the middle of downtown. Since their first year, the troupe has hidden an "Easter egg" phrase in each of its scripts. Want to know the secret phrase? Catch the Theatricals at one of their Playday performances, held the second Saturday of June.

Paragliders like to use the low, flat land around Mansfield as a landing zone. In 1990, Mark Shipman became the first to paraglide into Mansfield from his launch point on Chelan Butte, more than 20 miles distant. Rocket enthusiasts appreciate Mansfield too. The Washington Aerospace Club maintains a launch site just outside of town where amateur rocket scientists fly hobby rockets up to 14,000 vertical feet.

Mansfield feels like an American idyll. Framed by fields of wheat, the town occupies a modest square between a school, a park, grain elevators, and the railroad track. The town is not quite one-third of a mile squared, making it smaller than some of the surrounding fields.

The local Lions Club describes Mansfield as a place "you drive to, not through." It sounds like a joke: Is it an insult or a compliment? You won't visit Mansfield by accident. But, should a bluebird sky and a long summer drive or a sense of wonder at the thought of hundreds of rockets launched at once pull you onto Route 172, you'll be glad to discover this town.

The Mansfield School District, home of the Kernels, educates just fewer than 100 students in grades K–12. In addition to the usual course offerings, the school proudly provides opportunities for sports, music, drama, and IT education to students at all grade levels.

61

Population: 501
Founding: 1957

INSETS L to R: George Elementary serves nearly 200 students in grades K-4. Older students attend school in nearby Quincy. • The George Public Library is tiny but thriving. It offers a great selection of books and movies and a nice technology center. • After too many cars were lost over the edge of a small ferry operating at Vantage, the state built a highway for the convenience of residents on both sides of the Columbia. • A silhouette of George Washington, the town's namesake.

TOP: At the Community Hall, George carries on the traditions started by Charlie and Edith Brown.

George

Charlie Brown's Town

Coulee City claims the title of the first town in Grant County, and the town of Coulee Dam comes with an eponymous raison d'être. The town of George, Washington, couldn't be more different. The brainchild of area entrepreneur Charles Brown—Charlie, if you will—George might be the youngest town in the county. Born nearly 200 years after the country's founding and more than half a century after Washington became a state, the town of George chose to name itself after the first President of the United States.

In the 1950s, Charlie Brown imagined a city inspired by colonial times that would draw tourists and interstate travelers alike. The folksiest version of the town's origin story holds that Charlie Brown conceived the town out of whole cloth, from streets named for cherries to the annual bake-off of the world's biggest cherry pie every Fourth of July. As Brown's daughter noted, her father "had a new idea every morning!"

The streets of George are named for cherries, one of 60 crops grown across more than 1,800 farms in Grant County, contributing an annual value of $1.19 billion to the economy. In George, one might meet a friend at the corner of Rainier and Wild Cherry. The main boulevard through the tiny town is Montmorency, said to be the variety of cherry tree the man George Washington himself chopped down as a wayward child in Mount Vernon so long ago.

A less exciting, if more practical, story of George's founding reports that the need arose for additional towns in the massive irrigation district between Quincy and Moses Lake. All that space called for something middle-of-the-road, where farmers wouldn't have to go so far to get supplies. After citizens pushed back against a proposed federal site, the Bureau of Reclamation opened the bidding. Mr. Charles Brown was the only bidder. Working with a city-planning instructor from the University of Washington, Brown platted the town and became its first mayor, presiding over it until he died in 1975, at which point his wife, Edith, became the second mayor.

The City of George is a self-described "close-knit community." It's also a multiethnic one, with many Latino families. George feels like a place that welcomes citizens from many backgrounds, something that isn't felt in all rural communities. As the town website says, George is "very simply, a good place to live."

Home of the Sasquatch

Summer nights in George used to carry the song of the Sasquatch—the Sasquatch Festival, that is, one of the many concerts held at the natural amphitheater nearby. Formerly a winery called Champs de Brionne, The Gorge at George, as locals call it, is the Red Rocks of the Northwest. From its sloping lawn, Phish heads, hip-hop fans, and all manner of other festival-goers gather to watch their favorite musicians play against a backdrop of basalt cliffs rising over the Columbia Gorge. The Gorge, like Dry Falls farther north in Grant County, formed when the dam holding back Glacial Lake Missoula burst and flood waters surged through the landscape. A recent movie, *Enormous: The Gorge Story*, tells more of its history. Known for three-day festivals, George is a popular venue for camping and weekends of revelry. Cave B Estate Winery is nearby too. Night after summer night, 20,000 fans make the trek to this beloved venue.

By George!

Wind rushes through the Columbia River Gorge, sweeping up the cliffs toward Grant County and the tiny town of George. About halfway between Seattle to the west and Spokane to the east, it feels like little more than a truck stop. In fact, the truck stop in George, right off I-90, is a successful business. Eponymously named Shree's, it has a bust of the town's namesake, George Washington, in front of the pumps. A towering digital billboard proclaims the truck stop's owner, Shree Saini, to be the winner of Miss India Worldwide. "Need Motel/QSR space?" the sign asks. "Call Shree!"

But George is more than just a truck stop. There's a nice library with a great selection of books. The book club's picks occupy a special shelf, and here and there, you'll find selected works on display. A collection of Ursula K. Le Guin's poetry stands out, and in the Junior Nonfiction section, a book called *Queer, There, and Everywhere,* a young-adult book focused on LGBTQ history, stands displayed apart from its neatly shelved cohort. Signs in the library advertise reading groups in both Spanish and English, telling as much about the population as the selected books on display. During my visit, librarian Itzen was deep into a phone conversation about the prizes for this year's summer reading program. The person on the other end of the phone wanted to know what the prizes were, how much money would be spent on them, and who got to choose.

The George Community Hall is a nonprofit serving the Quincy Valley and promoting volunteerism, cultural sharing, and community. Every year, residents of George bake the world's largest cherry pie on the Fourth of July.

The library shares a building with a restaurant that doesn't seem to have a name, but whose sign advertises what's on offer: TACOS. Across the street from the library is a modern-looking fire station. The main road through town fronts another restaurant, a church, and a newish elementary school. There's no high school in George, so older students attend school in nearby Quincy. A few well-organized streets cluster around these businesses, but driving in any direction, the feeling of being in town quickly gives way to the wide open space of farmland. Houses become fewer and farther between. Irrigation implements tick out regular streams of water into greening fields, and tractors kick up dust in the distance. Looking east from the corner of Rainier and Wild Cherry, George Washington's silhouette graces the town's water tower. Signs from any direction point visitors to the Gorge Amphitheatre, tucked down in a canyon. To the west, hills rise above the Columbia Gorge, dotted with windmills. There's a lot to this little town, even if it passes by in the blink of an eye.

Just outside of George, at the edge of Grant County, the Columbia River cuts a path through the landscape. The Wanapum Dam inundated petroglyphs and required the relocation of the town of Vantage.

62

Population: 1,514
Founding: 1919

INSETS L to R: Some towns were built by the railroad, but Soap Lake was always a resort. • The whole town is visible from the hill at the South end of the lake. • To this day, local businesses tout the health benefits of bathing in Soap Lake's unique mud. • Sam Israel Paniyiri Square is named for the Seattle real estate investor who loved Soap Lake, which he said reminded him of Israel.

TOP: Soap Lake is too little to get lost in, but these signs are here in case you try.

Soap Lake

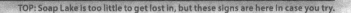

The Lake Effect

Since its earliest days, the story of Soap Lake has been a romance. In an undated photo, ostensibly from the first few decades of the 20th century, a wounded man approaches the rocky shore, leaning on a crutch. Thick bandages cover his left foot, and his left arm is in a sling. As though an angel of mercy, a barefoot woman stands at the water's edge, wearing something between a toga and a baptismal garment. She points toward the water, her other arm outstretched toward the suffering man, beckoning him into the water. At the bottom of the scene, someone has inked the phrase, "It will cure you."

Local mythology holds that "rival Indian tribes" treated the lake as a neutral zone and a place of healing. Indigenous people bathed in the lake to heal themselves and their animals of such ailments as rashes and snakebites, according to contemporary Soap Lake resident and amateur historian, Kathleen Kiefer. By the end of the first decade of the 20th century, sanitariums had sprouted up all around the lake, and according to one source, by 1940, one in 18 residents of the town had moved there seeking a cure for their Buerger's disease, a rare blood vessel disorder. The Veteran's Administration commissioned a study in the 1930s to determine whether the thick oils in the lake held healing potential for the disease, which afflicted large numbers of soldiers returning from WWI.

Soap Lake is meromictic, meaning that it contains different strata of minerals that never mix. Reports by the Department of Natural Resources dating before the construction of the Grand Coulee Dam describe the lake as producing a "tough foam" thick with oil which, left to stand, breaks down into an "evil-smelling black muddy liquid." The slick feeling left on the skin led to the eventual naming of Soap Lake, thought to be derived from the Native word *Smokiam*, which several sources interpret to mean "healing waters." Since the early 1900s, visitors and residents have sought relief by smearing themselves in the pungent mud, letting it bake to their bodies on the shore, and rinsing it off in the lake. Whether the lake actually contains healing properties remains a mystery, however.

Something in the Water

The two salinated layers of Soap Lake haven't mixed in 2,000 years, making the lake a unique living laboratory. In 2002, researchers from nearby Central Washington University won an $840,000 grant to study the microorganisms that live in the lake's unusual environment. The scientific community studying the lake received a recent boon when in 2014, more than 400 samples of lake water were discovered in the basement of a deceased Soap Lake resident, W. Thomas Edmonson. A former professor at the University of Washington, Edmonson had been collecting the samples since 1952. Researchers found that the samples provided evidence for the ways that Soap Lake's composition has changed since the construction of the Grand Coulee Dam. Building the dam and creating Lake Roosevelt closed off Soap Lake from the system of waterways carved by Glacial Lake Missoula's flooding at the end of the last ice age. As a result, researchers say, Soap Lake has gradually lost salinity.

A Century of Suds

Despite the changes to the lake's composition, Soap Lake still ranks among the world's best known mineral lakes, including the Dead Sea and Lake Baikal. The reasons for the decline of tourism in the area over the years are multifocal. The Great Depression limited people's ability to travel, and on the heels of the Depression came drought, lowering the lake's water level dramatically. At least one source associates the decline in tourism with the invention of antibiotics. Today, the town of Soap Lake aims to revitalize the once thriving tourism industry that built the town. Slogans on banners capitalize on the town's early reputation, noting, "There's something in the water," and "Soap Lake: The cure for the ordinary."

Scientific research on the lake continues as well. The Soap Lake Conservancy and Soap Lake Revitalization Team combine the efforts of engaged residents, as well as researchers from multiple universities, to study and protect both the economic and natural resources in Soap Lake. If not protected, the lake may become entirely fresh water within the next 100 years, scientists say. To date, local businesses and the city itself continue to promote the lake's "healing waters," advertising the lake's properties as curative for everything from circulatory problems such as Buerger's and Raynaud's diseases to psoriasis and rheumatoid arthritis. Testimonials on the Washington State tourism website support these claims with anecdotal evidence.

A 1941 report in the *American Heart Journal* noted that "in 66% of cases, gangrenous and ulcerative lesions" caused by Buerger's disease "healed themselves" after patients with the disease bathed in Soap Lake.

The town's revitalization includes a burgeoning local art scene too. The Masquers Theater, a Soap Lake institution since 1979, received a new building in the early 2000s, thanks to nearly $200,000 in donations from local supporters. Other arts projects that have inspired community effort include plans to build a massive lava lamp constructed of solar panels and lasers that display a nightly light show. (Call it Grant County's answer to the world's largest ball of twine.) To date, the lava lamp is still a dream, but this small town has been dreaming big for a long time. In 2019, the town of Soap Lake celebrated 100 years since its incorporation.

Signs in downtown Soap Lake help visitors find their way to the many available activities besides soaking in a mud bath.

63

Population: 562
Founding: 1890

INSETS L to R: Some towns work to achieve an Old West feel. Coulee City doesn't have to try.
• Coulee City lies in the path of the Cariboo Trail. In the 1850s, miners and prospectors utilized this ancient Indigenous route up the Okanogan river to reach the gold fields in British Columbia.
• Cariboo Trail Studio and Art Gallery is owned and operated by local artist Don Nutt.
• Signage at the Coulee City campground summarizes the town's history from pre-contact to its platting in 1890.

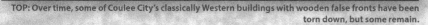

TOP: Over time, some of Coulee City's classically Western buildings with wooden false fronts have been torn down, but some remain.

Coulee City

A Proud Heritage

Platted in 1890, Coulee City is the oldest town in Grant County. Early on, its importance lay in its location along an easy crossing point on the Columbia River, making it a draw for travelers in the region. Nearby towns like Soap Lake, renowned for its namesake's restorative mineral properties, brought tourists through Coulee City, and the promise of agricultural success and jobs in rail and hydroelectric power brought workers.

Before 1937, Coulee City's official name was McEntee's Crossing, so named for Phillip McEntee, who established the first rail station and post office in the town. Coulee City served as home base for Grand Coulee Dam's engineers until 1934, when the US Bureau of Reclamation created the town of Coulee Dam for the dam workers.

McEntee came from Montana with a team of surveyors hoping to develop a road north from Ritzville. After finishing the road, he bought cattle and settled on the outskirts of today's Coulee City. Other settlers followed, and by 1888, there were two stores, a blacksmithery, and a saloon.

Before Washington became a state in 1889, livestock ranching dominated life in Coulee City. Railroad development changed both the physical and occupational landscape of the area, and many ranchers became traditional dryland farmers. The Columbia Basin Reclamation Project brought not only water but also much-needed jobs to the area during the Great Depression.

As the rail made its way west in the late 1800s, three lines came through Grant County: the Great Northern; Northern Pacific; and Chicago, Milwaukee, and St. Paul. Ranchers hoping to become farmers faced some difficulty in getting quality land, as the railways owned much of the desirable land along the water. Agriculture and tourism remained important to the development of Coulee City. A 1925 brochure lists citizens of Coulee City among the board members of the Grant County Fair Association, and a guidebook from 1962 notes several Coulee City businesses as advertisers hoping to draw folks to Coulee City while they explored the Columbia Basin.

In the first decade of the 19th century, Grant County cowboys rounded up 5,000 wild horses in the area and sent them by rail to buyers on the East Coast. Today's cowboys continue to show their stuff at the annual Last Stand Rodeo, on the circuit of the Professional Rodeo Cowboys Association. Today, the town's Chamber of Commerce promotes Coulee City as a great place to live, and notes that "Ours is a proud heritage; one those hardy and courageous pioneers would look on with favor."

Dry Falls

Just a few miles outside Coulee City on State Route 17 lies what remains of the largest waterfall in Earth's history. Dry Falls is a 3.5-mile cataract of basalt cliffs three times as long and as tall as Niagara Falls. At the end of the last ice age, a block of ice formed a dam here more than 2 miles wide and 30 miles long, ending in Glacial Lake Missoula. This ice dam failed repeatedly, and water scoured out Dry Falls and Lower Grand Coulee. Visitors to the area today can fish and boat in the lakes, hike basalt trails in what feels like Washington's own Grand Canyon, and observe nature in this refuge for shrub–steppe flora and cliff-dwelling fauna. Other canyons, or coulees, created by the ice age floodwaters in this region include Frenchman Coulee, Moses Coulee, Potholes Coulee, and Grand Coulee.

Living the Dream

A small American flag waves, tattered and faded, above the Pioneer Cemetery, just outside of Coulee City down a quiet dirt road on the edge of town. More graves than not have faded stones, and a dozen or more are marked but nameless, a simple wooden cross held together by a single screw. Nobody maintains the cemetery. A hornet's nest fills the mailbox that holds the sign-in notebook. The cemetery seems much larger than needed, as though the pioneers anticipated expansion.

Coulee City School, a modern and sizable building, has a sign advertising this month's character trait: courage. Students ride the bus in from as far away as Almira to attend high school here; for middle school, the Coulee City kids bus Almira's way. This way, both places keep a fundamental foothold in part of what makes a town a town: a school system.

A John Deere equipment sales company speaks to the local economy, as well as the lifestyle. Residents not only use farming implements in their daily lives, but they can also buy them right here in town.

Artist Don Nutt, owner of Cariboo Trail Studio and Gallery, was born and raised in Coulee City and has lived here most of his life. When asked

The unmaintained Pioneer Cemetery on the edge of town contains at least a dozen graves marked only by a simple wooden cross.

how things in Coulee City have changed, Nutt says the changes have been mostly demographic.

"People used to know each other," he says, "and most people were related." Now, Nutt estimates that half the residences in town are summer homes, owned by people who recreate at nearby Banks Lake.

Nutt documents the landscape of Grant County's high desert, as well as local history. His painting *Smoking Star* depicts the 1811 event of fur traders becoming the first white men to move up the Okanogan River from the Columbia. Another painting, *On the Graves of My Grandfathers*, depicts the journey of Chief Moses of the Columbia traveling with his people through their ancestral homelands, now known as Moses Coulee. In addition, Nutt produces artwork for the annual Last Stand Rodeo, which has taken place every Memorial Day weekend in Coulee City for nearly 70 years.

Nutt laments the loss of some of the false-front buildings that once made downtown Coulee City feel more like a town from the Old West, but he understands that unless the town can devote more resources to preservation, aging buildings become dangerous and require demolition. "Coulee City is kind of on the brink of being a ghost," he says. He imagines, though, that businesses like the John Deere sales outfit, as well as the rail and the campground, will keep the town going.

Though his family moved a lot when he was a kid, Don Nutt always knew Coulee City was where he wanted to end up. "I never imagined I'd be able to have an art gallery here," he says. "We manage to scrape out a living. It's a dream come true."

Dry Falls State Park is part of the Channeled Scablands, one of the several geographical features that make Washington State unique.

64

Population: 48
Founding: 1911

INSETS L to R: The post office in Krupp, open two hours per day, serves as an unofficial museum. • Once, Krupp had a city hall and a fire station • The post office in ' Krupp, open two hours per day, serves as an unofficial museum. Inside the town museum are hints of what the town used to be • Krupp is as silent as this empty sign frame suggests.

TOP: A HighLine Grain Grower elevator rises behind Krupp like a syscraper standing over ruins.

Krupp

The Password Is: *Marlin*

In 1892, the Great Northern Railway built a line through the rugged landscape known as Crab Creek Valley. Henry Marlin had settled in the valley fully 20 years earlier, followed by families with the names Urquhart and Walter. Prior to Great Northern's arrival, life in the valley moved to the rhythm of the ranch. Early settlers specialized in raising cattle and sheep. When the railroad came, a whole new settlement rose up to meet it. Great Northern named it Krupp. In 1911, the town of Krupp incorporated. Within a few years, residents sought to change the name to avoid an association with a German gun manufacturer by the same name. Instead, they chose the name Marlin, to honor the area's first settler, though it was George Urquhart who financed the town's initial development. Though the post office, rail depot, and grocery store all reflected the name change, it was never official. As a result, the town seems to have struck a somewhat clunky compromise. It's known as the Town of Krupp, Marlin, Washington.

By 1910, the town had a school, one of the first in the county. Ten years later, its population peaked at just more than 100 residents. By then, the livestock industry had given way to wheat production, which still drives the local economy, though it is smaller by the year. At one time, Krupp had not one but two of many of the types of businesses that typically make up a town: two saloons, two hotels, two lumberyards, and at least two churches, not to mention its own newspaper, the *Krupp Signal,* and assorted other businesses.

Repeated fires destroyed the town, and many residents moved to nearby towns. The school graduated its last class in 1964, closed in 1966, and was razed in 1970. The town managed to hang on to the First Presbyterian Church of Marlin, built in 1908, until 2013.

As recently as the mid-1980s, up to 75 people called Marlin home. They still had a grocery store and a community center, the old school gym repurposed. Today, the post office stands alone as a symbol of Marlin's municipal past. In the late 1990s, a family from Moses Lake bought some properties intending to renovate the town, but they didn't follow through. The Town of Krupp, Marlin grows smaller and smaller, but somehow it hangs on.

Monthly council meetings take place in the Central Washington Grain Grower's elevator, run by a volunteer mayor and council members who may have to interrupt the meetings to unload a wheat truck. More than a century ago, settlers turned these scablands into a lush, grain-producing valley. For all the change in its appearance, some things in Krupp—er, Marlin?—have stayed the same.

The Plain People

In 1536, Jacob Hutter was burned at the stake. A religious leader in the Austrian Anabaptist tradition from the alpine region of Tyrol, Hutter was persecuted for his missionary work on behalf of the sect's communal lifestyle and beliefs, which put the group at odds with both Catholics and other Protestants at the time. Today, an estimated 40,000 Hutterites live by the system espoused by the martyred Hutter. A few dozen of these, known as the Marlin Hutterites, are living in a community just outside of Krupp. Among themselves, they are "the plain people," so called for their simple clothing. Outside of Krupp, some derisively refer to the group as "the hoots." The Marlin Hutterites are farmers and pacifists. They do not evangelize. Within the community, they speak Hutter's Tyrolean dialect of German. They hope to keep their culture alive.

Signs and Wonders

Sagebrush takes root with stubborn opportunism on sun-washed basalt. Its leaves glint a soft silver under the still, hot afternoon. Walking through this landscape, one misstep is the difference between a pleasant desert hike and danger. These are the scablands. The ribbon of road spooling out its two-lane story misleads: life here is not gentle. It is precarious and exposed. There hasn't been a town for 20 miles. Then, a sign breaks the spell of emptiness: Krupp is 2.5 miles away. It seems like a mistake. No one lives out here. Then, another hint of civilization: the Marlin Gun Club. The sign is bright, white, and green against the dusty-colored high desert. No gunshots ring out. No marksmen are practicing. The road bends down, past a few ramshackle

dwellings into lush farmland. Grain elevators rise above a group of trees whose organization says "town." At the end of the field, an empty sign frame invites imagination. Maybe there was a time Krupp welcomed its visitors, but that feels like long ago.

Other signage tells visitors what Town of Krupp, Marlin is about. Someone named Ken is offering drilling services. HighLine Grain Growers,

The way out of Krupp is the same as the way in. Standing at the field's edge once more, looking through the glassless window of the used-to-be sign, the sky speaks a single word. From here, Krupp feels like an answer looking for a question.

a regional cooperative, seeks to meet the needs of multigenerational farm families and exercise good stewardship over the platform, following in the footsteps of those who came before. A bump over the railroad, and the platform is in the rearview mirror. Up ahead, through the windshield, is the past.

Sometimes, a very small town feels like a town because it has a library. A city hall doesn't hurt; in the absence of either, public art goes a long way. Krupp offers no such reassurances. City Hall stands vacant. Before that, it must have been a church. The double garage next to the old City Hall is recognizable in its former iteration only because of the ancient fire truck, wedged between the two buildings, collecting weeds.

Across the street, a low-slung building is lower by the moment. The roof is falling in. It's impossible to guess what the storefronts once contained. Through the filthy, cobwebbed glass, it looks as though 20 years ago, someone pulled everything off the walls and out of the drawers and threw it in a pile. Here and there, the broken ceiling throws a spotlight on the ruin. Broken sink basins lean against old computers. A mattress presses its bald-springed frame against a wall. Somehow, there's a post office. A bulletin board on the wall proves the town's existence in faded newspaper clippings and signage for Marlin Grocery. *We were here,* these artifacts say. Of course, someone must still be—the post office is open for business two hours a day, six days a week.

Upcycled tractor tire inner tubes serve as tree planters. The planters' intentional beauty strikes a contrast to the deep impoverishment of downtown. There are other signs of love. Through the splintered door of the corner building, someone has left out food for a cat.

65

Population: 3,054
Founding: 1909

INSETS L to R: The library, open five days per week, also serves as a food pantry and community center. • Benton County farmers have a short commute to the market. • Starting in 1910, the Walla Walla to Yakima line stopped in Benton City. • Benton County makes up a huge part of Washington's agricultural wealth, producing over 100 commercial crops.

TOP: Sunflowers brighten up a stone barn in Benton City.

Benton City

A Valley Held Dear

"Every worthwhile venture usually has had a very humble beginning." So begins the history of the settling of Benton City, as told by the History Committee of the Community Development Program of Benton City. Published in 1959, the work notes 41 businesses open in Benton City and an additional 14 in nearby unincorporated Kiona. The History Committee's work tells the story of Benton City from 1853, when "the first weary, bedraggled emigrants . . . called the Longmire Train" arrived from Indiana after enduring much "heckling" by local Indians and navigating the "tricky" Snake River. The account nevertheless credits the Yakama Native Americans, under the leadership of Chief Kamiakin, with helping the settlers across the confluence of the Columbia and Snake Rivers. Conflict with Native Americans, known as the Indian Wars, prevented much settlement throughout the 1850s. By the 1870s, the Northern Pacific Railroad Company was planning its course through the Yakima Valley. In 1883, the Cascade Division of the railroad laid tracks within a few miles of Kiona, near the future home of Ben-

ton City, allowing for the movement of products and goods east. The Historical Committee's history notes that "During the summer of 1885 there were over 37,000 head of cattle, over 4,000 horses, and nearly 30,000 head of sheep shipped by rail out of the Yakima Valley to markets in Montana and Chicago." As settlers arrived on the railroad, the cattle industry decreased, irrigation canals were built, and agriculture took over.

In 1909, railroad engineer F. L. Pitman bought 158 acres of land on the north side of the Yakima River for $422, platted the town of Benton City, and put up a railroad station. Within three years, 10 trains per day rolled through, and Benton City was the main junction between Walla Walla and Yakima. As initial plans to make Benton City a prominent rail hub faltered, residents looked for another way to keep their city growing. Pitman decided to make a bid for Benton City to overthrow Prosser as the county seat; Kennewick was also vying for the title. Both cities lost to Prosser, but continued expansion of irrigation meant that Benton City could count on a secure future as an agricultural center.

WWII reduced the population of Benton City, but the 1943 construction of the nuclear reactor in nearby Hanford brought new residents. After several decades of start-and-stop growth, residents formally incorporated Benton City in 1945. Within a generation, booming agriculture brought an increase in immigrants from Mexico. From 1970 to 1980, the population of Benton City doubled to just over 2,000 people.

Though the Hanford site brought jobs, it also polluted the soil. In 1986, Benton City had the highest levels of plutonium pollution in the area, prompting a decontamination effort. Hanford remains the most contaminated site in the United States. Despite this, and despite its impact on Benton City's soil, Benton City, Kiona, and the surrounding area has continued to increase its agricultural output, from peaches and cherries to wine.

The Nuclear Threat

Benton County is home to the Hanford Site, 27 miles up the Columbia River from Benton City. As part of the Manhattan Project, workers at the Hanford Site produced plutonium for nuclear weapons from 1943 to 1987. A few years after the reactors stopped producing, federal and Washington State authorities formed a multiagency agreement to clean up the radioactive waste threatening the local environment, including the Columbia River. Historically, the Hanford Site has been a key employer in the greater Tri-Cities region. The populations of Franklin and Benton Counties tripled in the years of the Hanford Site's development and war-era production. Hanford continues to employ many of the region's residents, though the focus of the work has shifted from production to cleanup. Workers are building a facility set to open in 2023 to glassify 56 million gallons of radioactive waste now held underground in tanks. Other efforts are underway to protect the land and the Columbia River from plumes of contamination caused by liquid waste that evaporated or seeped through holding pools into the

ground. A disaster at Hanford would likely result in devastation greater than that experienced after the earthquake that leveled Fukushima, Japan in 2011. The continued success of local agriculture, including Red Mountain's celebrated wine, likely depends on the successful mitigation of this problem.

The history of Benton City is also the history of Kiona, the unincorporated community just down the road. Proximity to the railroad meant early settlers developed Kiona first, though just three families, the Neils, Brownings, and Lightles, lived in Kiona prior to the construction of the irrigation canal.

Pastoral Paradise

High above the Yakima River, just down the main road from the Kiona-Benton City High School, the Benton City branch of the Mid-Columbia Libraries sits, overlooking Red Mountain, the smallest wine-growing region in Washington, and one of the most celebrated. The Red Mountain AVA, or American Viticultural Area, founded in 2001, comprises just more than 4,000 acres and 15 wineries focused on premium wine production. With a price per ton that is three times the state average, Red Mountain is an important part of the local economy.

Visitors to Benton City will find sweeping photogenic landscapes and pastoral agricultural scenes. Stop for coffee in town and check out the view from the library, and then take the Old Inland Empire Highway or any number of side roads to the lush farmland. Sunflowers stand sentinel over lush rows of peaches, cherries, and apples. The Farmer's Market is open every day but Sunday.

The Missoula Floods at the end of the last ice age caused sediment-rich soil in the Red Mountain AVA. Good soil, a long growing season, and precise irrigation result in the best possible product, like the fruit-focused wines made by three generations of the Williams family at Kiona Vineyards.

66

Population: 489
Founding: 1883

INSETS L to R: Mesa is just north of the confluence of the Columbia and Snake Rivers. • Prior to 1948, only dryland farming was possible in Mesa. • Mesa is in the South Columbia Basin Irrigation District, managed by the Bureau of Reclamation. • Mesa is home to Simplot, one of the nation's largest agribusiness companies.

TOP: Only 70 years until Mesa's citizens open the time capsule buried under this sign.

Mesa

The Town That Started Over

There's a reason that cities developed first along coastlines: Early industry made use of the easiest transportation and travel routes. Inland cities grew only as transportation did. Railroad companies forged tracks between regional hubs and recruited labor, but the promise of the railroad wasn't always fulfilled. In towns like Mesa, Washington, tracks emerge from an overgrown raised railbed, signaling the long ago hope that never saw fulfillment.

The Northern Pacific Railroad never had a depot in Mesa, developing instead in what would become the Inland Empire centers of Pasco and the Tri-Cities. Along the way, some Franklin County cities became ghost towns, despite a strong start. In the early 1880s, the city of Ainsworth, 26 miles south of Mesa on the Snake River, was home to as many as 1,500 people, including many Chinese immigrants recruited for the purpose of constructing the rail. Within a few years, the early industrialists relocated the railroad hub to the newly established Pasco, and Ainsworth faded away. Mesa, on the other hand held on—but its success has never been a sure thing.

From its founding in the late 1880s, Mesa proved to be a hard place to make a living. Part of the problem was access to water. Back then, the town went by the name of Bluff Wells, because it was one place in the otherwise dry Columbia Valley where a well existed, though the water was hundreds of feet deep in basalt and expensive and difficult to extract. Martha Poe homesteaded Mesa shortly after her arrival by covered wagon in 1887. Her husband had died of typhoid two years prior. Ten years later, Martha died, and her half-brother, Lanier Judson Wiltfong, took in Martha's three children and platted the town that would become Mesa.

Dryland farming in the decades prior to the post-WWII Columbia Basin Reclamation Project meant farmers' fortunes rose and fell with the weather. Several wet years and the promise of water attracted early settlers to Mesa, and the town grew to about 300 residents. When the weather dried up, the farmers began to leave. Amid the exodus, one farmer decided to stay on: Manton Poe, descendant of Martha Poe.

As his neighbors sold their land and homes, Poe bought them. Soon, he owned the entire town.

Poe stayed through the Great Depression. The Columbia Basin Reclamation Project and the construction of the Grand Coulee Dam brought irrigation to the area. The population of Mesa, once reduced to just the Poe family, began to grow. In August 1956, *Family Weekly Magazine* quoted Manton Poe as saying, "It's never too late for a man to start over, and that goes for a town, too." Today, the town is a shipping center for the local agricultural towns and Mesa, first Bluff Wells, and then Judson, continues to grow. Visitors, take note: locals pronounce it "Mee-sa."

A Modern Crisis

A century later, Mesa weathered a different kind of crisis. In 2016, Mesa's former mayor won a judgment against the city to the tune of $353,000, or twice the town's annual budget. As the story goes, the mayor filed the suit in 2003 after asking for records from a public meeting of the city council, which decided to revoke building permits that the mayor and her husband had obtained years before. The council declined her request. The former mayor suspected that the city government was retaliating against her. She persisted and, more than a decade later, won her case. A judge decided that the city should have provided the records in response to the mayor's first request. Later, the judge cut the amount of the judgment in half, reasoning that the amount of the initial judgment would place too great an impact on the city. Each of Mesa's residents had to pay $357.87 to the city to cover the cost of the judgment, which amounted to $5 per record for each day the city waited to provide the records. Superior Court Judge Bruce Spanner, who ruled on the case, noted that the judgment would "certainly sting the city but [would] not cripple them."

100 Years from Now

Just off I-90 into Mesa is a junction, at which point travelers turn north up the hill or south into the Coulee. Going north, the Mesa school comes into view, fronted by an expansive fenced playfield and colorful playground equipment. Just across the street is the headquarters of the Water Master, in charge of distributing irrigation. Well-kept homes stand in neat rows a short distance away. South of the interstate, a grain elevator towers over another collection of homes.

The old railroad bed here is barely visible. The rail ran along the river, through Mesa's pastoral beauty.

At the center of the junction, visitors are welcome with a soaring American flag, and a flourish of flowers lining the sides of a practical garden path. Below the sign, visitors will find a concrete vault that contains a time capsule. Residents of Mesa buried the capsule in 1989, when the population was 290 people. Since then, the population has continued to grow. Perhaps when they break open the capsule in 2089, Mesa will have doubled its population again. It seems a neat trick to perform in such a dry and difficult place. Then again, Mesa has done it before.

In 1989, the town of Mesa buried a time capsule. At the time, the town had 290 residents. How many people will live here in 100 years? Mesa is part of the fastest-growing county in the Pacific Northwest.

67

Population: 193
Founding: 1902

INSETS L to R: With fewer than 200 residents, Kahlotus still manages to maintain a local library. • The Kahlotus Coyotes play ball on the practice field at the center of town. • The Lower Monumental Dam, just outside Kahlotus, formed the Lake Sacagawea reservoir. • From the looks of it, the Kahlotus jail can hold one criminal at a time.

TOP: The welcome sign in Kahlotus depicts dryland farming in the rugged surrounding environment.

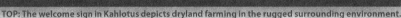

Kahlotus

A Town by Any Other Name

Franklin County takes its name from Benjamin Franklin, but there's some confusion about the name of Kahlotus, a small town located in the county's northeastern corner. Hans Harder, the German immigrant who first platted the town in 1902, named it Hardersburg, after himself. Harder and other settlers, including those with the names Moritz, Ebeson, Timmermann, Parkinson, and Hutchinson, came to Kahlotus in the 1880s. The Northern Pacific Railroad recruited many of these settlers during the creation of rail lines between Portland, Seattle, and Spokane. As with so many small towns, with the promise of the rail came settlers, and with settlement came industry. Kahlotus led Franklin County in shipping wheat, and the town began to thrive. The railroad bypassed Kahlotus, but many descendants of its original families call the town home today.

Five years after its platting, Hardersburg was renamed Kahlotus, though the origin of the name remains unclear. Some sources note it as a Native American word meaning "hole in the ground," or "stinking water" or "bad water," possibly due to

the highly alkaline water in the surrounding area. Other sources cite the Palouse tribal chief who signed the Yakima Treaty in 1885, whose name appears in many variations of the current spelling of Kahlotus.

The Columbia Basin Reclamation Project, which delivered irrigation to the Columbia Basin in the years after WWII, did not bring irrigation to Kahlotus as it did to other nearby towns. The local economy has historically depended on dryland farming, a highly efficient form of farming that relies on precipitation rather than irrigation.

Kahlotus sits just 7 miles north of the Snake River and the Lower Monumental Dam. Completed in 1969, the dam brought some irrigation to the area, but its chief impact was to make the Snake River more navigable and to allow for the creation of the Port of Kahlotus, one of the smallest ports in Washington State. The dam, the second of four on the Lower Snake River, helped provide a source of cheap power to the area. The construction of the dam wasn't without controversy, primarily focused on impact to native salmon runs. In addition, archaeological excavation in the area uncovered evidence of human habitation, the Marmes Rockshelter, as well as human bones dating back at least 10,000 years. This discovery took place shortly before the date on the dam's proposed completion date, but finishing the dam meant flooding this archaeologically important area. A public outcry ensued, and an effort was made to excavate the site prior to the dam's completion. In the end, the Marmes Rockshelter was inundated by more than 40 feet of water. In the event that the dam is destroyed someday, it's possible that the site may still yield important evidence.

Mid-Columbia Basin Library

Kahlotus is a small but mighty community. Its tiny main street is dressed up by public art in the form of murals and vibrantly painted signs welcoming visitors to town, along with fading advertisements painted on brick buildings long ago. Some years ago, local students undertook a project to beautify Weston Street, building facades that create an Old West effect. In Kahlotus, the largest structures are grain silos, marking the importance of agriculture to the area. A Connell Grain Growers silo towers above the downtown structures. Just beside it is the tiny Kahlotus branch of the Mid-Columbia Basin Library system. The little library, which has been serving the community since 1926, is another way of telling the story of Kahlotus, past and present. A sign on the door notes that books are available in both Spanish and English. The hours are limited, but the doors are open four days a week.

From Past to Present

To see the through line from Kahlotus's past to its present, look no further than The Farmer's Daughter. Mother-and-daughter owners Anne Moore and Candi Ranch describe their business as a convenience store, but that's only true if a convenience store is also a deli, general store, coffee shop, museum, and gossip mill. Located on the corner of one of Kahlotus' only intersections, The Farmer's Daughter is literally and figuratively the center of town. It's across from the football field, park, and school, and just down the street from the municipal buildings and the library. In 30 minutes at the store, 5% of the town's population came through to chat; get a coffee, snacks, or motor oil; and share news of the day.

A grain elevator towers above the Kahlotus branch of the Mid-Columbia Library, which is open four days a week and offers a selection of books in English and Spanish.

Visitors will find The Farmer's Daughter doing the work of a historical society as well. Laminated copies of the weekly *Kahlotus Record* offer a peek into the past. The issue from Friday, September 6, 1907, noted the opening of the Kahlotus school, declaring, "The aim is to build up a firstclass [sic] school this year. Industry and perseverance are our aims." In that year, there were nine grades at the Kahlotus school. Today, more than 60 students from pre-K to 12th grade attend the school.

Then, as now, the water supply was a concern. In 1907, the *Record* noted an ordinance to establish both water works and an electricity plant. Advertising promised relief from common ailments in ornate script. A section called "News of the World" promised "short dispatches from all parts of the globe."

At the turn of the 19th century, a subscription to the *Kahlotus Record* cost $1.50 per year. Some of the families who live here have been around since then, including the owners of The Farmer's Daughter. Though the *Kahlotus Record* is no more, Anne and Candi's social media posts tell of ongoing water shortages in the community and the occasional store closure for the Fourth of July or during the harvest. After all, as Anne and Candi say, " 'The Farmers Daughter' is not just the name of our store. It is also who we are."

The concrete-gravity Lower Monumental Dam is 100 feet high and nearly 4,000 feet long. Its reservoir is Lake Sacagawea. The project includes a powerhouse, a navigation lock, two fish ladders, and a juvenile-fish facility.

68

Population: 101
Founding: 1901

INSETS L to R: From a bird's-eye view, Hatton barely interrupts the farmland's squares and circles. • The railroad has defined Hatton since the town's founding. • By 1968, Hatton's population had declined two-thirds from its first census in 1910. • Fire and drought sacked Hatton in its earliest years. The town never recovered.

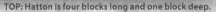

TOP: Hatton is four blocks long and one block deep.

Hatton

Jerkwater Town

Before the advent of diesel-engine locomotives, steam-powered trains required coal and water in almost equal measure. In 1927, the invention of large-capacity water carriers called tenders allowed trains to go upwards of 100 miles without resupplying, but before that, trains stopped every 7–10 miles to take on more water. As railroads advanced across the American West in the mid-19th century, water towers, wells, and ponds were essential infrastructure. Sometimes a town formed around the railroad. Other places were nothing more than a jerkwater; the train pulled into the stop, and an operator jerked a chain or lever to release the pump. If no infrastructure existed, workers might form a bucket brigade from a nearby pond. The term *jerkwater* eventually became derogatory, used to describe an unimportant place. Northern Pacific sank two wells in a location along its main line through Adams County; the railroad also built a section house and pumphouses. They called the place Twin Wells. When James L. Bronson arrived in 1888, Twin Wells was just a jerkwater.

Bronson left New York at the age of 20 with "the cash capital of fifty cents" and "a rich fund of common sense." He worked as a farmer, a miller, and a carpenter before moving to Twin Wells. Apparently he had only intended to stay the winter, "but in the spring he found the circumstances so favorable that he opened a mercantile establishment." That year, Twin Wells got a post office. Reportedly, the railroad superintendent asked the postmaster for a list of postal patrons. State Senator Sutton was one of the names. The postmaster was J. D. Hackett, also the railway agent. Hackett's wife was Belle Sutton. The superintendent combined the two, and the town had a new name—Hatton. Mrs. Hackett became the postmistress. More settlers came, and the town began to prosper as a wheat seller. In 1901, Hatton farmers sold 260,000 bushels. That year, Bronson platted the town.

Though Hatton had a new name and an economic base, its survival still depended on the railroad. Drought in the late 1920s and '30s led to population loss as dryland farmers sought better conditions elsewhere. When automobile travel and long-haul trucking replaced trains as the most efficient means of travel and transportation, towns without another economic center of gravity began a slow collapse. Writing of her early memories in school, Hatton resident Ruth Rickman Wahl recounted that the school "seemed very large to me." She started school in 1918. Though the rail was still going strong and the drought was a decade away, Hatton's population was already declining. Wahl writes, "I was all alone in the first grade."

Plot Twist

In 1947, a great drama came to Hatton. It was harvest season, and migrant farmers out of Texas came through looking for part-time work. Joe, Jim, and Kink came as a crew. Joe was the boss. They were honest men looking to get ahead. They didn't count on Fay Rankin, a local farmer's daughter. Fay fell hard for Joe, but Joe kept his head down and his nose clean. Meanwhile, Fay manipulated Jim to start skimming cash off the top. She was a modern woman, looking to make money of her own. Fay and Jim got married, and for a while the whole scheme kept all the players in the money, and no one in town was the wiser. Well, Jim got caught eventually, and the whole lot of them fled the state. Fay broke down and confessed her love for Joe to Jim somewhere around Nebraska. To find out the rest, you'll have to rent the movie. Scenes from *Wild Harvest*, starring Alan Ladd, Dorothy Lamour, and Robert Preston, were filmed in Hatton.

Hatton Was Here

In Hatton today, the fields barely stir. Birdsong is the only sound. Most of the homes are trailers, and many are decaying. A few modern homes with well-kept yards have satellite dishes and fenced-in yards with signs warning of guard dogs. The roads are unpaved. The old pumphouses are boarded up, but a grouping of grain elevators stands at the ready, should the train come by. In a 1921 photo, Ruth Rickman Wahl stands before the Hatton school with her 20 or so classmates. The school is long gone, as are the businesses and the hotel. A small home of indeterminate age serves as city hall. The

sign hanging from the porch roof looks like it was taken from the upline train—HATTON, in all capital letters on a simple white board. Next door, a John Deere riding lawn mower takes one of the parking spaces in front of a double garage. Over the garage doors, a large sign spells out Hatton's history: The railroad came. James Bronson built a store. Hatton boasted a population of 250 by 1904, says the sign.

Hatton's town hall is open three days per week. A sign over the building next door explains Hatton's history as a railroad town.

Then, drought. Fire. A movie was filmed here. Hatton had the longest-serving mayor, once. Harold E. Johnson was his name, and he served for almost 50 years, though the sign doesn't tell that part. An American flag flutters softly overhead. An almost entirely faded sign points the way out of town.

In Hatton, street signs are nailed to short wooden posts. On Second Avenue, a faded sign points the way out of town, to Lind (see the next profile).

Population: 564
Founding: 1888

INSETS L to R: Whereas Mesa buried its time capsule for a century, Lind will open its capsule after 50 years. • Lind's best "cappachino" spot appears to be closed for the season. • If combine drivers are bull riders, the seed trucks do the barrel racing. • Dave Govedare also created "Grandfather Cuts Loose the Ponies," visible from I-90 at Vantage.

TOP: Combine drivers battle to the (machine) death in Lind's annual demolition derby.

Lind

That's Lind, Spelled N-E-I-L-S-O-N

The history of any small town often makes a special note of the year it got a post office. Lind received its post office in 1889. In 1963, *The Lind Leader* published a description of the early mail service: "Prior to 1889 the settlers got their mail through the Ritzville postoffice [sic]. The postmaster there would put the mail on the train and the postal clerk would throw it off at Lind station, and the operator would place it where settlers could get it."

Such scenes remind us that history isn't just a matter of a costume change—things really were different. Before 1889, Lind station was "hardly more than a water tank, and a section house" for the Northern Pacific. Brothers James and Dugal Neilson put up a "bachelor's hall" in 1888, and the next year, they turned it into a store. The post office was established, with settler James Neilson as postmaster. Other buildings and businesses followed, including a bank and a saloon. The same year, Lind built its first school, hiring Bert Near to teach all six of the students. The Neilsons platted a four-block town. Lind was on its way, though local news coverage remained unimpressed. "The last time we saw Lind," wrote the *Centralia News*, "the town consisted of a million acres of sage brush, 400,000 jack rabbits, and a long stretch of railroad track."

In 1908, the Chicago, Milwaukee & St. Paul Railroad doubled the rail running through Lind, and the population followed suit. The Milwaukee Road ran 1,500 miles between Chicago and Seattle. Adams County had harvested its first bumper crop of wheat 10 years prior. Settlers, many of Volga German heritage, practiced dryland farming, working the land with teams of 28 horses to a combine. The Milwaukee Road stopped in each small town along the wheat-producing region, loading its cars with lentils, barley, apples, and wheat. When trucking replaced rail as the means of agricultural transport, the Milwaukee closed. The trail salvaged from its route leads through Lind.

The dirt road that ran up the center of town in 1906 is long since paved, and Hotel Lind is gone, but the people of Lind remember their history. In 1988, the town celebrated its centennial anniversary with a nine-day festival. For two years in advance of the celebration, hundreds of volunteers prepared. They raised money for a memorial sculpture, designed a new logo, and developed a motto: "Honor the past, live the present, guarantee the future."

With funding for the monument secured and an artist contracted, Lind built a park to hold the monument. The monument, designed by artist Dave Govedare, depicts Lind's history. In the upper-left corner, settlers arrive under a halo of sunshine. Farmed hills roll out before them, above a team of horses pulling a combine. Indicating the passage of time, mechanized combines take the place of horses. Overhead, the train runs above it all.

Below the sculpture, on a plaque titled "The dawn of a new century," Lind dedicates the monument and the park to the future by thanking the past: "We remember the railroad," it reads. "We remember the brothers, James and Dugal, who platted the town and left their surname in the N-E-I-L-S-O-N names of our streets. We only wish they'd left us a clue about the origin of the name of Lind. This part of our history seems forever lost."

Improvements to Dryland Farming

Rainfall in Russia's the Volga River Valley, where many Adams County settlers came from, averages 12 to 25 inches per year. Adams County seldom receives more than nine. In 1915, the county gave 320 acres, or two homesteads worth of land, to the State College of Washington in Pullman, to study farming in the area. The college, which would become Washington State University, started the Lind Drylands Research Station the same year.

Farming in Adams County works differently than elsewhere. In the early years, wind erosion led to soil losses. Today's farmers plant new breeds of wheat developed to withstand erosion conditions. It's planted up to 5 inches deep in the soil. Different varieties of wheat do better in different microclimates. What works in Pullman won't necessarily work in Lind. Senator and farmer Mark Schoesler notes, "If you bring it to Lind and it doesn't die, you probably have a winner." Thanks to research-based farming practices, today's dryland yields are more than five times the amount produced in 1915.

Derby Days

For road-trippers hoping to catch a small town at its best, Lind offers a definitive best time to visit: Derby Weekend. The 33rd anniversary was in 2020, which leads to the question: What did the people of Lind do on this June weekend 34 years ago? Today, thousands of people attend what has become a regional attraction organized by the local Lions Club, which sells tickets for 10 bucks.

The annual Combine Demolition Derby draws thousands of visitors to Lind.

The festival includes car and pickup races, a breakfast at the Grange Hall, and not one but two parades, one for the kids. Then the derby begins. Young men gather around old combines painted bright colors. The retired farm implements find new life as tools of destruction with names like mechanized WWE wrestlers. A bright-green machine goes by Pour Life Choices. It'll meet The Grain Digger and Red, White, and Booze in the arena later. The rules are simple: it's a fight to the death—of the combine. The grandstands are full of spectators. Massive tires spit mud into the first rows. Medics stand by with firefighting equipment. The derby continues until only one combine is operational. It's a spectacle, to be sure, but one filled with good feelings.

During the seed truck race, little '61—that's the truck's first year of operation—seems destined to lose. The bigger seed trucks outpace it. Then, the winner exits the arena too early. It can't seem to back up. Smaller than the rest, '61 pauses, the driver likely thinking the race is over. The crowd cheers, "*Go, go!*" The driver figures it out, keeps going, and pulls off an upset. The crowd goes wild. In the bleachers, a man stands up. "That's my truck," he says. "I gotta work on that transmission."

Artist Dave Govedare designed and built the Lind Memorial Sculpture, commissioned for Lind's centennial celebration in 1988. The concrete base contains a time capsule to be opened in 2038.

70

Population: 1,649
Founding: 1881

INSETS L to R: Local farmer and politician Daniel Buchanan donated over 500 books to start Ritzville's first library. • Taxidermied birds of prey wearing Uncle Sam hats adorn the tops of the stacks in Ritzville's Carnegie library, the only one of its kind in Adams County. • Birds occupy an old Pontiac service station in Ritzville. • Outside of the local Eagles' fraternal organization, a statue pays tribute to former F.O.E. president Klay M. McCrady as well as all military servicemen and women.

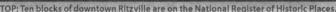

TOP: Ten blocks of downtown Ritzville are on the National Register of Historic Places.

Ritzville

Breadbasket of the World

The Alaska-Pacific-Yukon Exposition was the first World's Fair held in Washington State. The Exposition adopted artwork meant to symbolize Seattle's significance as a meeting point for east, west, and north. Styled after the Three Graces of Greek mythology, three women meet in the symbol, each holding a representative object; from the east, a steamship; from the north, a handful of gold; from the west, a railroad engine.

The year was 1909. Adams County was promoting itself as "the bread basket of the world" and a land where "the courage, intelligence, strenuous and persistent efforts of the hardy pioneer have wrested the hidden wealth from Mother Earth." For 20 years, Adams County had been promoting its county seat of Ritzville. Brochures from 1890 feature sketches of the high school in Ritzville, touting "Free education! Free farms! Free homes!"

Philip Ritz takes the title of first settler in Ritzville, though a few others preceded him in Adams County. Ritz settled in 1878. An early description notes, "Old timers say that Ritz took up land here

and secured all he could lay his hands on. . . . he was against immigration to the country, and wrote articles to the papers stating the land was barren and unproductive." Apparently, Ritz wanted the place all to himself. Still, when Northern Pacific made its way to the edge of the Channeled Scablands, Ritz took the contract to grade a railbed through his property. In 1881, Northern Pacific built a station there and named it Ritzville. The record suggests Ritz may have been involved in the naming.

As with the adjacent Lincoln County, wheat farmers of Russian-German heritage brought their experience farming the Volga River Valley to Adams County. Many came from the Odessa area, west of the Volga, which was a major shipping port for Volga River Valley wheat. As the railroad neared completion, a number of families moved to Ritzville from Canton, South Dakota, including the Harris, York, Bennett, and McKay families. The Bennetts arrived in 1880. In 1901, Mrs. Bennett remarked, "Twenty-one years have made a wonderful change in this part of the state of

Washington . . . The immigrant who now comes to Adams county is not a pioneer; neither has he come to the 'wild west.' "

In 1883, the few residents of the outpost requested and received recognition as a new county, as the Whitman County seat was a full 80 miles away. Even by train, that was a long journey to conduct business. Ritzville, the only settlement in the newly named Adams County, became the county seat.

Reading with Raptors

Ritzville is home to the only Carnegie library in Adams County, built in 1907. While Andrew Carnegie furnished the buildings, he required that any city receiving a library in his name donate the land and commit to maintaining it using public funds. Further, Carnegie didn't pay for the books to fill his libraries. Critics called the projects "bookless libraries." Ritzville's own Carnegie library is full of books and is open six days per week. Taxidermied birds of prey wearing little Uncle Sam hats perch atop the cases. According to one librarian, the golden eagle on display was shot down by her aunt, who called the game warden first to warn him she was going to have to shoot it. The librarian had worked there for years before she learned that story and couldn't believe it when it turned out to be true.

Anything Is Possible

Ritzville describes itself as part of the Othello "micropolitan" area. The Columbia Basin Reclamation Project finally brought irrigation to Adams County in the early 1950s, and Othello's population boomed. Between 1950 and 1960, Othello's population increased by more than 400%. Ritzville saw just more than 1% growth in the same time period. Still, Ritzville is the county seat, ensuring its stability into the future, and its position along I-90 makes it a popular stopping point for travelers between Spokane and Seattle.

Nearly 100 years after fire destroyed the town, Ritzville experienced another disaster: Mount Saint Helens erupted in May of 1980.

Though the volcano was 300 miles away, its ash plume fell directly over Ritzville, dropping up to 6 inches on the town and stranding 2,500 travelers. For five days, the town hid behind closed doors. While the cleanup took days and risked the health of residents and passers-through alike, ultimately, the volcanic ash was good for business—it improved the soil.

Ritzville's Carnegie library is rare in two ways. It's Adams County's only Carnegie library, and it's still used for its original purpose.

The entire 10-block downtown Ritzville has been placed on the National Register of Historic places. The buildings in this part of town date to the building boom in the first decade of the 20th century. After the fire, the town rebuilt out of brick. Despite further development, the town's key businesses have always occupied these buildings.

Today, in Ritzville, many buildings stand empty, though the town's development association has devised clever signs to explain: "This space is not empty," signs say, "It's full of possibilities." Pigeons roost in an old service station. Red brick shows beneath the faded white paint. On the other side of the tracks, grain elevators rise, a reminder that some things stay the same. In Adams County, wheat is still king.

Sculptures are Ritzville's most frequently occurring form of public art. This representation of Ritzville's founder, Phillip Ritz, stands at the corner of Main and Washington Streets.

71

Population: 208
Founding: 1878

INSETS L to R: Visitors to the Palouse Falls may experience a sense of geologic time. • One-stop shopping is less a choice than a fact in Washtucna. • Washtucna is tucked behind a highway in the glacier-scraped Scablands. • Snyder Park offers free books and a place to sit and read.

TOP: Washtucna leads with its claim to fame, the official state waterfall.

Washtucna

Triangulating History

George Bassett and his parents crossed the Great Plains to Helena, Montana, in 1866. A dozen years later, he and wife Alice Lancaster went west again. They became Washtucna's first non-Indigenous settlers. A general history includes Bassett's time as the first postmaster in Adams County and that he and Alice moved to the area to raise horses. Bassett is responsible for naming the town Washtucna, after a Palouse chief. (The word *Washtucna* is thought to mean "many waters.") A local's telling of history holds a bit more detail. In her recounting, Washtucna local Catherine Harder Peot noted that the Bassetts "set the tone of social life on the local scene."

Before incorporation, the town had a hardware store, a hotel, and a saloon. From 1902 to 1903, the population increased sixfold and the town incorporated. Farmers shipped wheat on the Oregon Improvement Company's new line, and Bassett's farm was the well-known end point of an annual roundup of wild horses. Charles Booth, Washtucna's first mayor, sponsored the first irrigation projects on the Palouse River, but the project stalled when production was limited to the immediate area of Washtucna. "I can remember the ditch extending beyond Washtucna," Peot writes, "but the flumes leaked and the water sank away." Later, the Bureau of Reclamation declared the project unusable. "Of course," notes Peot, "in those days no one thought of concrete ditches."

Washtucna's fortunes rose and fell with agricultural output, but when the railroad closed, the town began an inevitable decline. By 1970, only 24 students graduated from Washtucna, and the school had to combine several programs with other schools. Today, the nearest grocery store is in Ritzville, 30 miles away. Opportunities for new revenue and jobs are scarce, and those that do come up aren't always preferred, such as a recently installed regional landfill nearby.

A few short paragraphs can capture, at best, a very incomplete history. Railways chart a path from station to station, but sometimes the stations catch fire or fall into disuse. The details get lost under the weight of the main plot points: wheat, rail, promise, decline. For all the apologies she makes for the holes in her *Abbreviated History of Washtucna*, Catherine Peot's account offers a measure of what Washtucna must have felt like in the early 1900s:

"We all went to the Fourth of July celebrations in Bassett's Grove, the present site of the city park. We were all dressed up in dresses off the bolts of dotted Swiss, batiste, or gingham from the general store. People were friendly. Somebody generally made a speech and firecrackers and giant smokers were going off like mad. Teams were tied at the hitching racks. The hotel and various other places, notably the livery stable, were gathering places for the men folk and the roughnecks. There was a local band and other accouterments [sic] of the times. The women and children visited and picnicked and ate. There were foot races and horseshoe throwing and like contests. The evening hours were for dancing. There was the invariable baseball . . . Of course, there was the flag raising and all sang 'America' and 'the Star Spangled Banner.'"

Maximizing the Land

Highway 26 cuts a straight line from Hatton to Washtucna through a patchwork farmscape. Strict lines divide fields into fertile and fallow. Fields like this may reflect the USDA's Conservation Reserve Program (CRP), whose policies pay farmers not to use all of their land for production. The CRP covers millions of acres of farmland in the US, totaling about 7% of planted land. Washington farmers have enrolled 1.4 million acres in the CRP. Congress initiated the program in 1985 with the goal of preventing soil erosion and another Dust Bowl. Opponents of the program include fertilizer and equipment producers and other businesses specializing in farm products. CRP policy has led to increased wildlife habitat, and studies link increased biodiversity in the insect population to healthier soil. Even the land needs rest.

Small Town, Big Effort

Washtucna is nestled into a valley backed by terraced basalt. The wind waves across a soft ocean of green grass. Kids play in Snyder and Bassett Parks. The espresso shop at the end of town does a brisk business. The grocery store's front door is long since padlocked, but the cash register stands on the counter as though all that's needed is someone to knock the dust off the place and put a few things on the shelves. Downtown is a string of boarded-up buildings, but men are working in the old Sonny's Tavern, cutting boards to build with. The community bulletin board paints a lively picture. The Lions

The USDA's Conservation Reserve Program (CRP), started in 1985, utilizes unplanted farmland for wildlife habitat and soil protection. Research shows that the CRP's efforts may have prevented subsequent Dust Bowl eras in the US despite lengthy droughts.

Club is active, and the library holds weekly events. On the docket this week are judging the most beautiful yard in town and a "Not-So-Newlywed Game."

In recent years, Washtucna schoolkids got involved in the state legislature when they advocated to recognize the Palouse Falls as the state waterfall. Teachers Janet Camp and Amy Whipple created curricula about the history of the waterfalls and led a field trip to Olympia, where five students testified before a House committee. Students cited the historical and geological significance of the falls and its importance as a tourist destination and local asset.

The effort garnered much local support. In a letter to the legislature, area farmer Alex McGregor noted the falls' significance to the Palouse Indian Nation, whose culture includes a creation story of the falls. Lewis and Clark met with the Palouse nearby, McGregor pointed out, and important military actions happened in the area.

After months of work, the students won their campaign. The House passed the bill, and Senator Mark Schoesler sponsored the bill in the Senate. Governor Jay Inslee traveled to the Palouse Falls to sign the bill. While there, Inslee named Cooper Jessop, the youngest in his class, Washingtonian of the Day. The hardworking students of Washtucna Elementary won another prize for Washington that day too. The Palouse Falls is the first official state waterfall in the country.

Welcome to BASSETT PARK
This area is the heart of what birdwatchers call a "desert oasis". Washtucna's ornamental and native plantings and the park's running water attract a large variety of birds during the spring and fall migration when they travel between northern breeding and southern wintering areas.
HISTORICAL ATTRACTION

In Washtucna, the rolling Palouse meets the Channeled Scablands. Nearby, the Palouse River runs over the 200-foot Palouse Falls toward its confluence with the Snake River.

72

Population: 318
Founding: 1902

INSETS L to R: The birth dates of those laid to rest in the Ivy Cemetery go back to the 1850s. • Sunflowers beautify fire-damaged walls in the Prescott Plaza. • Libraries rock, and the Prescott library is especially rocking! • The Touchet Valley Unity Wall project displays work from local artists across the valley.

TOP: Past meets present at the corner of Second Avenue and D Street in Prescott.

Prescott

The Names They Left Behind

The story of Prescott begins with German immigrant Ferdinand Heinrich Gustav Hilgard, a famous and perhaps infamous player in the development of Puget Sound and beyond. When he arrived in the US in 1853, he took a new name: Henry Villard. He learned English, became a journalist, and ingratiated himself everywhere he went, with the goal of becoming just the sort of industrialist he eventually became.

Backed by German financiers, Villard took over a struggling transportation business in Portland and bought the Oregon Steam Navigation Company, which he turned into the Oregon Railway and Navigation Company. It would be this company that eventually dominated transcontinental rail development in the Pacific Northwest, with Villard as president and majority stockholder of Northern Pacific Railway and perceived savior of the failed Seattle & Walla Walla line. When Villard took over as president, he brought his friends on as directors, including C. H. Prescott of Portland, who became the company's general manager. In 1881, Prescott determined the site in Walla Walla County

as a good location for division offices and named the town after himself. The Oregon Improvement Company, part of Villard's empire, took charge of platting the town the next year. Later, the company moved its offices to the town of Starbuck, in neighboring Columbia County.

Apart from leaving his name behind, C. H. Prescott didn't leave a lasting mark on the town. H. P. Isaacs, another industrialist with Northern Pacific, established a flour mill in Prescott, one of several he owned in the area. Again, while the rail and mill surely provided jobs for settlers in the area, the industrialists who owned the properties seem not to have left a cultural legacy behind. Others, whose contributions may not have launched the town's economy, nevertheless impacted the Prescott area in ways that feel much more personal.

Benjamin Flathers was a farmer in the area not yet named Prescott in the middle of the 19th century. Together with his wife, Malinda, Flathers operated a "halfway house" on Mullan Road, itself an important contribution to the area. In the pre-railroad era, when cross-country travel was exceedingly difficult, the US military created the

Mullan Road, making for an easier traverse from the Missouri River all the way across the Rocky Mountains to Fort Walla Walla on the Columbia River, 600 miles away. Mullan Road's purpose was to move troops easily, but it was accessible to everyone. Today, parts of I-90 and I-15 use the old Mullan Road. Benjamin and Malinda Flathers offered respite to travelers along that road. In 2015, in a ceremony held at Prescott Elementary School, locals led by a civic group called Walla Walla 2020 dedicated a historical marker to honor the Flathers' contribution. Both Malinda and Ben Flathers are buried at Ivy Cemetery.

Wallula's Complicated Legacy

On civic group Walla Walla 2020's list is the need to recognize the importance of the Wallula Historic Site. Located at the confluence of the Columbia and Snake Rivers, about a 40-minute drive west of Prescott, the Wallula Site, was an intertribal gathering place for the Walla Walla, Cayuse, and Nez Perce peoples. Lewis and Clark camped here on their way toward the Pacific in 1805, and the North West Company built a fur-trading post nearby about a dozen years later. Steamboats and railways followed, and pressure increased on the land and relationships between the Indigenous population and the settlers. The Walla Walla Treaty of June 9, 1855, took more than 6 million acres from Indigenous populations who'd made their homes along the Columbia and Snake Rivers.

Life in the Touchet Valley

Driving east on State Route 124 from the Tri-Cities toward Waitsburg takes travelers past Burbank, Eureka, and Lamar. The first sign of Prescott is the Ivy Cemetery, indicated by a wrought iron archway and a surreal beauty. The cemetery's sign is starkly white against the deep golden wheat and a bluebird sky. A single road cuts through the field toward a patch of green trees that have shaded the final resting place of Prescott residents since its pioneer days. The Touchet River, pronounced TOO-she, meanders nearby, and a vibrant wall of art tiles cre-

ated by area students notes the interconnectedness of towns in the Touchet Valley: Prescott, Dayton, and Waitsburg.

Under blue skies and the proverbial amber waves of grain, the Ivy Cemetery just outside Prescott has provided a simple and elegant final resting place since its earliest pioneering days.

In town, the highway winds past the outdoor city pool and the shared junior and senior high school and through a progression of short streets, most of which are simply named A through G, First through Fourth. The whole town is not quite half a mile square, bordered by Whetstone Creek on the north and the Touchet River to the south.

Near the corner of Second and D, between the library and the Tuxedo Bar, is The Prescott Plaza. After a fire gutted the building, the people of Prescott decided to create a community gathering place rather than leave the space empty. Sunflowers stand tall against the charred walls, and tables made of giant wooden spools line a central promenade leading to a stage.

To the left of the plaza, The Tuxedo Bar does a brisk business with everyone from bikers journeying across the state to Waitsburgers and residents of other nearby communities. Just down the sidewalk to the right of the blaze, multicolored stained glass welcomes visitors to the sparkling and bright Prescott Library, boasting multiple technology stations, a spacious reading room, and access to statewide interlibrary-loan systems, according to the young librarian on duty. As in many small towns, Prescott's library is a center of community activity and a great place to strike up a conversation with a local. When asked what used to be in the large building near to the library, a local man named Lawrence wasn't sure. He hadn't been here that long, he said. When did he move to Prescott? "Oh, about 18 years ago." On a trip between Seattle and Spokane, Prescott is a bit out of the way, but it would be worth the detour to drop in on "taco Wednesday" at the Tux, maybe bump into Lawrence again, and catch up on what's been going on in this sweet small town.

The business between the library and the Tuxedo Bar and Grill burned down. Rather than leave the space empty, the people of Prescott created a beautiful community gathering space, The Prescott Plaza.

73

Population: 193
Founding: 1869

INSETS L to R: Creating the Bruce Memorial Museum was the Waitsburg Historical Society's first project. • Idyllic downtown Waitsburg. • "The Waitsburg Story," a work in bronze by artist Wayne Chabre, depicts Weller Library founder Fannie Weller across from Edward Bruce, whose parents pioneered Waitsburg. • Waitsburg is an increasingly popular destination for foodies and wine enthusiasts.

TOP: In Jeffrey Hill's "The Waitsburg Trilogy," the town's founders walk past the *Waitsburg Times'* offices.

Waitsburg

Wait's Mill Town

There are railroad towns and mining towns, fishing towns, and trading towns. Waitsburg was first a mill town. Sylvester Mather Wait, the founding father of Waitsburg, was born in Vermont in 1822. By the time he turned 30 years old, he'd made it across the country to Oregon, where he married Mary Hargrove. Wait first operated a mill and ran a dairy farm in the Rogue Valley in Oregon. It was a time of frequent conflict between the US government and local Indian nations. In 1855, local miners massacred 28 Native Americans camping near the Table Rock Reservation. The miners hoped to start a war that would lead to gainful employment as paramilitary volunteers, as the mine had seemingly run dry. The Rogue River Treaty had been signed just two years prior, supposedly guaranteeing an end to the hostilities between the US government and the Rogue River nations.

As a result of the conflict in the area, Wait lost the mill, sold the farm, and in 1864 moved to the Touchet Valley. He arrived with $1,500 and a dream of starting over. Earlier settlers Dennis Williard and William Perry Bruce, who'd homesteaded there a few years prior, donated land to Wait, and in 1865, he started a gristmill at the confluence of the Touchet River and Coppei Creek. Shortly thereafter, residents voted to rename the town Waitsburg. Sixty years had passed since Lewis and Clark had traveled through on their return trip from their expedition. Another decade would pass before the Nez Perce people came through on the trail named for them as they fled the US cavalry, abandoning their homelands, resisting being forced onto reservations, and seeking peace in Canada.

In 1853, Washington became a territory. Sylvester Wait built his five-story mill just a dozen years later. This time, Wait's mill succeeded, creating an economy for the town. Wait bought wheat from local farmers and sold it in far-flung markets. By the time the town was platted in 1869, 100 people lived in Waitsburg.

As goes the story in many early towns, however, a fire burned through Waitsburg in 1881. The population had reached 250 residents, and they rebuilt. By then, Wait had sold the mill, but he had solidified his legacy as the founder of Waitsburg. The new owners of the mill expanded the business to locations as far away as Milton, Oregon. Changes in technology in the 20th century brought electric power to the mill, replacing the water-powered system. The Waitsburg mill remained operational until 1957 and was a symbol of the success and growth of Waitsburg, whose population continued to expand until the turn of the 20th century. The Waitsburg Historical Society sought to preserve the mill, but a fire destroyed it in the fall of 2009. Just a few years prior, the mill had earned a place on the Washington Trust for Historic Preservation's list of most endangered places. For a town that's done so much to preserve its history, the destruction of the mill represented a significant loss.

The Waitsburg Times

Wait's mill isn't the only important institution in town. In fact, local journalism has been a successful enterprise in Waitsburg for even longer than the mill. In weekly publication since 1878, *The Waitsburg Times* is one of the oldest publications in Washington. At one point, the owner and publisher of the paper was also the mayor, Tom Baker. *Time* magazine covered the unusual story of a local politician owning the local source of news in a story called "Press Lord" that ran in 1983. According to the article, local residents found the situation unremarkable. When questioned for the magazine, their answers demonstrated the close-knit nature of the town. "It's easy for Tom," one said. "His newspaper is only two doors down from town hall." Another commented that it was "[Tom's] turn."

Preserving the Past

In the 1970s, the Waitsburg Historical Society formed in an effort to preserve the Bruce House. William Perry Bruce, one of the early settlers who donated land to Wait for the mill, built one of many impressive homes that went up in the postfire years, when Waitsburg's population was booming. The Historical Society has restored the house and named it the Bruce Memorial Museum. With just 15 minutes' notice, a docent will meet visitors and provide a guided tour of the museum and explain much of Waitsburg's history.

One such docent is Anita Baker, wife of former mayor and publisher Tom. The Bakers moved to Waitsburg in 1963 for the opportunity to own a newspaper. Anita describes herself as the "Bruce House Boss." She knows the history of this place just as well as if she were descended from its original families. On the tour, she focuses on family connections. There's a chart explaining the connections between early citizens of Waitsburg. Here's

In 2015, the city commissioned three bronze sculptures depicting scenes from Waitsburg's history. *The Waitsburg Three*, by Jeffrey Hill, honors the town's three founders, Sylvester Wait, William Bruce, and William Preston.

a piece of fabric, one of four pieces each of Sylvester Wait's four daughters took from their mother's wedding dress. Though the past is very much present, Anita says Waitsburg is changing. "Suburbs don't have a Main Street," she says. City life in Walla Walla is just 25 miles away.

Waitsburg has the distinction of being the only town in Washington to operate based on an iteration of its original territorial charter.

Population: 133
Founding: 1882

INSETS L to R: George Drouillard, this park's namesake, was a civilian member of Lewis and Clark's expedition. • W.H. Starbuck worked for the railroad, not the coffee chain. • The historic Mullan Road crossed the Snake River at Lyon's Ferry near Starbuck. • Washington has the nation's largest Grange association.

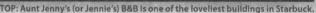

TOP: Aunt Jenny's (or Jennie's) B&B is one of the loveliest buildings in Starbuck.

Starbuck

The Railroad Giveth

In an 1880 annual report to its stockholders, the Oregon Railway and Navigation Company notes its plans for the Tucannon River Valley. Proposed construction included extending the Columbia and Palouse Railroad by 28 miles and constructing a branch line from Starbuck to Pomeroy and Pataha, for a total distance of 31 miles. The railroad stood to gain financially by providing transportation from these "very rich wheat district[s]." The report lists W. H. Starbuck of New York City as a board member and vice president. The railroad transported less wheat than anticipated that year, but the report noted, "Immigration to the North Pacific coast regions by our own lines of steamers . . . was larger . . . and of a much better class than ever before." The railroad "reaped a direct benefit."

Starbuck, named for the railroad man, was little more than a train station to begin with. By the time the OR&N completed the Pomeroy line in 1885, Starbuck had several businesses and a handful of citizens. Most of the people who lived there were railroad men and their families. In 1893, W. H. Starbuck gifted a bell to the Presbyterian

church and officially named the town. Soon, the town saw two dozen trains every day. The Bank of Starbuck opened in 1904. The next year, the railroad had a $20,000 payroll in Starbuck. In 1910, the town built a school with indoor plumbing, and within a few years, more than 200 students were in attendance.

Early descriptions of the landscape describe the steep grades trains had to climb in Columbia County toward the Snake River. "There is some difficulty in explaining these lands," notes an 1889 account. "They are a succession of knolls. . . . The prairie farmer of Illinois would call them hills; but in New England and New York they would be called magnificent plains."

Harsh winters on the plains led to crop failure. Raising cattle and sheep were a safer bet, but crop failures meant food shortages, which affected the livestock too. The new Mallet locomotives powered trains up the region's steep grades without the "helper trains" that Starbuck specialized in. In 1914, the High Line Bridge near Lyons Ferry further reduced train traffic in town. The Bank of Starbuck collapsed at the start of the

Great Depression in 1929. Farmers went into debt. By one account, "In 1932 the shops were closed . . . the natural process of disintegration is being accelerated by wreckers, who are moving the town piecemeal to Walla Walla."

The Works Project Administration provided some jobs in road and facilities repair, and some farmers and ranchers stayed, but in 1956, the high school closed, and a few years later, the railroad station followed. Dayton, 15 miles away, became the county seat and center of commerce in Columbia County, and Starbuck became the sleepy backcountry town it remains today.

Lyons Ferry

Just across the Snake River from Pataha, Lyons Ferry State Park is a 10-minute drive from Starbuck. Lyons Ferry, first called Palouse Ferry, operated from 1859 to 1968. Before cars and trains, ferries allowed for safe passage over the river. People used Lyons Ferry for entertainment, fishing, and even transporting their sheep between grazing lands. One area farmer, Mervin DeRuwe, crossed "2,000 to 3,000 sheep at a penny a head." The military used the ferry too. The Mullan Road, which connected Forts Walla Walla and Benton, used the ferry as part of its route.

The bridge over Lyon's Ferry today first crossed the Columbia at Vantage. The Wanapum Dam, built in the 1960s, increased water levels, requiring a higher bridge. Rather than demolishing the existing cantilevered truss bridge, the state dismantled it and stored it before reassembling it at Lyons Ferry. Though it was common to disassemble and move truss bridges, Lyons Ferry is one of the largest. Today, the 168-acre park at the confluence of the Snake and Palouse Rivers offers camping, swimming, fishing, and more than 50,000 feet of shoreline.

A Town on Wheels

Columbia County farmers continue to produce wheat, asparagus, and peas, and have recently added garbanzo beans and lawn grass seed. Starbuck is home to Grange No. 1032, part of a movement of farmers founded in 1889 working closely with the progressive and labor movements to fight for improved living conditions in rural areas. The railroads often exploited farmers, promising big payouts and cut-rate shipping. Farmers leveraged their properties to buy into the railroad, but the railroad turned their backs on all but the biggest producers. The Grange advocated for farmers' rights in this and other political matters. Today's Granges continue to advocate for farmers' interests at the state and local levels and to maintain social ties in small communities like Starbuck.

Daniel Lyons and John Markley purchased the ferry at the Snake and Palouse Rivers from Edward Massey in 1893. When Lyons died, his wife, Olive, purchased Markley's share. W. C. Cummings purchased the ferry in 1926 but kept the name Lyons Ferry.

In 1945, Congress passed legislation authorizing four dams on the Lower Snake River. Two of these, the Lower Monumental Dam and Little Goose Dam, were close enough to Starbuck that the town experienced a population explosion. "Trailer parks and businesses on wheels flooded the town," and the population went from 200 people to 1,000 "almost overnight." Today, signs of the later boom are invisible to the outsider.

Columbia County City Hall took over the bank building in the 1930s and still inhabits the building today. They're open from 9:30 to noon on Tuesdays. Aunt Jennie's Bed & Breakfast and Rebecca's Lodge restaurant hint at a service economy, but it's hard to imagine there are many customers. On a warm summer afternoon in Starbuck, there's not a person to be seen, though a few cars pass by. Barely a breath of air stirs the maple leaves. But then, the grass in the tiny park around the memorial bell is freshly cut. The bait shop's open. This town isn't a ghost yet.

Rebecca's Lodge restaurant is one of a handful of businesses on **Main Street** in Starbuck.

75

Population: 313
Founding: 1888

INSETS L to R: During the Great Depression, when construction materials were scarce, Clint Dobson was resourceful. • Grain elevators often make the first impression for visitors to rural Washington towns. • The Ice Age Floods Museum offers tourists an interesting and educational experience. • Facing the decline of their town, the people of LaCrosse choose to see possibility.

TOP: Murals in LaCrosse tell the town's story of wheat and rail.

LaCrosse

History in the Details

If the point of learning about history is to know something about who we are, there's only so much that can be learned from a list of postmasters and the dates of the first general store, when the rail came through, and how quickly the town reestablished itself after the first great fire. Even according to local historians, "The Palouse towns all began in somewhat similar fashion." Railroads, settlers, kids, schools—the points plot a familiar curve. The book, *Writ in Remembrance: 100 Years of LaCrosse Area History,* goes beyond the familiar to include a personal history of LaCrosse, rich in detail.

Howard Jennings Wigen's grandfather owned stock in the hardware store and the First State Bank. Wigen remembers three grocery stores, two garages, a drugstore, a livery barn, and stockyards, among other businesses. Town was "an exciting place for a country boy," he writes. The luckiest girl in town got a job working at the soda fountain at the drugstore, and the luckiest boy in town was her boyfriend. Apart from seeing westerns at the showhouse, young people in LaCrosse had the most fun driving to the railroad tracks and drinking beer until fights broke

out. Wigen recalled that "tank towns," as they were called, for the water tanks where the steam-driven trains refilled, were about a day's drive apart for a team and a wagon. Wigen died in 2003, followed in 2009 by his wife of 57 years, June. His contribution to the history of LaCrosse takes the form of a letter to his granddaughter, Jennifer.

A surveyor from LaCrosse, Wisconsin, is said to have named LaCrosse, Washington, after his own hometown. (Local lore has it that the original LaCrosse was named Prairie de la Crosse, after the game played by Indigenous peoples that developed into the modern-day sport of lacrosse.) A brief effort to rename the Palouse-area town of LaCrosse to Dunlor, a portmanteau of Dunphy, a railroad engineer, and Taylor, the first postmaster, failed when townspeople objected to the confusion created by having a station and a town with different names. In 1888, the train came through LaCrosse for the first time, and by the next year, it was hauling wheat, the Palouse's primary agricultural product. The town of LaCrosse incorporated in 1917. About equidistant from Spokane and the Tri-Cities in Washington and Lewiston, Idaho, the area now known as LaCrosse was originally part of the territory inhabited by the Palus people, said to be culturally related to the Nez Perce. The Palus did not recognize the Yakima Treaty of 1855 and refused to move to a reservation.

Family of Giants

Millions of years ago, lava flowed from vents in the earth, cooling quickly into basalt. The rolling wheat fields of the Palouse give way to scrublands marked by columnar basalt, and suddenly, the earth opens up. Palouse Falls, formed from erosion, is one of the remaining active waterfalls from flooding at the end of the last ice age. The Palus and Nez Perce tell a different story. In their depiction, five giant siblings lived along the Palouse River, oiling their hair with oil from a beaver's tail. When they ran low on supplies, they attacked Big Beaver, who lived upriver. Big Beaver clawed the rocks and smashed his tail into the ground, creating the Palouse Falls and surrounding geographical features. His claw marks mar the falls' basalt face to this day, and his heart, a massive stone, lies where he died, felled by Coyote's song, at the point where the Palouse River joins the Snake River.

Small Town, Big Effort

The community of LaCrosse has taken a particular interest in the Ice Age Floods, and in 2019 opened a museum dedicated to telling the geologic history of the area, as well as the ways that history has shaped the culture and industry of LaCrosse and other towns across the Palouse. The museum puts LaCrosse in partnership with the Ice Age Floods Institute, an organization that since the late 1980s has worked to study the causes and impacts of the floods and raise public awareness about them across the Northwest states.

In the mid-1930s, money was tight and construction materials were expensive, so LaCrosse resident Clint Dobson built houses from basalt stones he gathered in the fields around town. Dobson built seven structures in total, including a service station and six homes Dobson rented to rail and farm workers. The stone houses, now listed as among the most endangered historic buildings in the state, represent Depression-era resourcefulness. Today, all but one of the houses remain. LaCrosse Community Pride (LCP) is working with the Rural Communities Design Initiative at Washington State University to restore them to new life. Potential uses for the restored buildings include lodging for tourists and hunters. Though the current museum resides in one of the small houses, plans are in the works to move the museum to the larger service station after its restoration. The timeline for the restoration project depends on LCP's ability to secure funding.

OPEN, reads the sign through the gleaming windows of LaCrosse's grocery store. The townspeople know this sign means the difference between a town that's willing to let itself die and a town that fights to live.

LaCrosse Community Pride was formed to "prove the pessimists wrong," as prominent area farmer Alex McGregor put it, after LaCrosse lost its grocery store, earning it media coverage as an example of the death of small-town life in America. Since then, the group has managed to rally the community to reopen the grocery store, which now shares a building with a library and community center. Peggy Bryan, a longtime LaCrosse resident who recently retired from the Whitman County Library system, has led much of the effort, according to Jeff Andrus, president of LCP. Visitors are likely to find him at the Ice Age Floods Museum, showing tourists the beautifully produced video about the floods and the history of LaCrosse. Andrus, who has lived in LaCrosse for most of his life, knows McGregor (Farmer McGregor!) personally. The history described in the video is the history of his very own life. Half a dozen assembled tourists fill the metal folding chairs listening to McGregor narrate the through line of geologic time. "He worked really hard to get the vocals just right," Andrus says of his friend.

Clint Dobson's stone houses draw photographers and architecture enthusiasts to LaCrosse. Visitors can learn more about the houses and the geologic and cultural history of LaCrosse and the Palouse at the Ice Age Floods Museum.

76

Population: 70
Founding: 1910

INSETS L to R: Lamont's community church. • Lamont Middle School serves about 40 area students in grades five through eight. • Lamont's Community Center hosts everything from the town's two annual gun shows to November's Turkey Bingo. • Lamont's city park shares a name with the hometown of the fictional Beverly Hillbillies. Coincidence?

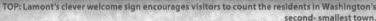

TOP: Lamont's clever welcome sign encourages visitors to count the residents in Washington's second-smallest town.

Lamont

Layover Town

The Depression-era work by James Agee and Walker Evans, *Let Us Now Praise Famous Men,* sings of the unknown and unnoticed American sharecropper. In reportage and imagery, Agee and Evans sought to reveal the hardscrabble resilience of Dust Bowl America. Their work was important in part for the way it contrasted with an already entrenched trope of American mythmaking: the story of the singular, great man. In a 1912 work, *History of the City of Spokane and Spokane County, Washington,* writer Nelson Wayne Durham proclaims Daniel Morgan one such man. "Though a young man," Durham wrote of Morgan, he "stands forth prominently in the ranks of the successful." Durham credits Morgan with building and promoting the town of Lamont as part of his work for the Spokane, Portland and Seattle Railroad, owned by James J. Hill, who'd built Great Northern. Of Lamont, Durham wrote, "It is a model town on a magnificent site and Mr. Morgan proposes to make it 'the greatest little town in the United States.'" At the time, Durham records Lamont as having about 600 residents and "every convenience of a city of many thousands." By other accounts, Lamont's population has never exceeded 165, which it reached as of the 1920 census. Morgan became the president of the bank and mercantile, and he owned a 1,000-acre farm in Whitman County, yet he stopped short of naming the town after himself. Lamont takes its name from the vice president of the Northern Pacific Railway, Daniel Lamont.

Lamont was first a layover town. Rail workers traveling between Spokane and Pasco spent the night in Lamont until 1913, when, after a fire, the railroad began compelling laborers to work through from one end to the other. Though the railroad chose to minimize its use of the Lamont station, through the 1950s, steam-powered trains still stopped there to replenish their water tanks. In the end of that decade, new diesel-powered trains began refueling in Pasco, and the rail abandoned the fueling station based in Lamont. Since then, the town's population level has risen and fallen by a few families every decade or so, but mostly fallen, to its current level of fewer than half the number of residents it had a century ago. The rail is long gone, removed after Burlington Northern, its final owner, decided not to upgrade the seldom-used route. The State of Washington now owns the railbed and has converted it as part of the Rails-to-Trails historic-trail system. The Columbia Plateau Trail makes its way through Lamont in an unpaved trail rough with rail ballast and rich in scenery that hasn't changed much since the early days when men like Morgan and Hill raced to lay tracks faster and farther than their rivals, leaving towns rising and falling in their wake like the dust.

The World of Lamont

In search of a road less traveled than US 195 North from Pullman or I-90 East toward Spokane, an adventurous traveler might choose a detour on State Route 23 and find herself momentarily in Lamont. The two things she'll notice first and remember are the grain elevator and the welcome sign, which notes Lamont's population in hash marks instead of numerals. Below that, a smaller sign proclaims that Lamont is "a nuclear-free zone." Steve Lacy, once mayor of the town, maintained a blog for several years that offers insight to the accidental tourist. In one post, titled, "Iconic Lamont Town Sign Goes Missing!" Lacy questions why anyone would steal a sign from a town "dead on its feet," but he simultaneously rejoices that the town must be moving up in the world if they've got something worth stealing. Though many of Lacy's articles are whimsical or entirely fictional, the blog offers glimpses into the struggles and successes of one of the tiniest towns in the state.

Connected at Every Level

Though home to fewer than 100 residents, Lamont operates on a municipal-governance system consisting of five elected council members and a mayor. Effectively, nearly 10% of the town works in local government. Maps dating back to Lamont's platting in 1910 show the town as a compact grid formed along a stretch of rail cutting diagonally through large squares that represent land owned by people named Reid, Swannack, Melville, Kelly, and Shields. Today's map might look similar: The town itself is a blip of organization surrounded by the large, wild ranches of Whitman County.

Like many school districts in rural Washington, Lamont's merged with the district in its neighboring town, Sprague. Students attend middle school in Lamont and for high school and elementary school, they ride the bus to Sprague, about 10 miles away.

For ranchers in the area, some of whom own and work several thousand acres of land, success fluctuates with local and international beef markets. Over the years, ranches expanded as smaller farm operations closed, and they contracted as ranchers were forced to sell off land to manage expenses like sending kids to college. When talking about the impact global politics has on local agriculture, picture a rancher in Lamont, hoping to sell more beef in Asian markets and that the weather will be favorable. Lamont has fewer grain producers than it used to by nearly half. Many of the Lamont Grain Growers Association's 130 members live as far away as other states and even other countries. Though profitable, the association recently decided to merge with the Ritzville Warehouse Company, which they hope will lead to more opportunities for grain growers to market their product.

Not everything about Lamont's future feels uncertain. Recent news stories about the town detail the interconnectedness of this small community. One story highlights the way the town came together when one of the neighbors fell ill. It was harvest time, and there was a limited window in which to do the work. Whole families paused work in their own fields to help their friend. It's a small-town ethos. In places like Lamont, everyone's in it together, and they have been since the beginning. The neighbor who fell ill? His last name can be found on the original town plat.

Lamont's town sign gives an accurate count of its population, which is so small that it can be noted in hash marks. Lamont also wants visitors to know that nuclear weapons and power plants are banned within its limits.

77

Population: 537
Founding: 1904

INSETS L to R: General Mills towers above St. John's downtown • Whitman County has been the nation's number one wheat-producing region since 1978. • St. John's Heritage Museum tracks the region's success, from the price of wheat to school consolidations. • Katerina Wiley's mural accurately depicts the lay of the land on the Palouse.

TOP: Downtown St. John.

St. John

The Price of a Bushel

Whitman County has been the country's number-one wheat-producing region since 1978. The historical museum in St. John shows that farmers had been tracking the price of wheat for nearly a century by the time Whitman County's wheat production rose to its current prominence. In 1890, two years after Edward Talert St. John donated the land and platted the town, hard red wheat sold for 70¢ per bushel. Within 30 years, St. John had nearly the same number of residents it does now, and wheat had risen to 87¢ per bushel. Gasoline, by then another trackable commodity, cost 30¢ per gallon at the time. With the Depression, the price of gas fell, but wheat continued to rise, and St. John's population dipped but rebounded. Between 1950 and 1960, wheat rose from 64¢ cents to $2.19 per bushel, while gas stayed at the low price of 31¢ per gallon. This is how a farming community remembers: What was the price of wheat when, and how were we living because of it? A 1901 history of Whitman County describes St. John as a "very pleasant little country town," originally a railroad outpost then with four general stores and other businesses ranging from lumber yards to a butcher shop.

Though wheat farming has sustained St. John since its earliest days, farming on the Palouse presented challenges unique to the region. Whereas the wheat fields of the Midwestern prairies lay flat as far as the eye can see, the dunes of the Palouse roll like waves in a cross-current. Ice age glaciers ground the bedrock to a fine silt. Floodwaters carried that silt across the landscape, and the wind blew the rich sediment, called loess, into the dunes that make up the Palouse. The steep slopes of the dunes reach grades of up to 50%, and the loess runs up to 50 inches deep. Because of the landscape's crests and hollows, farmers on the Palouse couldn't make use of early combines and threshers, which required level ground. Soon, smaller machines and self-leveling combines allowed area farmers to join the technological revolution in agriculture.

After years of painstaking restoration and research, St. John's Heritage Museum opened in 2013. Its walls and exhibits tell the story of St. John in maps, photos, and documents. The town remembers what it was like in the earliest days, when the

Oregon Washington Railroad and Navigation first came through; it remembers how Edward T. St. John left his wife and children in Texas, following gold rush dreams to California. The town documents every one of its 23 school consolidations, and it honors the stories of its fallen soldiers. Underneath it all runs the through line—the price of wheat, and the life that price affords.

History and Herstory

Winston Churchill famously said, "History is written by the victors." As a visit to any historical society will reveal, the victors of many a small town are the men. Women's contributions show up in model kitchens and old clothing. Occasionally more information surfaces; next to a book that lists the names and biographies of WWII veterans, a photograph might show the women who went to work in the factories while the men were at war. In keeping with the comprehensive nature of its storytelling, St. John's historians remember Joy Margaret Bonnington, a St. John local and a nurse, who enlisted in the Navy in 1943.

Stationed in Santa Barbara, California, Bonnington worked caring for the needs of soldiers coming back from the Theater of the Pacific. Bonnington was part of the first contingent of nurses to serve the wounded in this part of the country. She was one of only eight nurses caring for a base of thousands of soldiers. Bonnington was an operating room nurse, but part of her job was to listen too. Local historians suggest that nurses like Bonnington played an important role prior to the identification of PTSD. Discharged in 1946, Bonnington went on to enroll in the University of Washington on the GI Bill. She married, had four children, and spent decades working as a nurse. Among its heroes, St. John remembers Joy Bonnington.

Pretty Good at Survival

The General Mills granary towers over St. John. Murals painted by schoolchildren adorn building walls in the colors of wheat through the seasons. The Lamont Bank of St. John is still up and running, more than a century into its existence, despite multiple robberies and the Great Depression. Though many people drive the hour to Spokane to take advantage of Costco and Walmart, St. John's own Empire Foods continues to thrive, and the hardware store next door is busy. In St. John, a full round of golf with a cart costs less than the price of lunch in any neighboring city, but businesses and residences still have access to high-speed, fiber optic internet service, thanks to the St. John Telephone Company. Small towns like St. John walk a fine line between survival and what happens when a town can no longer sustain itself. Thus far, St. John is surviving. As longtime mayor K. B. Trunkey put it, "We seem to be doing pretty good at that."

St. John's Heritage Museum opened in 2013 after more than four years of painstaking restoration. A gallery of black-and-white photography showing the history of farming in the area is the museum's centerpiece.

The owner of a local coffee shop and gift store has time to chat between customers. She moved to St. John after getting married in Spokane, and she and her husband raised their five children here. Her youngest just moved to Spokane to go to the university, and according to her mother, she's afraid to take the bus, preferring to drive. The bus schedule is hard to figure out, and the people on public transport can sometimes be frightening, her mother reports. It's no wonder the entire town of St. John occupies less than a single square mile. There are roughly 400 times the number of people in Spokane as St. John. I wonder if Spokane is a scary place for a small-town girl. Like it or lump it, St. John is small and steady. Maybe that's why the name of the store is Welcome Home.

St. John recognizes local artists who beautify the town. Katerina Wiley's mural won her a gold award in the local chapter of the Girl Scouts in 2018.

78

TOP: A manicured rose garden beautifies the park beside Rosalia's library.

Population: 550
Founding: 1870

INSETS L to R: The Milwaukee Bridge calls attention to Rosalia's beauty. • The Texaco station is on the National Register of Historic Places. • For any history buff, Rosalia is a must-visit stop on the Palouse Scenic Byway. • Rosalia is one of many small towns in Washington facing economic decline.

Rosalia

Conflicting Histories

"The embryo town needed a railroad to give it impetus forward." W. H. Lever's 1901 history recounts Rosalia's development alongside the railroad. The town, named for Rosalia Favorite, wife of the town's first postmaster, owes also to M. E. Choate, J. E. Kennedy, J. M. Whitman, and others, who, Lever argues, "under trying difficulties and privations wrought the development of Rosalia and the surrounding country."

Even in a book that aims to be a love letter to 100 small towns, it's important not to look through too-rosy lenses. Chief among the difficulties and privations suffered by Rosalia's earliest white settlers were the events at what is today called Steptoe Butte in 1858. Conflicting accounts note the events; even the names given the battle are different.

Lever writes that the men under Colonel Edward J. Steptoe's command beat a hasty retreat, "beset by hordes of Indian foes, almost without ammunition and facing, as it seemed, the certainty of being cruelly massacred."

HistoryLink, a website based in Washington State and consisting of scholarly articles written by regional historians, refers to the battle as The Steptoe Incident. In his history of Whitman County, historian Phil Dougherty writes that Colonel Edward J. Steptoe's task was to enforce the treaties Governor Isaac Stevens had made between the territorial government and various Indigenous nations, many of whom had refused to sign, including the Palouse, Yakima, Spokane, and Coeur d'Alene Tribes. In May of 1858, Steptoe sought to force the tribes into submission. A day after Steptoe's small contingent set out, several tribes collaborated in an attack, killing and wounding troops. Here, Dougherty's reporting ends. Only so much space can be given to a single incident—even an important one—in the retelling of an entire county's entire history.

The fighting took place alongside what is today called Pine Creek, formerly known as Tohotonimme. The Battle of Tohotonimme, according to the Coeur d'Alene Tribe, "brought the Colonel's men to within their last few rounds of ammunition before they were able to slip away under cover of dark." Eastern Washington tribes had won no small victory, but a few months later, Colonel

George Wright defeated the tribes with a contingent of 700 men.

Any place's history will be different depending on the storyteller, and no single history is complete. Disparate accounts exist regarding exactly what happened, down to disputes about where the battle took place. Nearly 50 years after the incident, the Daughters of the American Revolution erected a monument at Steptoe Butte, inscribed with the story that Chief Timothy of the Nez Perce helped the US Army evade the tribes. Though Nez Perce scouts worked with the US, no evidence supports Chief Timothy's betrayal, leading most to consider the inscription a false account.

Bridge to Beauty

From a distance, the Rosalia railroad bridge is a visual anchor, the way, in a vast expanse, a single structure can seem to pull the sky down toward the land. Its concrete arches suggest leaping movement over the road and the creek. Up close, it is no less impressive. Its form becomes a frame for a focused view of the Palouse. The bridge is Washington State's only example of a multispan concrete arch bridge built specifically for rail. Engineers rarely chose concrete to bear the heavy impact of rail loads. The Rosalia bridge calls to mind similar bridges in Spokane, both built around the same time. Those bridges span the Spokane River. The Rosalia bridge's placement in the midst of a quiet field inspires a contemplative moment. Cliff swallows flit in and out of their mud nests built in the concrete joints. Built in 1915 to carry the Milwaukee Railroad line, the bridge now offers a pastoral stroll. To visit the bridge is to contemplate one's smallness; it is a monument amid a landscape yet more monumental.

Battle Days

To an outsider, Rosalia makes a cheerful first impression. Bright murals in Spartan Legacy Park offer a welcome and a pictorial representation of the town's most important sites. The Howard Street Clock is in the picture, preserved from its former incarnation as Portland's official timekeeper. The mural has the Texaco station, the best-preserved example of a service station of its era in Washington State and now Rosalia's visitor's center. Next to the station, the mural shows the Steptoe monument and a church. In the background, the bridge presides over the town.

The Milwaukee Bridge arches over Pine Creek in view of the Steptoe battlefield. Long abandoned by the rail, the bridge is now accessible to all as part of the 285-mile Palouse to Cascade State Park Trail, also known as the Iron Horse Trail and the John Wayne Pioneer Trail.

Visiting Rosalia is like stepping inside the mural. The sky is a robin's-egg blue and the earth a gently rolling golden sea. Roses tended alongside a wrought-iron arch invite a visit to the memorial for local veterans. Grain silos rise just beyond the blooms.

The recession of the early 2000s hit towns like Rosalia hard. Already suffering from dwindling population numbers as younger generations left farming life, the recession led to more closed businesses and cuts to crucial services like policing. The future is uncertain, but tourism may provide for future economic opportunity. Rosalia is a town for history buffs. The biggest event of the year is Rosalia Battle Days, an annual June celebration commemorating the 1858 battle. In 2019 the weekend-long celebration marked its 50th anniversary. Like many towns on or near the Palouse, Rosalia claims to be "the gateway to the Palouse byway." It's a title that should be shared, in hopes that all the small towns along the byway will benefit from the draw of the Palouse's undeniable beauty.

A 1914 monument commemorates the conflict outside Rosalia. One of its inscriptions reads, "In memory of the officers and soldiers of the United States Army who lost their lives on this field in desperate conflict with the Indians in the Battle of Te-Hots-Nim-Me May 17, 1838."

79

Population: 422
Founding: 1888

INSETS L to R: The farmer in this mural appears to be growing America itself. • With 170 sunny days per year and summer temps in the 80s, a pool is a nice amenity. • Downtown Oakesdale represents a century's worth of architectural trends. • Oakesdale School District serves about 115 students in grades K-12.

TOP: Oakesdale has a number of buildings on the National Register of Historic Places.

Oakesdale

A History in Brick and Wood

Thomas Oakes was general manager of the Northern Pacific Railroad, which lay tracks across James McCoy's homestead in what is today Oakesdale, in the McCoy Valley, just northwest of the Spokane Indian Reservation. One source reports that from its early days, Oakesdale enjoyed the most "favorable situation" of any town in Whitman County, given its placement along not one, but two railroad lines, the comparatively gentle roll of its hills, and its youthful energy. By 1888, the town had "about three hundred inhabitants and one hundred good, substantial buildings," including a school. The International Hotel caught fire in 1892 and took most of the town with it, save a few buildings spared by firefighters from Tekoa, who heard of the disaster by telegraph. Oakesdale did not despair. "With an energy which mocked disaster," they rebuilt, using brick, this time. Many of those brick buildings remain today.

The National Register of Historic Places recognizes three buildings in Oakesdale as historically important. The Edwin H. Hanford House, three stories of brick, reflects the work of an important

regional architect, as well as the community contributions of E. H. Hanford, a fish salesman who came to Oakesdale from Chicago in 1889 and cofounded the first bank. He became one of the most prominent landowners in the county and led the way in orchard cultivation. City Hall, built in 1892, was one of the first buildings the town erected after the fire. Initially used as a hotel, it has been the city's center of governance since 1928.

The one building any visitor might guess holds import in the town's history towers over the rest. The J. C. Barron Flour Mill once held a steam-generating plant, elevator, and warehouse in addition to a gristmill. Though it now sits on a concrete foundation, the rest of the mill is built from shiplap, fir, and cedar. Its narrow, weather-worn boards draw both the gaze and the imagination.

J. G. Porter built the mill in 1890, and Northern Pacific immediately built a spur track to service it. The mill somehow avoided the fire that destroyed the rest of town and became a regionally important business. In the mid 1890s, the mill ran 24 hours per day, producing a daily yield of 80 barrels of flour. Joseph Barron bought the mill in

1907 and replaced the steam-powered system with electricity. Closed finally in 1960, the J. C. Barron Mill was the last to operate in the Inland Empire.

Rural Realities

The pastoral beauty of the Palouse obscures the less-beautiful reality that rural life isn't easy. A 2016 study of poverty in Whitman County undertaken by the League of Women Voters of Pullman found that Whitman County residents experience poverty at higher rates than the state average, even when adjusting for college students at Washington State University, who make up a statistically significant percentage of residents. The statistics gathered from state agencies reveal that residents of rural Whitman County experience food insecurity and a lack of access to services like healthcare and childcare. Fully a third of rural Whitman County's poor are children; another third are elderly. Taken together, these groups paint a picture of a vulnerable and needy population in which up to 19% of low-income households report going hungry in the last year. The numbers vary from town to town. In Oakesdale, 37% of students qualify for a free or reduced-price lunch.

Oakesdale School Childcare Center offers assistance for working families and shares with Tekoa a specialist to help homeless and impoverished students. Nearly two dozen families make use of the local food pantry. Oakesdale residents in need of medical care must travel either to the clinic in Tekoa or the hospital in Colfax. While Oakesdale has a modest grocery store, the study finds that the next nearest large supermarket is 36 miles away. The study asks, "Who are Whitman County's poor?" The answer may be that they're not always visible, but they are there and in need.

Nighthawk Pride

A good way to get a sense of any place is to climb to the highest point and look down. The city park in Oakesdale sits on the crest of a hill between the school and downtown. Looking down the long flight of stairs that ascend the hill, past the flags variously representing the country, the state, and the military, the town of Oakesdale sits in a neat grid of old brick fronted by tidy sidewalks. The flour mill stands at the end of town, and beyond that, just past the exit sign for the highway, the Oakesdale cemetery occupies a treed swath of green in the yellowing fields. It's a sleepy town and a peaceful view. Depending on the day, the top of these stairs would make a great place to meditate in silence or to have the best possible seats for a parade.

Joseph Barron, Jr. started working at his father's mill in 1909 at the age of 18 and took over the business in 1955. Despite the unlikelihood of being able to compete with large-scale commercial operations, the younger Barron claimed to have "flour in his blood."

In June 2019, 12 members of the 17-person Oakesdale High School Class of 1969 gathered for their 50-year high school reunion. The group took part in a parade for the annual Old Mill Days celebration, presided over by Oakesdale High's own Jeanne Ellis, age 100½, who graduated in 1936 and has lived in Oakesdale all her life. After a long hiatus, the Old Mill Days celebration is back, and it's a hit. From the vantage point of the park, you might see folks enjoying beer brats from a local recipe and hot rods cruising down the street for the car show. The state volleyball and track champions are part of the crowd, as is the state-level boys' basketball team. This is Oakesdale, Home of the Nighthawks.

From the park above Oakesdale, visitors get a glimpse of the town's history and a suggestion of its present struggles. The flour mill recalls prosperity; Crossett's is one of the few remaining businesses.

80

Population: 778
Founding: 1888

INSETS L to R: The funds needed to preserve the old Milwaukee trestle topped $1 million. • Tekoa is closer to city conveniences than it feels. • Walter Dorsey ran Dorsey's Chevrolet in Tekoa for 45 years. • Roof lines in Tekoa mimic the lines of the surrounding Palouse.

TOP: Public art in Tekoa ranges from an Art Deco theater to agricultural murals.

Tekoa

The Beginning of the Line

Tekoa has inspired appreciation since its earliest days. W. H. Lever's 1901 history describes the town as "a veritable dream of loveliness," a landscape "replete with feminine pride in her newly-wrought garment of green." Better farmland cannot be found, he asserts. Its water system was "the best," and its "fine six-room school-house" is evidence that "its people are friends of education." All this, and the town had "quite a large payroll."

Those receiving the payroll worked for the Oregon Washington and Northern Railroad. Tekoa went from a few claims homesteaded by David and George Huffman and John McDonald in the 1880s to a thriving town of nearly 1,700 residents by the 1920 census. Lever writes, "When it was definitely known that Tekoa was to be a junction, many places of business were opened . . . in anticipation of the expected transportation facilities." As goes the railroad, so go towns across Washington State.

Settler Daniel Truax platted the town in 1888, dividing it into 20-acre parcels. Frank Connell built a trading post to continue trade relations with the Nez Perce Indians. Tekoa's own website notes this trading post, as well as the Whitman Massacre, may have limited early settlement in the area. The site's accounting of Tekoa's history doesn't name the Nez Perce or Cayuse people but refers generally to Native Americans and explains, "Long before the first white settlers came to Tekoa, the area was part of what was known then as Great Oregon Country . . . explored in certain areas by Lewis and Clark, David Thompson, Father Desmet [sic] and Ross Cox."

Given its history, one might expect, then, that Tekoa would instead be named Coxville, Trauxville, or Huffman's Junction. Daniel Traux's wife, "standing on the porch of her house on the west bank of Hangman Creek," thought to name the emerging settlement after the biblical town south of Jerusalem, whose name means "city of tents." Other biblical references to Tekoa seem to fit the town as well. They variously describe Tekoa as the "extreme edge of the inhabited area," and the place where a "wise woman" was found to mediate between King David and Absalom. Tekoa incorporated in 1889.

A Most American Thing to Do

There are many ways to end a sentence that begins, "I wonder what people did before . . . " Digital natives will ask what we did before the internet. Before a universe of information was at our fingertips and Netflix delivered binge-watching, before TV and radio and Encyclopaedia Britannica, people gathered in small communities across the country for cultural festivals lasting days or weeks. These were the chautauquas. In the late 19th century, as the railroads raced to complete transnational lines, kicking up towns in their wake, a movement started in New York and soon spread all the way to the West. Chautauquas, first started in Chautauqua, New York, were festivals meant to inform and entertain. Authors lectured, politicians spoke, vaudevillians performed, and everywhere, people flocked to the tents. *From Bunch Grass to Grain,* a local history of Tekoa, mentions chautauquas and medicine shows at the opera house as two forms of entertainment, as well as the occasional circus. By some estimates, in the early 1920s, 40 million Americans participated in chautauquas held in more than 10,000 locations country-wide. Teddy Roosevelt famously called the traveling shows "the most American thing in America." The movement fell away during the Depression, but in recent years, a group called the New Old Time Chautauqua has restarted the tradition. The NOTC is working in partnership with Washington State Parks; their 2016 tour marked the first chautauquas in the region since 1925, a year in which the chautauqua came to Tekoa. The NOTC and Washington State Parks include Native American voices, too, partnering with the Confederated Tribes of Colville and the Lummi Nation.

Slippery Gulch Life

More than other tiny towns in Whitman County, Tekoa is picturesque. Positioned on a rise in the hills at the foot of Tekoa Mountain, the town offers vistas over the wide Palouse. A mural over the Tekoa museum and library depicts a train station in early Tekoa. The train steams down the track tucked between rolling hills. The Milwaukee trestle, built by the Chicago, Milwaukee & St. Paul Railroad in 1909, spans the hills, very much the way it looks to a visitor today, standing just a block away from the mural. Advertisements for writing camps and reading programs testify to the centrality of the library in city life. A paper alien in the library's window demands, "Take me to your readers!" The curved roofline of one building cedes to a roofline of descending notches, like a set of stairs.

> The railroads saw the Palouse as a pathway to the Rocky Mountains and a ticket to economic success. Agricultural products and natural resources rumbled over the 975-foot-long, 115-foot-high railroad trestle above Tekoa to the tune of millions of dollars annually.

The combination of shapes mimics the mountain, here soft with agriculture, there sharply treed. Across a small park built in an empty space in a row of connected buildings, the art deco marquee of the recently restored Empire Theatre promises performing-arts events that will draw a regional audience. Tekoa is one stop on the Palouse Scenic Byway, and like other towns on the loop, Tekoa has signs that tell visitors what's nearby. The town of Latah, in Spokane County, is just 7 miles away, and Oakesdale is a dozen miles in the other direction. On the other hand, why not stay in Tekoa? "Imagine living in a town where folks are extra friendly," they advertise. Tekoa offers services from grocery stores to a medical clinic, and despite the boarded-up evidence of economic decline, it has numerous thriving businesses, including restaurants and a coffee shop. The noon whistle still announces lunchtime in Tekoa every day. A dream of loveliness, indeed.

The Empire Theatre reopened in 2000 after five years of volunteer labor for its restoration and more than four decades of disuse. Originally a movie theater, the Art Deco space is now a regional performance hub for local talent and visiting artists alike.

81

Population: 998
Founding: 1888

INSETS L to R: The view from Kamiak Butte rewards a visit during any season. • Bicycles parked unlocked in a front yard in idyllic Palouse reveal the town's friendly nature • The first burial in Greenwood Cemetery in Palouse was in 1877. The tree-filled cemetery doubles as a park, offering views of Palouse in all directions. • In June, the Palouse is a saturated green that softens to gold by the fall.

TOP: This sculpture stands in Heritage Park, on the site of an old service station.

Palouse

Whitman Before the Wheat

When the air and the earth warmed, and the scrubby vegetation of the Columbia Plateau began to thaw, the Cayuse people left their multigenerational longhouses and headed for the river, where they'd find the spring salmon returning and harvest camas root. In the 1700s, after acquiring horses for the first time, the Cayuse expanded their territory from the Columbia Plateau to the Great Plains and California, claiming The Dalles in southeastern Washington and becoming, by one account, regional "monarchs." The Confederated Tribes of the Umatilla Reservation, to which the Cayuse now belong, notes the territory controlled by the Cayuse as stretching deep into British Columbia and encompassing the entirety of what is now the state of Idaho. They traded goods and cultural elements with other tribes; when Lewis and Clark first encountered the Cayuse, they traded with them too. As with other multicultural encounters, the Cayuse expressed interest in the culture of the whites exploring their land and were hospitable to missionaries.

Into this environment walked Narcissa and Marcus Whitman, Presbyterian missionaries from New York. Relations between the Whitmans and the Cayuse were positive. Whitman was a respected doctor whom the Cayuse regarded as a medicine man. Records show that the Cayuse celebrated the birth of the Whitmans' daughter in 1837. The Whitmans sought to culturally assimilate and convert the Cayuse. The missionaries encouraged the Cayuse to cultivate the land but did not compensate them after turning their land into a cornfield.

After a few years, Whitman's missionary board ordered him to close the mission, but he did not. Meanwhile, the Cayuse and other Indigenous groups were increasingly disturbed by the intrusion of a seemingly endless stream of white settlers. As many as 4,000 came in 1847 alone. As a consequence of the settlement, a measles outbreak killed nearly half the Cayuse, and Dr. Whitman was powerless to stop it. In response, a group of Cayuse men killed the Whitman family and several others. This conflict is noted as the first of many Indian Wars in the Pacific Northwest that coincided with the treaties signed between territorial governor Isaac Stevens and various Indian Nations. The Cayuse, Umatilla, and Walla Walla peoples ceded more than 6 million acres of land in the Walla Walla Treaty of 1855. Wheat farmers flooded in, and towns sprang up alongside train tracks across southeastern Washington. William Ewing was the first settler in the town of Palouse. The land the Cayuse used to occupy, along with the Palus, Nez Perce, and many others, received a new name: Whitman County. Marcus Whitman was born in 1802, a descendant of John Whitman of England, whose last name was originally spelled differently: Whiteman.

Kamiak Butte

Between Pullman and Palouse, 3,600 feet above the loess, Kamiak Butte rises like a rogue wave in a soft green ocean. Under the long, cool shadows of ponderosa pines on the butte's northern slope, warblers, nuthatches, golden-crowned kinglets, and red cross-bills trill and call. About 130 species of birds live here, as well as nearly 200 species of plants and dozens of mammal species. As the 3.5-mile Pine Ridge Trail ascends and turns toward the south, the forest gives way to the sun's warmth. The vast Palouse region comes into view. From the peak, hikers can see the cities of Pullman and Moscow to the south and Steptoe Butte 15 miles to the northwest. Kamiak Butte's name honors Chief Kamiakin of the Yakama Nation.

The Friendliest Little City

State Route 27 wends through seemingly endless fields until signs of civilization suddenly appear. First-time visitors might wonder what sort of character the town ahead has. Will it be a town that takes care to preserve and celebrate its past? Will it be a town that shows evidence of forward thinking? A short bridge over the Palouse River later, the city of Palouse provides the answers: it is both. Just outside of town, a large solar array basks in the sun. Signage proudly notes that the solar farm has reduced well-pump electricity requirements by 58%. As of this writing, the project has generated more than 309 megawatt hours, avoiding the release of 185 tons of carbon dioxide and offsetting nearly 30,000 gallons of gasoline.

The town of Palouse welcomes visitors with friendly faces and abundant public art, from mosaic work to preserved advertising adorning building walls in the backdrop of the sculpture seen here, of a boy pushing a girl on a swing.

In town, a printing museum and an old railroad trestle tell parts of Palouse's past. The museum's history itself reads like that of many small railroad towns. The museum represents a lifetime of work by Dr. Roy M. Chatters, a nuclear engineer who collected newspapers and printmaking equipment. The museum opened in 1976 only to close after floods rendered the building unsafe. Heroic community efforts restored the place, and the museum opened again in 2003. Once, the Spokane and Inland Empire Railroad crossed over the town; today, the tracks are gone, but signage on the old concrete bearings keeps the memory alive.

Palouse is a community that feels friendly and quietly busy. Volunteers work along the Plant Identification Trail. Children ride scooters down the street and stand over the river, pointing out little fish swimming under the bridge. Mosaic art glitters on the side of a restaurant, and people sit outside the café drinking coffee. In Hayton Green Park, families picnic near the veterans' memorial and offer conversation. As in many small towns, Palouse has little distinction between its residential and commercial areas. Neighbors walking to the grocery store stop to chat over low fences. The town feels like the landscape it's named for—a place to let your attention relax and wander, where no demands are made on a person except perhaps to say hello.

The fields that make up the Palouse were once the ocean floor. Kamiak Butte was formed of hard quartzite lifted up by volcanic forces. It takes its name from Yakama Indian Chief Kamiakin, who reluctantly signed the 1855 treaty that created the Yakama Indian Reservation.

82

Population: 345
Founding: 1878

INSETS L to R: The Palouse encompasses a wide geographical region including southeastern Washington, northeastern Oregon, and central Idaho. • Jacob's bakery opened recently in the space of a renovated former brewery, which even earlier was the home of Uniontown's opera house. • Like many small towns, Uniontown's library shares a building with the town hall. • Barrel-vaulted masonry is characteristic of Romanesque architechture, in vogue in Europe from the 10th through mid-12th centuries.

TOP: The fence along the Dahmen Barn's property is made of more than a thousand wheels.

Uniontown

Producers on the Palouse

German Catholic farmers were the first Europeans to settle the Palouse region and what is now Uniontown. History notes 1873 as the first year German immigrants settled in the area. Just a few years prior, the US government's westward expansion had moved beyond negotiating with Indigenous nations. For almost a century, the US government had acknowledged Indian sovereignty in nearly 400 treaties across the country, but the 1871 Indian Appropriations Act abolished treaty-making in favor of creating reservations by "agreement" with individual tribes and often groups of tribes. The law thus opened Indian lands for the taking. Europeans, largely from Germany and Switzerland, settled the Palouse, and their farming techniques turned the region into America's breadbasket.

Thomas Montgomery left New York in the final years of the Civil War, arriving in Uniontown four years before the Indian Appropriations Act and filing a homestead claim three years after it, in 1874. By the end of the decade, he'd established a post office and platted the town. Other early arrivals, notably L. J. Wolford, Roy Woodworth,

and a Dr. Cole, had such a hard time getting along with Montgomery that they founded their own town, Colton, whose name is a portmanteau for Dr. Cole and Wolford's son, Clinton. Today, Uniontown and Colton share a school district, and a sign on the way into Uniontown proclaims it HOME OF THE WILDCATS, the mascot of both the Washington State University and the Colton schools' sports teams.

Montgomery continued to create enemies, and eventually he was murdered, just nine years after filing a homestead claim. Despite his brief and controversial contribution, Uniontown remembers Montgomery fondly. A memorial stone in his honor stands in Holzer Park.

The settlers weathered the economic downturn known as the Panic of 1893, briefly putting on hold plans to build a magnificent church out of brick and stone. They resumed construction in 1904, and in 1905, St. Boniface Catholic Church became the first to be consecrated by a bishop in the state of Washington. St. Boniface is in the Romanesque style, with barrel-vaulted masonry in the interior and exterior towers predating the Gothic style that took hold in the middle of the 12th century.

Uniontown remains a center of agriculture, and since its founding has been a social and cultural center, as well. Of particular interest is Uniontown's history as early adopters: They had phone service in 1886 and set up internet service in 1997.

The Dahmen Barn

In 1935, local farmer Frank Wolf built a barn just north of Uniontown on Highway 195 for the Dahmen family, who used it as a commercial dairy operation for nearly 20 years. Today, the Uniontown Community Development Association maintains the barn as a community space focused on artistic education and performance. Grants from the National Endowment for the Arts and the Art Place Foundation have contributed to the expansion and renovation of the venue. The striking fence that surrounds the barn consists of more than 1,000 wheels from every kind of machine, artfully welded together in a visual representation of both the history of the barn and the community effort that created it.

A Gem Amid the Jewels

What's the opposite of finding a needle in a haystack? Visitors to Uniontown will feel more like they've found a diamond in a bowl of emeralds. Highway 195 runs right through the center of town on its way north to Pullman from the Snake River on the border of Idaho, compelling visitors to stop at the tasting room for Wawawai Canyon Winery, Whitman County's oldest vintner. If it's too early for wine, stop in at Jacob's, a café housed in one of Uniontown's oldest buildings. Formerly a brewery and before that an opera house, Jacob's has been beautifully refurbished. Visitors with time to wander might find themselves with a pastry in one hand and a cup of coffee in the other, heading up the hill to see St. Boniface Catholic Church. Marilyn and Lee Jackson's retrievers, Katie and Kylie, will leap and bark, but they only mean to hand off their favorite ball in hopes of a game of catch. The Jacksons bought the old convent turned bed-and-breakfast a few years back, from the first owners after the church. The church

almost tore the place down, as it had become expensive to maintain and renters had caused damage to the interior. "Like the old song goes," Marilyn says, "they were going to put up a parking lot—not that they need one."

The Dahmen Barn is a former dairy farm turned art studio, gallery, and performance center, thanks to the efforts of the Dahmen family, the Uniontown Community Development Association, and countless volunteers.

Though they're still newcomers to Uniontown, Marilyn and Lee know a lot about their neighborhood. To the right of the convent lives John McCann, the bookbinder for WSU's graduate theses and dissertations. In his mid-eighties now, McCann operates J & S Bindery out of his garage, accessed through a garden path overflowing with poppies and greenery. "His wife was a master gardener," says Marilyn. To the left of the inn is the church, and to its left is Uniontown's oldest building, a two-story house owned by a WSU history professor.

Maybe, as its website says, it's Uniontown's prime location smack in the middle of the "Quad Cities" of Pullman, Lewiston, Clarkston, and Moscow—two in Idaho and two in Washington—that makes it such a great place. A visitor who takes the time to walk the small downtown and have a few conversations will learn the truth: It's the people who make Uniontown feel so special. Many of the town's buildings are on the National Register of Historic Places, so owners can't change much about the exteriors, Marilyn says. "I've got a bullet hole in my dining room window." She supposes it was from when Jacob's was a bar. A bar fight must have come uphill. "I imagine all the nuns holding their rosaries," she says. (One supposes the nuns were doing that anyway.)

Hang around taking pictures long enough, and someone will invite you to see the inside of St. Boniface. "We'll be praying, but come on in," they'll say.

Wawawai Canyon Winery is the project of retired biology professors David and Stacia Moffett. Their son Ben, who studied viticulture and enology, is the chief winemaker. Wawawai Canyon is the oldest bonded winery in Whitman County.

83

Population: 1,410
Founding: 1886

INSETS L to R: Downtown Pomeroy. • On a sunny day in Pomeroy, it's difficult to tell where the mural ends and the sky begins in this lovely park between buildings. • Pioneer Plaza in downtown Pomeroy features a mural, memorial wall to area veterans, and fountain all beneath a sheltered picnic area. • A closer look at the memorial wall.

TOP: Congress named Pomeroy the seat of the county named for President Garfield.

Pomeroy

Soil, Climate, Resources, and Opportunities

Pomeroy occupies fewer than 2 square miles along Pataha Creek in the Pataha Valley, midway between the foothills of national forest and the Snake River. When Joseph and Martha Pomeroy arrived in 1864, they found only a few other settlements. Parson Quinn's settlement was about a day's travel away, and there were several ranches held by Indigenous people, including Tamootsin, called Chief Timothy. Tamootsin later converted to Christianity and by some accounts assisted Colonel Steptoe in evading the Nez Perce.

The Pomeroys set up a ranch and a way station to feed and resupply travelers. In 1914, Martha Pomeroy, by then Martha Pomeroy St. George, recounted her early life for a feature in *The East Washingtonian*, a newspaper in publication from 1884 to 2018, when the *Dayton Chronicle* purchased it. Pomeroy recalled that she and Joseph were "as poor and hard up for money as any one [sic] that ever came to this country." Despite meager resources, they managed to scrape out sustenance not only for themselves, but for others. "When the travel was heavy we made some money," St. George said.

Her account also makes reference to relationships between the white settlers and the Nez Perce. "I was afraid of the Indians for a few years," St. George writes, "but got over that feeling." She describes trading huckleberries, game, and salmon. At the time, women's work meant raising and educating children, as well as working on the farm. St. George summarized, "I was a very busy woman."

The Pomeroys platted the town in 1878 and, within five years, Pomeroy held the county seat of the newly formed Garfield County, named for recently assassinated President Garfield. Wheat and pea farming and ranching drove the town's early economic development, and the arrival of the Oregon Railroad and Navigation Company meant more efficient export of Pomeroy's product.

Demand for grain increased through the periods of World Wars I and II, and Pomeroy was a railway hub for shipping grain. In 1942, The Blue Mountain Cannery began processing peas for nationally known Green Giant, becoming the county's first large food-processing company. When the value of peas failed to keep pace with the price of freight, the company closed. The Robert Dye

Seed Ranch purchased the facilities and in short order became the nation's largest producer of processed bluegrass seed.

An Art Nouveau–style advertisement from 1908 persuades settlers to consider Garfield County, promising "Soil, Climate, Resources, and Opportunities." In the early days, "It was slow work for one or two men to make a farm," Martha Pomeroy St. George remembered. When she and Joseph arrived, "not a furrow had ever been plowed." Today, agriculture continues to drive Garfield County's economy, and though the number of farms has significantly decreased, the size of the remaining farms and the wealth they generate have increased.

The Nez Perce Trail

Chief Joseph of the Nez Perce is quoted as saying, "The earth and myself are of one mind. The measure of the land and the measure of our bodies are the same." What does it mean, then, to leave home? Can the body leave the mind, or vice versa?

In 1855, territorial governor Isaac Stevens signed a treaty with the Nez Perce. Within a few years, prospectors discovered gold on the recently formed reservation and began exerting pressure on the land and its inhabitants. A new treaty restricted the Nez Perce to a smaller parcel of land, but not all chiefs agreed to the new terms. The nonsigning Nez Perce refused to leave, even as white settlers flooded into their ancestral lands. In the summer of 1877, the US threatened to send the Army after the Nez Perce; the tribe fled, following the trail they had traditionally used to cross the Rockies and hunt buffalo.

The Nez Perce Trail, now a registered National Historic Trail, crosses through what is today Pomeroy. The National Park Service notes, "It is up to us to respectfully use the trail while remembering that it is part of our heritage. To the Nee-Me-Poo (the Nez Perce), the trail is part of their sacred land, land they still use. If we want those who come after us to have a sense of the trail history, it is up to us to preserve and protect it." For their part, the Nez Perce, through spokesperson Frank B.

Andrews, note, "We the surviving Nez Perces, want to leave our hearts, memories, hallowed presence as a never-ending revelation to the story of the event of 1877. This trail will live in our hearts."

An "unblinded" Justice graces the top of the Garfield County Courthouse in Pomeroy, one of just 14 similarly rendered statues of Justice in courthouses across the country. Four of them are in southeastern Washington.

Monumentally Friendly

Garfield County is the smallest of Washington's 39 counties by population, with only 0.1% of the population of the largest, King County. Yet despite the county's comparatively small numbers, the town of Pomeroy has a monumental atmosphere. Pomeroy is home to two museums, and the entire downtown area has been on the National Register of Historic Places since 2003. Pomeroy became the official county seat in 1884. Its courthouse, originally built in 1901 and refurbished in 2010, reflects the Queen Anne style of architecture. Signs in a park note the historic ground where Lewis and Clark met Chief Big Horn of the Nez Perce Tribe in 1806. In the downtown area, Pioneer Plaza holds an impressive monument to Garfield County veterans, its multiple walls inscribed with the names of servicemen and women who served in conflicts from the Spanish-American War to the Vietnam War. Even small spaces in Pomeroy feel monumental. The walls in a small park adjacent to a brick building are the same color as the summer sky, lending an air of grandiosity to the small, well-maintained space.

Public sector jobs make up a portion of Pomeroy's employment, with the US Army Corps of Engineers maintaining hydroelectric projects on the Snake River and the Umatilla National Forest nearby. Still, employment is unsteady in Pomeroy, and since the recession of the early 2000s, employment has declined. Interesting economic opportunities may be on the horizon. Columbia Pulp, a recent venture started in Dayton, employs nearly 100 workers in making paper products from straw, an abundant waste product of wheat farming in the area.

HISTORIC GROUND
Lewis and Clark met Chief Big Horn, of the Nez Perce Tribe, at or near this point, on May 3, 1806.

A memorial wall in Pomeroy's downtown Pioneer Plaza pays tribute to the town's servicemembers from the Spanish-American War through the Vietnam War.

84

Population: 1,251
Founding: 1881

INSETS L to R: Asotin occupies the land from river bank to butte's edge. • A spiral staircase on the north side of the bridge leads to the creek below. • After losing the first courthouse to fire, Asotin repurposed a 1905 hotel as a new county court. • Though the canyon has some class IV rapids, the river flows peacefully past Asotin.

TOP: At its deepest, Hells Canyon is 2,000 feet deeper than the Grand Canyon.

Asotin

A Superlative Place

Asotin is the most and the best. Asotin County is one of the smallest counties in Washington by population and size, in the most southeastern corner of the state, touching both Oregon and Idaho. The city of Asotin lies at the confluence of Asotin Creek and the Snake River, the largest tributary of the Columbia. The landscape is rugged, formed of gullies and buttes, in the country's deepest river gorge, Hells Canyon. The Blue, Bitterroot, and Coeur d'Alene Mountains that surround it are Washington's oldest geological structures, formed between the Carboniferous and Cretaceous periods between 360 and 65 million years ago. No wonder Asotin became the county seat.

Early settlers established both Assotin City and Asotin, and when the latter grew more quickly, the two cities combined. The new city of Asotin was 30 miles from Pataha, then the interim seat of Garfield County, and in 1883, the territorial legislature took a section of Garfield County and created the new county of Asotin to recognize the far-flung development. Pataha went on to fight Pomeroy for the county seat in Garfield County,

and Asotin soon found itself in a similar fight, with Clarkston.

Clarkston, the largest city in Asotin County, developed several years after Asotin, when the Lewiston Water & Power Company irrigated Jawbone Flat, making farming possible in the comparatively dry valley. Nearly overnight, Clarkston bloomed. Farmers planted fruit, vegetables, and grain, and raised dairy and cattle, and the population began to climb. In 1899, the Lewiston–Clarkston Bridge opened to the public, replacing ferry service and drastically easing transport over the Snake and between the two cities. At the time, it was the largest wagon bridge in the state.

Given its increasing importance, Clarkston began making bids for the county seat. In 1936, the Asotin County courthouse burned down; Asotin residents presumed that Clarkston was to blame. The two towns are only about 6 miles apart; at the time, that was a long journey. Even in the 1930s, many people in Asotin preferred to travel by horseback, whereas in Clarkston, cars outnumbered horses. Asotin is so far-flung that electricity didn't reach the entire county until after WWII. In the days before the internet, doing business involving the county government, whether filing a land claim or a marriage license, meant traveling to the county seat. Despite Clarkston's repeated challenges, Asotin managed to hang on to the county seat, securing its relevance into the foreseeable future.

Early Encounters

Lewis and Clark's Corps of Discovery followed the Snake River through Hells Canyon in the fall of 1805 and again on their return trip in the summer of 1806. There, they encountered the Nez Perce people. Pictographs, petroglyphs, and scratchings in rocks at the Snake River Archaeological site reveal evidence of Indigenous habitation in the area dating to 2,000 years and as many as 11,000 years ago. Lewis and Clark's journals reveal their impressions of the Nez Perce. The men reported offering medical care to the Nez Perce, whom Lewis and Clark described as impertinent, insolent, and stingy with their resources. On the other hand, they describe a man whose name they record as "We-ark-koomt" favorably, both writing that the man "has been of infinite service to us." The explorers then employed the man to liaise on their behalf, writing "through him we now offered our address to the natives." We-ark-koomt is better known as Apash Wyakaikt, or Chief Looking Glass. Local legend holds Lewis and Clark gifted Wyakaikt with a looking glass; he misunderstood the men to be naming him, not the object, and even passed the name on to his son. In 1855, Apash Wyakaikt signed the Treaty of Walla Walla on behalf of the Nez Perce.

Remote Paradise

The interstate system bypassed Asotin, further isolating the town in the 20th century, but these days, Asotin is a destination in its own right. The Hells Canyon recreation area offers fishing, hunting, and outdoor sports, and Asotin boasts that the town is the Jet Boat Capital of the World. A paved path offers access to the riverfront, and signs posted along the way describe the history of the Nez Perce, Lewis and Clark, and the development of the valley.

Asotin sprawls across hills and valleys, much resembling the city seen on archival postcards and images from the turn of the 20th century. Turning toward the river off Highway 129, the town that emerges feels both old and new. Teens bow hunt at Evans Pond. A young woman on a horse makes comfortable, slow progress toward town.

The Snake River carved Hells Canyon over 6 million years out of rocks formed from ancient volcanoes. Asotin sweeps down from soft buttes to the river's edge.

Neither scene feels out of place. Across from the high school, Chief Looking Glass Park offers a wide green expanse by the Snake River. Laughter and boat engines fill the air with the sound of kids tubing and fishermen casting. Across the water, Idahoans relax on the beach.

The word Asotin comes from the Nez Perce word *Has-Hu-Tin*, or "eel," for their prominent presence in the river. In its earliest iteration, the town site was a popular gathering place for the Nez Perce, who chose it for its favorable weather conditions. "No wind, no snow." Asotin, it seems, has the best weather, for both recreation and agriculture. In recent years, enterprising agriculturalists have sought to bring back one of the valley's earliest agricultural products—wine. Clarkston's Basalt Cellars testifies to the potential of the area for vineyard development. Perhaps soon, Asotin will add best wineries to its list of superlative categories.

In 1919, the steel and concrete Asotin County Memorial Bridge replaced a wooden bridge built in 1902. The brass plaques affixed to the pillars serve as a memorial to area veterans.

85

Population: 910
Founding: 1902

INSETS L to R: Odessa's churches are each architecturally distinct. • A tank guards the armed forces memorial at the town cemetery. • The Bavarian style of Odessa's city hall pays homage to the town's Volga German heritage. • The Odessa Inn's roof has seen better days, but its paint is still pure sky blue.

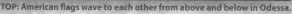

TOP: American flags wave to each other from above and below in Odessa.

Odessa

Cultivating Home

Russian Empress Catherine the Great founded the port city of Odessa in 1794. Thirty years earlier, she invited immigrants to settle in the region around the Volga River, just east of where she would establish Odessa, on the banks of the Black Sea. Catherine offered free land and exemption from military service, among other benefits. She wanted to cultivate the vast and uninhabited Volga River area and populate it as a hedge against potential invasion. Thousands responded, including Germans fleeing the impoverished aftermath of the Seven Years' War.

The German immigrants farmed wheat in the rich Volga River valley and shipped their products out of Odessa for nearly a century until Czar Alexander II unmade Catherine's promises, revoking privileges and, for the first time, drafting the long-settled German-Russians into the czarist military. Facing this and other persecutions, many German-Russians fled for the United States and took up land claims under the Homestead Act. By 1920, more than 100,000 Germans from Russia were living in the US.

Great Northern capitalized on the exodus. In 1892, the railroad began laying a sidetrack through George Finney's timber claim, which he'd established several years prior. In a calculated appeal, Great Northern called the line Odessa Siding and offered free passage to immigrants. Meanwhile, Finney donated his land and platted the town. In 1898, Odessa received its post office, and it incorporated in 1902. Between 1901 and 1902, Odessa's population increased by a factor of eight. The vast majority of its immigrant population were Germans from Russia.

In 1900, the town of Odessa shipped 600,000 bushels of wheat. Despite the advent of steam-powered threshers, farming remained labor intensive. In the heat of summer, men arrived in towns across Washington State, banking on a job working the wheat harvest. Each farm needed 20 men, and every combine required a team of nearly three dozen horses. By 1940, diesel-powered equipment began dramatically increasing the possible yield. Farmers who plowed 5 acres per day prior to the technology were able to plow 100 acres with diesel power. The harvest from the entire state of Washington was 50 million bushels in 1936. Thanks to a range of developments in agricultural technology, by 1985, that number had increased to 150 million bushels. By the middle of the 20th century, Lincoln county was among the top three wheat-producing counties in the entire country. In 2018, Washington wheat farmers produced 153 million bushels.

The year Odessa incorporated, the *Seattle Post-Intelligencer* reported that "there was no Odessa beyond a sign post and a water tank in 1900. There is quite a good deal to Odessa now." Today, the railroad tracks cut diagonally through town, between Rocky Coulee Brewing and Odessa Foods. The HighLine Grain Growers elevator rises above the tracks, a pile of railroad ties at its foot.

Imagine a family of Germans from Russia arriving in 1901, stepping off a train into a vast land rich with potential. Generations before, their ancestors had done a very similar thing, moving from Germany to Russia, cultivating the land. Imagine arriving in an unknown place on a summer day and finding that your new home shares a name with the one you've left behind: Odessa.

Cash Crops

Lincoln County is second only to Whitman County in terms of wheat production, but in 2012, voters passed Initiative 502 by a margin of nearly 10%, leading to an explosion of the newest cash crop— cannabis. The next year, a group of entrepreneurs, including a few men who grew up in Odessa, opened Kush Valley, specializing in high-quality cannabis and cannabis concentrates. Their estimated earnings are in the neighborhood of $300,000 per month. Statewide, marijuana ranks just ahead of cherries and behind hay in terms of its production value. Apples still claim the top spot, with wheat taking second place. Kush Valley joins more than 1,500 cannabis producers and 540 retailers in Washington to date, generating more than $5 billion in annual sales and more than $740 million in tax revenue.

Small-Town Snapshot

After the county seat of Darrington, Odessa is the biggest little town in Lincoln County. Though its population is more than three times that of Sprague, Odessa is a town, while Sprague is a city, due to its population of more than 1,600 residents at its 1890 incorporation. Odessa had fewer than 900 residents when it incorporated in 1910.

Odessa held its first annual Christian Rock Freedom Festival in 2019, featuring music, and art, including a sculpture of a guitar covered in license plates.

Odessa occupies the center point between Soap Lake and Darrington on a lonely stretch of State Route 28, which parallels I-90 and I-2, splitting the difference between them. Odessa's nearest neighbors are the unincorporated communities of Irby, Lamona, and Mohler, dwindling communities named for ranchers, merchants, and stagecoach drivers. Meanwhile, Odessa's population has remained relatively stable since its founding.

The local school district, educating more than 200 students in grades K–12, has earned awards as a Washington State School of Distinction, and in 2015, the US Department of Education recognized high school science teacher Jeff Wehr as Teacher of the Year. The Odessa Memorial Healthcare Center is regionally important both in terms of access to medical care and employment. With a full calendar of events year-round, anytime is a good time to visit Odessa. The most popular event of the year is Deutschesfest, a weekend-long celebration of Odessa's Volga German heritage that takes place the third full weekend of September. A local newspaper, *The Odessa Record,* has kept track of area events since 1901.

The town Visitors Guide notes that Odessa is "a quiet, crime-free, and prosperous community," and advertises the town as the perfect place for anyone "tired of gridlock, smog, and just too many people." On signs around town, a shock of yellow wheat centers the town's logo, framed by its slogan: "We like Odessa," it reads. "So will you."

In the parking lot of the cemetery in Odessa, just in front of the entrance to the center that hosts funerals and memorial celebrations, a military tank sits in front of a memorial to veterans and military servicepeople. Lush fields surround the scene. The US flag flies high above.

86

Population: 884
Founding: 1889

INSETS L to R: Highway 2 cuts through the middle of downtown. • The community garden occupies most of a city block. • The Alibi brings in patrons with a sense of humor. • A quote from C.S. Lewis's Aslan the lion gives garden visitors something to contemplate.

TOP: This town celebrates all beloved Wilburs.

Wilbur

Goosetown

Among the thousand-plus pages of their 1904 *Illustrated History of the Big Bend Country*, historians Steele and Rose note Wilbur as "one of the most promising and enterprising towns" in the Big Bend. Founded in the basin of an ancient lake, Wilbur became a reality when the railroad coming through central Washington created the need for a town in Lincoln County west of Davenport, the county seat. The undisputed founder of the town is Samuel Condin, whose name is just as often misspelled Condit, and whom everyone knew anyway as "Wild Goose Bill." At first, it seems all Wild Bill did to start the town was to occupy the land. Officials in Washington, D.C., established a post office on Condin's land and gave the post his middle name, though in the early days people referred to the place as "Goosetown."

Given Wilbur's proximity to both the county seat and the northern Washington mining claims, a town sprang up within a few years. At one time, there were as many as 32 mining claims in the Wilbur area. Condin platted the town in 1889, and when railroad surveyors came to scope out possibilities for building a road and a railbed, Condin allowed them to manage the organization of the town he'd platted and much of the surrounding land. The town developed swiftly. The 1904 record of this period describes three sawmills running at maximum capacity in order to supply lumber needed for the development of the rail and the town. Local news reports in 1889 noted that "Five new buildings have been completed within the past week; six more are in the course of construction. . . . There is no doubting the success of Wilbur. A grand and glorious future is already secure."

Like so many early towns, Wilbur lost everything to fire, twice. The first, in 1881, caused the deaths of a local mother and her three children as well as several thousand dollars in damage. The town rebuilt, only to meet more devastation by fire 10 years later, when a department store owned by the Hay brothers went up in flames, to a loss of more than $150,000, the equivalent of more than $4 million in inflation-adjusted terms. Recalling the damage, *The Spokesman* in 1923 notes, "True to the undaunted spirit of the pioneer, each loser started business again within a few hours." The town installed a spring-fed water system shortly after the second fire and rebuilt the lost structures. Wilbur's population peaked around the time of the construction of the Grand Coulee Dam and in the decades since then has achieved sustained population levels of about twice that at the time of its founding.

Strange Visitors

In 2007, it happened at Jim Llewellyn's farm. "I thought the less you said, the more it would go away." Five years later, the same thing happened to Cindy and Greg Geib. "If it's man-made," they asked, "do they do this with helicopters?" In 2018, the Chamber of Commerce recognized the repeat events with an award that reads, "Thanks to the aliens who made Wilbur their vacation destination!" A year later, the aliens struck again. Lincoln County is second only to Whitman County in terms of wheat production, and settlers have been planting the crop since 1880. Crop circles, patterns of flattened wheat, have appeared since 1993. Investigators into the phenomena include the Seattle-based Unexplained Northwest Investigation Team and, headed by Peter Davenport from nearby Davenport, the National UFO Reporting Center. Local newspapers, brewers, and restaurants have all capitalized on the trend, which brings tinfoil-clad agri-tourists and paranormal enthusiasts to Wilbur after each visitation.

Big Bend Country

Wilbur sits just at the top of the Big Bend, where the Columbia River starts a wide turn west toward Wenatchee before heading south toward the Tri-Cities, roughly four hours away by car. Highway 2 runs from Seattle to Spokane and smack through the middle of downtown Wilbur. Travelers who decide to stop in and stretch their legs will be rewarded by Wilbur's small-town charm.

The Visitor Center offers information and invites photo opportunities. An enormous sculpture of Wilbur and Charlotte from E. B. White's *Charlotte's Web* sits outside the center's steps. Flanking the building from the other side is a stagecoach pulled by massive wooden geese and driven by

a figure representing Wild Goose Bill, "a Frontiersman, Miner, Wrangler, Packer, Freighter, Cattleman, Road and Bridge builder, Merchant, Land Owner, and Ferry Owner/Operator," according to pamphlets in the center which ask, "Wilbur? Where's Wilbur?"

In downtown Wilbur, the Eden community garden occupies a lush space diagonally from City Hall. Granite and basalt walls rising in the background show how the town is nestled into the scablands.

A stroll around town reveals more public art, from ironwork sculpture to colorful murals. Just a block off downtown, the Big Bend Historical Society has taken up residence in an old church, and they manage a display of farm equipment in the center of town. The Eden Community Garden flourishes with squash blossoms and roses. Before hitting the road, stop in for a beer at Constantine's Alibi, Wilbur's pub. The sign outside advertises "Free beer, topless bartenders, and false advertising." Astute observers may notice that the sweet, friendly town of Wilbur doesn't take itself too seriously.

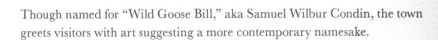

Though named for "Wild Goose Bill," aka Samuel Wilbur Condin, the town greets visitors with art suggesting a more contemporary namesake.

87

Population: 1,734
Founding: 1880

INSETS L to R: The courthouse in Davenport blends Colonial Revival and Romanesque architecture. • The museum has exhibits on the railroad, Indigenous cultures, and historic local businesses. • Perhaps an unlikely choice for a mascot in a region where wildcats and eagles seem to dominate, students at the Davenport High School compete as the mighty gorillas. • Davenport recognizes its champions on its beautiful town welcome sign.

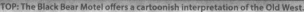

TOP: The Black Bear Motel offers a cartoonish interpretation of the Old West.

Davenport

A Regional Hub, Then and Now

Davenport is more than a small town. At nearly 2,000 residents, it's the largest town in Lincoln County, and it's the seat of governance in the county. These facts, combined with the services offered in Davenport, from medical care to education, make it a regional hub. The importance of the area where the town now resides dates from long before its name was Davenport, or Cottonwood Springs before it.

Lincoln County lies just south of the Colville Reservation, between the Spokane River; the Columbia River; and the various lakes, canyons, and plunge pools formed at the end of the last ice age. Pre-contact, what is now the town of Davenport was a popular campsite along a well-used trail running east–west between the rivers. A sign in Davenport's City Park recounts the shared use of the trail by Indigenous people and settlers and notes the natural springs and lush cottonwood growth nearby, which led to the first English name of the town—Cottonwood Springs.

The first white men in the area were fur traders, followed by gold miners. The first permanent non-Indigenous resident noted in Davenport's history is Aloysius Harry Harker, who arrived in 1880. The Nicholls family arrived shortly after. A few years later, a man named John C. Davenport founded a town he named for himself nearby. John Davenport built his town quickly and lost it almost as quickly to a fire; surviving businesses moved downhill to Cottonwood Springs, which adopted the Davenport name.

Davenport fought a short-lived war with Sprague over the title of county seat, and an opulent courthouse rose on the tallest hill in town, surrounded by a great iron fence that the town dismantled during World War II and offered in contribution to the war effort. The courthouse today is a replica of the original building, which succumbed to fire only to see a complete rebuild within a year, replete with restored iron fencing.

The Northern Pacific Railroad Company roared into Davenport in 1889, warranting a new depot for the rail that would serve both freight and passengers. As the town grew, wheat became its industrial identity, and the town's success rose and fell according to the relative success of the harvest. Construction of the Grand Coulee Dam brought workers to Davenport as with other regional communities, diversifying the town's industry and workforce. Soon, the town added medical services to the growing list of the resources it offered the region. Wheat, the rail, hydroelectricity, and medical services remain important to Davenport's economy today, but the oldest by far is wheat. One can trace a through line from the earliest area farms to today, with some farms having exceeded 100 years of continuous operation, often by the descendants of the families that started them.

The Mitten

There are three possibilities for buildings in towns that have been around for a century or more. Sometimes a building is the same as it always was—churches usually fall into this category. Fire takes a lot of buildings, and when reconstruction isn't possible, the buildings disappear, sometimes even from local memory. Then there are a lot of places that used to be something else.

The Mitten was an ice-cream parlor with wooden booths and wrought iron tables and chairs. There was a fireplace on the south wall, and in the 1930s, according to local history, all the high schoolers gathered at The Mitten. Owners Al and Oliver allowed students to run a tab until they could pay with their allowances. Prices went from 5¢ for a Coke to 35¢ for a banana split, remembers Laurence Jayne. Helen Ehlenfeldt remembers visiting The Mitten after seeing a silent movie at the Blue Mouse.

The Mitten family sold to the MacMillans and then again to brothers-in-law Albert Leipham and Oliver Barnes. A few decades later, The Mitten became The Hangar. The museum in Davenport keeps memories of The Mitten alive.

Gorillas in the West

Rolling fields of wheat and barley fall away as Davenport comes into view. The turnoff to Lake Roosevelt, a popular recreation site, is just outside of town. On the south end of town, the Black Bear Motel welcomes visitors to the place where "the pavement ends and the West begins." The motel reflects the environment of Davenport's earliest days and evokes a Wild West ethos, complete with

a jail and marshal's office, a blacksmith shop, and a trading post, guarded by two wooden Indians. Next to the hotel, the town's welcome sign boasts of Davenport's All-State Academic awards. Davenport's stately courthouse stands atop a hill, flag waving, and from its steps, most of the town is visible.

The Black Bear Motel welcomes visitors to Davenport with an eye toward the Wild West days of Lincoln County's earliest European settlements.

Though small, Davenport is thriving. Morgan Street, the main road through town, has restaurants, antiques shops, and medical services, as well as city buildings and a grocery store. A block farther into town, the Lincoln County History Museum tells the stories of Davenport's beginnings, as well as those of Sprague, Almira, and others including towns like Peach, which was inundated by the Grand Coulee Dam construction. The museum pays loving tribute to Native American artist George Flett, whose work the museum displays.

The preschoolers bustling through the museum may not know about the old Mitten diner, and the high schoolers doing a science project may not know their town was once called Cottonwood Springs, but when asked, the kids say Davenport is a great place to live. It feels like a place moving into the future.

The museum is shaped like an old barn, but there's an electric vehicle charging station in front. A small skate park inhabits the lot behind the very old police and fire station. Just up the hill are more homes from just about every decade in the last 100 years, as well as the high school. Davenport's the kind of place where just about everyone can walk to school. Unusual for the Pacific Northwest, whose schools often choose a regional animal like the cougar or eagle for a mascot, Davenport High School's mascot is the gorilla. A massive emblem of their gorilla graces the top of the highest grain elevator that stands along the railroad tracks right behind the football field. Standing on the field looking up, one can almost hear the young athletes of Davenport beating their chests.

Davenport's courthouse stands proudly atop a hill on the east end of town. From its steps, nearly all of the town is visible.

88

Population: 446
Founding: 1883

INSETS L to R: Sprague still has its own grocery store, though bigger stores in nearby Spokane likely pull shoppers from Sprague. • An old fire truck from Lamont stands beside Dorothy Giddings' antique shop. • Mary Queen of Heaven Catholic Church exemplifies Gothic Revival architecture. • This tile wall, surrounding the base of a gazebo in a downtown Sprague park, features stories from Sprague's history.

TOP: Old advertisements and a new art-tile wall tell Sprague's story in the city park.

Sprague

Hoodooville

From I-90, the white steeple of Mary Queen of Heaven Church peeks over the sage-covered hills, giving the impression of an arrow pointing toward Sprague Lake and the basalt cliffs beyond. Once a major junction and construction headquarters of the Northern Pacific Railroad, Sprague takes its name from John W. Sprague, a railroad superintendent. In its early days, after its establishment as a sheep camp but before it became a town, Sprague's name was Hoodooville, after an early settler known as Hoodoo Billy.

In a park located in the center of town, a tile wall tells much of the story of Sprague's history. Though Hoodoo Billy was influential enough to name the place, he doesn't feature on the wall. The painted tiles recognize the family of D. W. Matheson, whose wagon arrived in Sprague three years before its incorporation. Visitors can trace the town's development from sheep-shearing center to boomtown replete with multiple saloons and nearly 2,000 residents. The two fires that devastated Sprague share one tile; after the fire of 1895

destroyed most of the railroad's property, Northern Pacific decided not to rebuild. The fire of 1925 dealt another blow. Between the two fires, Sprague lost the county seat to Davenport, which has held it ever since.

Lincoln County was formed from Spokane County in 1883, the same year Sprague incorporated, and Sprague expected not only to be the county seat but also for the county to share the name Sprague. Davenport took the honor first, and in subsequent elections, Sprague, Davenport, and Harrington all sparred for the title. Sprague won this time, but the vote was suspect, as the number of votes exceeded the number of residents. Officials speculated that Sprague had made use of passengers coming through on the train, children, and the names of the deceased to stuff the ballot box; however, Sprague lobbed the same accusations at Davenport, whose votes also exceeded their population. The decision fell to Sprague's favor, but Davenport came back and won the fight in 1896. The US Air Force briefly took up residence near Sprague in the mid-20th century, but the town has steadily lost population since the railroad relocated the terminus to Spokane after the first fire.

What a Wonder

The Channeled Scablands are rightly noted as one of the Seven Wonders of Washington State. Ice age floods scoured the soil from the bedrock, and water flow stronger than that of all the rivers in the world put together, cut coulees from Spokane to Vantage. Outdoor enthusiasts can hike the Columbia Plateau State Park Trail across 130 miles of this landscape. Those who do may run into historical vestiges less worthy of admiration. In Sprague's southeastern corner, a watershed known as Negro Creek has been the subject of renaming campaigns for decades. Older maps show an earlier, even more offensive name for the creek. To date, the name stands. According to the Washington State Committee on Geographic Names, renaming the creek is not currently under consideration.

Endangered but Hanging On

Dorothy Giddings and her husband, Gary, bought land in Sprague in the 1980s when they went to work at Hanford. She was the only woman, she says, among what seemed like 3,000 men. "You did your job. You were one of the guys," she says. "Pretty soon, they'd forget you were a woman. There were the flirty ones too. You ignored them," she says. "You put on your attitude and you went to work." Dorothy worked in quality control, doing things like checking welds. She trained to work specifically at Hanford. Dorothy was the second generation in her family to work at the nuclear site. "When Daddy worked there during WWII, the work was all a secret," she says. By the time she worked there, the work had moved from production to cleanup. Hanford remains the most dangerous and toxic nuclear site in the country.

Today, Dorothy operates an antiques store, Dot's Farm Junk. You'll find her paging through old magazines in the sunshine. Gary runs the shop down the street, for larger items like cars and elevators. Photography clubs come by often to photograph their haul. The building Dot works in is in tough shape. She's hung a sign in the window advising shoppers to proceed at their own risk as they explore the property, which dates to 1897. A few years ago, the adjoining building collapsed, prompting locals to seek and receive designation for Sprague on the Washington Trust for Historic Preservation's list of endangered places.

The view of Sprague from its historic downtown shows a community-made tile wall that serves as art, history, and advertising, as well as a well-preserved mural and in the distance, the Catholic church, Mary Queen of Heaven.

Across the street from Dorothy's shop stands Kathy's Family Foods, Sprague's only remaining grocery store, owned by Kathy and Rich Bluhm. Here, in the old First National Bank building, shoppers can purchase staples as well as liquor, and they can play the state lottery. Without the grocery store, Sprague would have virtually no businesses, and residents would have to go several miles down the road for produce and meat.

A 2010 report by the Center for Rural Affairs notes the increasing numbers of food deserts in rural America; these are communities in which residents cannot meet their nutritional needs in their immediate area. The report cites USDA data showing that in 803 counties across the country, residents are at least 10 miles from a grocery store. The loss of a grocery store has immediate and lasting impacts on a community and has been shown to disproportionately affect elderly people. With so much at stake, Kathy's Family Foods can count itself an important reason for Sprague's continued survival.

Kathy and Rich Bluhm operate Sprague's only remaining grocery store. A Center for Rural Affairs report notes that the ease of getting to nearby cities and the advent of superstores like Walmart are two reasons that small towns risk losing their local grocery store, often an important institution in a small community.

89

Population: 1,073
Founding: 1900

INSETS L to R: Industry has always been a prominent feature of Republic. • Murals throughout town provide an illustrated walking tour. • The fossil beds at Stonerose hold some of the oldest known examples of roses and maples. • Nearly a century after Republic's first gold mining days, Hecla began mining the town's Golden Promise vein.

TOP: Republic is proud to have "air you can't see and water you can't taste."

Republic

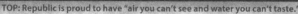

Eureka!

Imagine the way a single star might tell the story of the known universe. In the same way, the discovery of gold in the area now called Republic is more than the story of the birth of one town.

In 1848, James Marshall discovered gold flakes in the American River in California. Marshall was working to build a sawmill for John Sutter, a wealthy landowner who'd assumed control of 50,000 acres of Indigenous land. Records show that Sutter kidnapped Indigenous people and forced them into slave labor. Shortly after Marshall's discovery, the Treaty of Guadalupe awarded California to the United States. Within months, would-be gold prospectors were pouring into California. Many of them came from Oregon; in fact, within the next four years, two-thirds of the white men in Oregon traveled to California in search of gold.

Washington wasn't yet a state or even a territory, but it was already sending timber to support California's exploding population. As the gold rush dwindled in California, prospectors began looking elsewhere. All the future states of the Pacific

Northwest had their turn. Some prospectors chased the Fraser River rush; 30 years later, the Klondike Gold Rush drove 100,000 people to the Yukon.

Before the discovery of gold, Ferry County was home to many Indigenous nations, including the Okanogan, Colville, San Poil, and Lake. President Grant created the Colville Reservation in 1872, consolidating many area nations under one umbrella. In the next decade, the discovery of gold in the area led to an influx of prospectors. The patterns of the California Gold Rush of 1948 replayed themselves.

In 1891, the government bought half the Colville Reservation, hoping to find gold. Five years later, they found it. The government gave notice that the Colville Reservation was open for business, and miners responded, building a mining camp they called Eureka. By then, the Colville Reservation had already been severely eroded by settlers legally disenfranchising Indigenous people as a result of the General Allotment Act that ran from 1887 to 1934.

By 1898, the town of Republic was platted, and it boasted 2,000 citizens. City planners voted to change the name from Eureka to Republic, as Washington already had a Eureka. There were fires and a smallpox scare. Some of the mines closed in 1901, and the promised railroad failed to appear. The next year, the railroad finally came through, but mining production lagged, and Republic's economy shifted focus to the abundant timber. By 1925, the town had fewer than half the number of residents it had at its founding. Republic sits just north of the Colville Reservation's remaining lands.

An Unusual Lagerstätten

Admission is $10, $5 for kids. A hammer and chisel set costs $5 more. Wear boots and long pants, and bring something to protect your knees from the sharp shale. At the Stonerose Fossil Site in Republic, visitors can play junior archaeologist, uncovering fossils buried 50 million years ago, during the Eocene Epoch.

Once, the town of Republic was a lakebed. Over time, volcanic eruptions in the region filled in the lake, burying fish, insects, and plants in thick layers of shale, mudstone, and sandstone. The earliest gold miners to the area discovered fossils buried alongside the mineral wealth. Stonerose is among the world's leading fossil beds from the era.

Visitors can take up to three fossils of their choice after evaluation by experts at the Stonerose classification center. If a visitor uncovers a previously undiscovered type of fossil, paleontologists at Stonerose will classify it and credit the visitor who found it in any subsequent publications.

Golden Promises

Republic has a history of resilience. When mining incomes dipped in the 1920s, some residents turned to distilling liquor or smuggling it from Canada. Not long after, the Depression that sank the American economy generally redounded to Republic's benefit as the price of gold surged upward and mines reopened.

Hecla, a mining company based in Coeur d'Alene, Idaho, since 1891, owned the prosperous

Knob Hill Mine in Republic, which produced until 1995. Near the entrance to town, a monument to Hecla stands just in front of a mural depicting the meeting grounds for Interior Salish Tribes. Taken together, the monument and the mural are a good cross-section of Republic's identity.

After a fire in 1983, Republic rebuilt itself in the style it calls "Western Victorian." There are no stoplights in Republic, but there are three hotels and plenty to see and do. A 25-mile trail takes visitors along an old Burlington Northern railbed.

In recent years, Republic has seen an uptick in tourism. The Stonerose Eocene Fossil Site and Interpretive Center draws more annual visitors than live in the entire county, and hiking and camping opportunities abound. Positioned at the nexus of a number of scenic byways, Republic is a popular spot for bikers, both motorized and non. Curlew Lake offers fishing and waterfront resorts. Though the mines are closed and seem sure to stay that way, for one weekend every summer, Republic reprises its history in a celebratory fashion. Prospectors' Days brings visitors from around the region to pan for gold and witness a shootout, as well as more modern activities like a fun run, a parade, and live music. The festival seems both a callback to the past and a promise for the future: perhaps Republic's prospects haven't run out yet.

Thousands of visitors tour the Stonerose Eocene Fossil Site and Interpretive Center annually, and most find a souvenir fossil to keep. Tourism to Stonerose has helped boost a struggling economy in Republic in the years after mineral and timber extraction dwindled.

90

CAMAS VALLEY

Population: 285
Founding: 1889

INSETS L to R: The local tavern takes a multifocal approach to advertising. • The Lucky Duck Pond is open to junior anglers. • The "world's smallest museum" in Springdale is indeed about the size of a garden shed. • Originally a lunch stop on a train line, Springdale today might be a lunch stop on a drive between Spokane and Republic.

TOP: The name "camas" refers to the plant and appears on valleys, schools, and towns.

Springdale

Claiming and Taming

Under the Donation Land Claim Act, settling the land had a specific definition. Claimants could take 320 acres for free, or double for married couples. In exchange, the claimants agreed to live on the land for four consecutive years. After 14 months of occupancy, they could purchase the land for $1.25 per acre. It sounds like a simple proposition, but in 1850, there were no prebuilt subdivisions or even old farmhouses. In order to live on their newly claimed land, settlers had to build a place to live. Before they could build homes, they first had to clear the land.

Clearing the land was a daunting task. A 1924 pamphlet describing the process notes, "Stands running more than 100,000 feet per acre were not at all uncommon. . . . Many of the trees were 200 feet in height and from four to eight in diameter at stump height." After cutting the timber, in order to cultivate the land, settlers had to clear the stumps. "Stump farming" was the hardest form of labor. A 2001 history of the West notes that settlers were "at once hopeful and desperate, many with no farming experience . . . some people would try anything if

it carried the faintest glimmer of landownership." Later on, railroad and logging companies industrialized this work, but the first settlers in southern Stevens County had to do it themselves.

Springdale's first homesteader was C. O. Squires. His sawmill was the first nonresidential building in the town. The Spokane Falls & Northern Railway built through Stevens County in 1889, and Springdale rose up to meet it. Mark Shaffer and Charles Trimble built the first store. Squires initially named the town after himself, calling the place Squires City, but the rail station and post office were known as Springdale. Springdale got its own water system in 1902 and incorporated the following year. By 1904, alfalfa hay and timber were the primary industries, and 400 people called Springdale home.

Home on the Grange

City dwellers might only ever encounter a Grange at a county fair, where Grangers arrange their products in artistic displays. However, Granges are more than farming collectives. The Grange in Washington started in 1889 when local farmers raised objections to the proposed state constitution. The Grange rallied farmers to reject the new document on the grounds that it would create "an office-seeking class, the most worthless class that can exist," and that it would "foster machine politics of the most corrupt and offensive character." The Grange quickly positioned itself as a political gatekeeper, but it didn't succeed in preventing the state constitution.

The Grange fought for the Sherman Antitrust Act and was the sworn enemy of railroad companies that exploited farmers. As the number of farms in the state increased, the Grange followed suit.

The Grange has historically allied itself with progressive policies. The organization advocated for workmen's compensation laws and better working conditions, as well as women's suffrage. In the first decades of the 20th century, political differences split the Grange into factions, but the organization continued to function, turning its attention to public land use and utility ownership. Today, as corporate farming continues to scale up, the social relevance of the Grange is shifting. While membership has declined, there is a Grange chapter in every county in the state.

Blink and You'll Miss It

The whole town of Springdale is visible in a single panoramic glance. The post office shares a building with the computer center and the grocery, hardware, and liquor store. Storefronts serve as makeshift bulletin boards. Backwoods Pizza & Grill is advertising the next car show, a post–football game party, and W. G. Jeff's 40th birthday celebration. A few doors down, Geronimo's promises shaky bartenders, fat cooks, and a great breakfast. A more permanent sign on the side of the bar reads, "We have a stage, but it won't get you out of this town."

Across the street, one of three schools in the Mary Walker School District sits next to the Lucky Duck Pond, open for fishing to youth only. A trail leads to the pond, where kids stand fishing off a

small bridge. The Kountry Korner offers hamburgers and video rentals. The Grange Hall occupies the intersection of Main Street and Second, where State Route 231 dips into town.

Springdale is just about equidistant from Spokane to the southeast and Colville to the northwest. County-wide, the biggest employers are Boise Cascade, Walmart, the county itself, and the Colville School District. It's fair to say that most people who live in Springdale don't work there. On the other hand, some people who leave find their way back.

With 50,000 members, the Washington State Grange is the largest in the nation. The state's first Grange started in Waitsburg in 1873. The Camas Valley Grange in Springdale is Chapter 842.

Mary Walker School graduate Desiree Sweeney has given back to her home community. As the CEO of Northeast Washington Health, Sweeney helped Springdale get a new dental clinic. In an interview with *The Chewelah Independent,* Sweeney said, "I wanted to invest in the community that invested so much in me."

Newcomers to Springdale include bison ranchers Jessie Turney and Andrew Winter, owners and operators of the Win-Tur Bison Farm in Springdale. With the bison, Turney and Winter brought agri-tourism to Springdale. They offer farm tours and a meet-and-greet experience with their nine bison. "We will always keep our core group of nine," Turney notes on the farm's site, "and will sell or butcher the off-spring [sic]."

Though tiny, Springdale has many amenities found in larger towns, including a store and restaurant, and this downtown oasis, the Lucky Duck Pond.

91

Population: 1,595
Founding: 1891

INSETS L to R: Volunteers are standing by at the Visitors Center next to Happy Dell Park. • A recent grant allowed for the construction of a large new community event space at the library. • Take this sign seriously. The Town Grouch is a beloved honorific. • Boise Cascade operates a plywood sawmill in Kettle Falls.

TOP: The Old Apple Warehouse is a relic of Kettle Falls before the Grand Coulee Dam.

Kettle Falls

A Changed Way of Life

Nothing impresses like nature, except perhaps the man-made structures that disrupt it. Picture an entire town lifted off its foundations. Imagine massive gates closing on a dam called the "Eighth Wonder of the World." The water begins to rise behind the dam, quieting the thundering falls. Ten communities relocated during the construction of the Grand Coulee Dam. Kettle Falls was the largest. The most important salmon fishery on the Columbia and a historic meeting place for Indigenous peoples east and west of the Rocky Mountains was lost forever.

Canadian explorer David Thompson is much venerated as the first non-Indigenous person to explore the Columbia River. Reaching Kettle Falls in June of 1811, Thompson observed the lives of the people he met. "The arrival of Salmon throughout this river is hailed with Dances and many ceremonies." Thompson recounted that the village served as "a kind of general rendezvous," noting the presence of several different nations. The fishermen used spears and J-shaped baskets called *Ilth-koy-ape* to harvest the salmon, and Thompson referred to both the place and the people by that name. French

Canadian explorers would later rename the place Kettle Falls for the deep, pot-shaped depressions the river cut into the quartzite.

The Hudson's Bay Company established Fort Colvile, a military and trading post, nearby in 1825. Missionaries began visiting the area in the next decade, and settlements began to develop around ranching and sawmills. In 1872, President Ulysses S. Grant established the Colville Reservation, consolidating and relocating more than a dozen Indigenous nations. A group of Spokane-based businessmen designed Kettle Falls as a resort in 1891, anticipating Great Northern's path through the area. The railroad located to the north instead, and Kettle Falls declined until the Grand Coulee Dam's construction forced it to relocate. Eventually, the new Kettle Falls merged with Meyers Falls. The dam went up, and the 300 residents of Kettle Falls relocated and rebuilt. The life of every person, plant, and creature in the area had changed forever.

Incomprehensible and Noncompensable

Archival photos show Indigenous people fishing at Kettle Falls before the dam. Then, the rapids were thick with salmon. Artist Paul Kane described the fish as "one continuous body . . . more resembling a flock of birds than anything else in their extraordinary leap up the falls." The Jesuit priest Pierre-Jean de Smet described watching a harvest of thousands of fish per day using spears and baskets. David Thompson, observing the fishermen, noted, "Deep attention is paid by them to what they believe will keep the salmon about them . . . [the salmon] form the principal support of all the Natives of this River, from season to season."

The US Bureau of Reclamation built the Grand Coulee Dam in order to irrigate the Columbia Basin for agricultural development. Its concerns did not include the future of the Kettle Falls salmon fishery. While some dams include fish ladders to allow passage and minimize habitat disruption, the Grand Coulee Dam did not. In any case, no fish ladder technology can help salmon surmount a 550-foot structure. Before the dam's completion, Indigenous people gathered for a Ceremony of Tears to mourn the tremendous loss. Jim DeSautel of the Colville Confederated Tribes noted, "The river was the central and most powerful element in the religious, social, economic, and ceremonial life of my people. Suddenly, all of this was wiped out."

Mostly Friendly

Kettle Falls wants to be one of Washington's top 10 small towns. The Kettle Falls School District, the City of Kettle Falls, and more than 20 other sponsors brought in a kind of consultant to help. Ron Drake is a contractor from Arkansas. His book, *Flip This Town,* has inspired something of a movement in small town revitalization. Drake visited Kettle Falls and listened as residents of all ages shared their ideas and concerns. Students suggested improvements like bike lanes, and Drake agreed that Kettle Falls could be more walkable. When business owners expressed concern that the twice-daily trains held up traffic for 20 minutes at a time, Drake suggested they see it as an opportunity.

"Make appetizers 20% off" during that time, he said. "Try to make it a point of interest, just one of the quirks about your town."

Hydroelectric power at Meyers Falls, the oldest water-based power generation site west of the Mississippi, operates a "run of the river system." There is no dam here, nor large power houses. Instead, some of the river water diverts through a pipeline to a turbine. The turbine generates electricity without disturbing the ecosystem, and the water returns to the river.

Visitors to Kettle Falls will get a chuckle out of the town's welcome sign, which lists the population as "1,640 friendly people and one grouch." Being that grouch is a point of pride in Kettle Falls. Citizens run for the position of Town Grouch annually, and the city makes the appointment during its summer festival, Town and Country Days. Recently appointed Town Grouch Adam Huff touted his community involvement, having returned to the area with his young family after graduating from Western Washington University in Bellingham. Like any other politician, Town Grouch hopefuls give stump speeches at events that Kettle Falls uses to raise money for charities or pay for swimming lessons for local kids. Who doesn't want to support a good cause while drinking locally made microbrew and listening to grouchy candidate speeches? Ron Drake recommended the town lean into its quirks. Check.

His other recommendation was that Kettle Falls do a better job telling its story. The visitors center and Kettle Falls Historical Center are doing that work. And, for those who know what to look for, signs of Kettle Falls' story are all over the place. Take Old Kettle Road to the Kettle Falls swimming beach trailhead. In the campsite called Locust Grove, a short flight of concrete steps interrupt an otherwise grassy expanse. A sidewalk makes an orderly, unnecessary path through the trees. As though in counterpoint to the forever disappeared falls, remnants of the old town insist: We were here.

Kettle Falls' slogan is "The Town That Moves!" Their recently adopted logo features a waterfall pouring through trees. The Kettle Falls Historical Center offers interpretation of the lost Kettle Falls fishery and other sites in the area. The visitor center occupies a restored train depot.

92

Population: 183
Founding: 1862

INSETS L to R: Get fresh-pressed cider by the gallon, half-gallon, or cup at the Marcus Cider Fest. • Residents can find town news on a bulletin board at the Marcus post office. • A mural and a sunflower garden brighten the lot next to the post office. • It's difficult to tell whether this building is mid-construction or demolition.

TOP: Though Town Hall is just down the road, the Marcus post office feels like the hub of town.

Marcus

From Trading Post to Town

The Hudson's Bay Company (HBC) moved its fur trading operations from Spokane to just north of Kettle Falls in 1825. They named the new post Fort Colvile, after Andrew Colvile, governor of the company. The HBC had just merged with the North West Company, which had recently purchased the interests of the Astorians. Alexander Ross wrote of the new location, "The place is secluded and gloomy; unless the unceasing noise of the Falls in front . . . can compensate for the want of variety . . . there are very few places in this part of the country less attractive or more wild."

According to a 1904 history, the HBC "exercised autocratic ownership and controlled completely all the continuous Indian tribes and monopolized their trade." The fur trade flourished for another two decades. In 1846, as trade declined, the 49th parallel became the official division between British and American land, placing Fort Colvile on the American side. In 1871, the HBC abandoned the fort, having sold its interest to the US government. The Americans established a military fort in its location and changed the

spelling to *Colville*. "The name Colville has . . . been given to river, valley, mining district, Indian tribe, military post, and town."

To the publishers of the 1904 history, Fort Colville was already "ancient history." Still, they took pains to describe it in detail. "Time has destroyed these ancient structures, but there still remain on the spot numerous small flat stones which formed the chimneys of these houses. . . . A slight depression in the ground shows where in the long ago, stood the company's brewery. . . . Upon entering either room the first thing that attracts the eye is a fireplace. These are composed of clay, and a space in the floor at the bottom, about three feet square, is made of stone and brick. . . . Standing in one of the rooms is a large hard wood desk, of ancient design, undoubtedly brought from England nearly a century ago."

Marcus Oppenheimer was 18 years old when he and his brothers, Samuel and Joseph, came to the US from Germany, moving first to Kentucky and then Missouri before following the Oregon Trail to The Dalles. In 1862, Oppenheimer filed a homestead claim in Stevens County at Fort

Colvile, where the British were on their way out. There, he and his brothers started a general store, catering to miners headed north. Business thrived, and Oppenheimer named the town for himself: Marcus. By 1910, Marcus was a shipping hub, thanks to the Spokane Falls and Northern Railroad and Great Northern. Marcus is the only town in Washington named for a Jewish immigrant.

Moving Marcus

Marcus relocated during the construction of the Grand Coulee Dam. A WPA press release from 1940 noted that "Most of the 3,000 persons who were forced to move accepted their fate philosophically. . . . Many felt that this forced evacuation released them from a bondage that held them in the great canyon where tradition and custom bound them inevitably to a life of drudgery and poverty." The drudgery and poverty the WPA means are the results of the Great Depression.

In archival photos stored at the University of Washington, F. E. "Sunny" Horn, Marcus' mayor, stands on a hill and points across the valley. Below his outstretched arm lies the town. At the time, Marcus was home to about 600 people. It had a hospital, a movie theatre, and several small businesses. Orchards, grazing lands, and farms filled the valley. Everything had to move or be submerged.

When the dam went up, the federal government, under the Bureau of Reclamation, paid homeowners for their land but didn't compensate them for having to relocate. Today, when the reservoir draws down in spring, the bones of the old Marcus are visible. Ed Frostad remembered the old town. In 1985, he remarked, "Sometimes I just can't help but wonder if things might have been better up here if they hadn't built the dam." At the time of relocation, hopes were high. The photo of Mayor Horn is captioned, "There will always be a Marcus."

Life After the Dam

Eleven towns relocated to avoid inundation by the Grand Coulee Dam's reservoir. Some, like Kettle Falls, recovered. Others, like the town of Peach,

disappeared forever. Marcus occupies a sort of middle ground. The street names call out to the town's apple-producing past, before the dam drowned the orchards. Winesap, Rome Beauty, and Delicious Street intersect with Overlook Boulevard, aptly named for its expansive view of the Columbia River.

At the annual Cider Fest, Marcus residents press apples on machines. Sherman Creek, Emery's, and Riverview are a few of the apple orchards nearby.

State Route 25 is Cider Street as it runs past Marcus. On Cider Street, a cider press sits under a picnic shelter amid ponderosa pines by the highway, behind a banner depicting apples and the American flag. The first Saturday of October each year, the Marcus Cider Fest raises money for the local volunteer fire department. Marcus residents press more than 1,000 gallons of cider on homemade machines. Most other weekends, one imagines, Marcus is pretty quiet.

Despite its grandiose name and the spectacular view, Overlook Boulevard is a one-lane gravel path. People park their cars on the grass to the side of the road; their front doors are steps away. A stately old wooden church occupies a tidy yard. In an overgrown field, a large building is in the process of construction or demolition; it's hard to say which. The wide floor plan and high ceiling suggest a community center. The general store isn't open anymore, but there's still a post office in one corner. The bulletin board outside is FOR OFFICIAL TOWN USE ONLY. Control noxious weeds, it says. No setting off fireworks. The computer lab in City Hall is open four days per week.

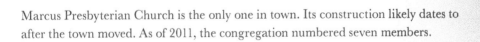

Marcus Presbyterian Church is the only one in town. Its construction likely dates to after the town moved. As of 2011, the congregation numbered seven members.

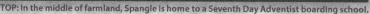

93

Population: 278
Founding: 1872

INSETS L to R: Like many communities in the area, Spangle's economy depends on the price of wheat. • Farming offers hands-on educational opportunities at the Seventh Day Adventist school in Spangle. • Spangle is off the beaten path, but it's still on a highway. The 195 runs between Spokane and Pullman. • The Liberty School District serves more than 500 students from six rural communities.

TOP: In the middle of farmland, Spangle is home to a Seventh Day Adventist boarding school.

Spangle

The Family That Migrates Together

An early bulletin from the Washington Geological Survey notes Pine Grove as "a station on the S. & I. E. Ry, 5½ miles south of Spokane, in central Spokane County; elevation, 2,292 feet." The Spokane and Inland Empire Railway, nicknamed "The Bug," connected rural farming communities along the Palouse on electric passenger trains from 1907 until 1939. In 1877, long before The Bug began its service, Washington territorial delegate Thomas Bents recommended renaming the community at Pine Grove in honor of the Illinois-born founder of the town, William Spangle.

The Spangles came as a troupe. After serving in the Civil War, William, George, and Henry Spangle left Illinois with their families. They took the train to San Francisco and then traveled by ship to Portland. When they made it to Walla Walla, they picked up wagons, which took them the rest of the way. A history dating from 1900 notes that when the Spangles arrived, they found few other settlers, but that "passing to and fro were a good many Indians," described as "peaceful and friendly." The Spangles arrived in then Pine Grove

in 1872; by then, the Battles of Steptoe and Four Lakes were long over. It's possible that the Spangles encountered the skeletal remains of horses that Colonel George Wright's troops slaughtered by the hundreds in 1958. Wright's campaign, including the lynchings at Hangman's Creek, had quelled Indigenous uprisings in the area well in advance of the Spangles' arrival.

William Spangle felled timber, and his sons helped him build a log cabin. Over the years, the house became a way station for travelers, who called it "the old castle." Spangle started a hardware store selling farm tools, and he ran the post office. Other early merchants in town were E. M. Downing, James Machete, J. T. McFarling, and J. M. Grant. Northern Pacific came through in 1886. By then, Spangle was in full swing, with two hotels, several granaries, a weekly newspaper, *The Spangle Star,* and a brick school.

In 1900, people thought Spangle would grow into a business center. Spokane became the regional center of commerce, while towns like Spangle stayed small and focused on raising wheat and cattle.

Best Riders in the World, No Bull

One might not expect much in the way of excitement in Spangle. Now and then, a train derails, or a brush fire starts. Sometimes a terrible crime occurs. Most of the time, one imagines, it's a sleepy little place. In 2019, 72-year-old George Chica, a local cowboy, decided to change that. Chica offered $10,000—and a custom belt buckle—to the winners of the first ever mechanical bull riding "world championship," held in Spangle. On the day of the contest, 24 entrants faced off in front of a crowd of 300, more than the number of people who call Spangle home. Two of the top four riders were women. Laura Moore won the grand prize with a 57-second ride.

Gateway to the Palouse

Spangle's about as quiet as you'd imagine a town of fewer than 300 people. Two-lane roads cut through the northwestern edge of the Palouse, often signed with a warning: ROAD MAINTAINED DURING SUMMER ONLY. Graffiti and trash under the railroad trestles attest to a youthful presence, and the fields are plowed in tight rows, but the landscape feels empty. There's not a cell phone tower or a farmhouse in sight. Dozens of minutes go by without another car passing. Birdsong and your own footsteps on the blacktop are the only sounds cutting through the silence.

The pavement turns to gravel. Up a brief incline, grain elevators rise above railroad tracks. The Producers welcome visitors to another rural community. Blue sky cuts through Spangle's stenciled steel welcome sign claiming the town as "Gateway to the Palouse," like so many others. No fewer than three signs, all within a few feet of each other, note the town's establishment date as 1872, six years before its incorporation. A few cars sit outside The Harvester, a restaurant that seems impossibly big for the population it serves.

In town, a smattering of small homes and trailers stand a car's length off the narrow road. There's a collision repair shop, the city hall offices to the side of a double garage, and the Spangle Saloon. Drive over the tracks and across the bridge and you're out of town nearly as soon as you arrive.

In the late 19th century, the multistate agricultural area known as The Palouse was growing at a faster rate than Puget Sound, which today is Washington State's most populous region.

Follow Old US Highway 195 out of town, and an organization of more modern buildings comes into view. There's a greenhouse and a sign that says THE FARM. A 40-foot container van sits by the side of the road, painted with the slogan, "True education trains young people to be thinkers and not mere reflectors of other people's thought." The Farm is a project of the Upper Columbia Academy, a residential high school owned and operated by the Seventh-Day Adventist Church. The campus has the feeling of a land grant university, with its brick edifices rising out of cultivated hills and valleys. Just more than 200 students attend grades 9–12 at the school, which charges just less than $20,000 annually. Most of UCA's graduates go on to four-year universities.

Not far from UCA, Liberty School District is a public school with an enrollment of 500 students from middle school through high school. Students bus to Liberty from Spangle, Latah, Waverly, Plaza, Fairfield, and Mount Hope. In the distance, a capital *L* for "Liberty" marks a water tower on a rise of farmland. Then there is only the land, a ripple of water now and then, an occasional trestle over the road cutting through the stubbly field of next year's harvest.

Rural-area students near Spangle who don't attend the Upper Columbia Academy likely attend Liberty High School, which serves rural students in an area covering 300 square miles.

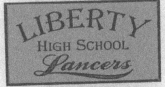

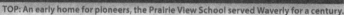

94

Population: 106
Founding: 1879

INSETS L to R: In 1889, the Washington State Beet Sugar Company opened a factory in Waverly, employing 150 workers. • The Waverly School has been repurposed as the Masonic Lodge. • The name "hangman" has persisted, though the creek in question is also called Latah Creek. • Lewis and Clark first mapped the creek with the name "Lau-taw River," translated from the Nez Perce as "place to fish."

TOP: An early home for pioneers, the Prairie View School served Waverly for a century.

Waverly

A Complicated Past

The town of Waverly received a post office and a name in 1879. Then, while other Inland Empire towns met the railroad and began to flourish, Waverly remained a lonely outpost. An early history describes it as a "little village, quiet and serene . . . remote from the scenes of turmoil and strife." However, Waverly's most prominent feature speaks to a history that is anything but bucolic.

Hangman Creek winds through Waverly. Uncultivated land approaches the creek's edge. Farmed acres stop for a treeline, a rocky butte, and a soft marsh. The water looks as though it might spill over its edges, glimmering gently past farmhouses. The name was long ago changed to Latah Creek, but it's still widely known as Hangman, and for a reason. The Spokane Historical Society isn't pulling any punches in its description: "This is the site of a murder."

In 1858, the Spokane and Yakama Tribes resisted treaty terms, and violence erupted in eastern Washington. When the Tribes defeated Colonel Steptoe's 150 men, Colonel George Wright sent hundreds more in their place. Chief Owhi, whose son,

Qualchan, was wanted for murder, tried to negotiate with Wright, who took Owhi hostage. Not knowing Wright had imprisoned his father, Qualchan entered the camp on his own peace mission, along with his wife, son, and brother. Wright ordered Qualchan hanged. The next day, Chief Owhi tried to escape and was shot and killed. In three days, Wright ordered the hangings of more than a dozen people, all of whom had approached with a white flag, symbolizing their peaceful intentions.

By the time A. D. Thayer homesteaded on Hangman Creek, evidence of the violence was long gone. Two decades later, Waverly began to flourish. The Washington State Sugar Beet Factory, established in 1898, employed 150 men. *The Waverly Optimist* reported in 1899 that laborers made $1.50 per day, while "skilled superintendents" earned as much as $7,500 per year, or more than $250,000 in today's dollars. A dam across the creek fed water to the factory. Soon, the railroad came, and multiple grain producers established warehouses and elevators in Waverly. In 1900, the population had blossomed to 895. Ten years later, the sugar beet factory closed, and the bloom began to wilt.

In Waverly today, Hangman Creek Bar and Grill is closed and boarded up. Peeling signage in the windows upstairs advertise Miss Elsie's 5¢ baths and Doctor Yankum's dentistry services. Concrete memorials at the park's edge remember beloved townspeople and war veterans. In 1935, the Spokane County Pioneers Association established a memorial at the site where the hanging tree once stood.

School's Out

In 1910, Washington State had more than 2,700 school districts. Not quite a century later, that number has declined by about 90%. Spokane County had some of the first schools in Washington, dating to the 1830s. The first schools often took place in settlers' homes until a community secured funding for a dedicated building. The first schools constructed were log cabins, like the settlers' homes themselves. As the population increased, communities often abandoned their log cabin schools in favor of wood frame and later, brick schools. As the student population grew, schools diversified, distinguishing elementary and junior-high education programs and locating them in their own schools. By 1915, Washington boasted 500 high schools.

The boom in school construction continued until the Depression, when a lack of funding put the brakes on school spending. Despite funding scarcity, many new schools were built in the 1930s as part of the Works Progress Administration. Even with the government-sponsored infusion of capital, by the end of WWII, school consolidations in rural areas had begun in earnest. After the war, urban centers grew at the expense of rural communities, and by 1946, nearly all one-room schools had closed. The Prairie View School in Waverly is one of these.

From 1904 to 1938, the school served as many as 40 students in a year. The simple, wood-frame building boasted an iron stove for heat and a curved stage for the teacher's desk. Prairie View is the oldest example of its kind in Spokane County. Long since fallen into disuse, the school malingered in a cottonwood grove, its porch sagging, wind rushing through its empty windows. Then, in 2013, preservationists decided to move and restore the decaying school.

With a fundraising effort that garnered thousands in private donations, the Southeast Spokane Historical Society led the effort to preserve the history of public education in eastern Washington. Today, the school has a new foundation and a new roof. A modern door stands between the weather and the schoolroom. The clapboard siding is original, but the windows are brand-new. If left abandoned, nature would have taken the school back. Over years of snow and neglect, the roof would have collapsed, and then the walls. Instead, the Prairie View School stands on the corner of South Prairie View Road as it curves out of, or into, town, like a greeting or parting message for visitors.

The town of Waverly doesn't have any schools of its own. The former school, built around 1930, closed in 1961, shortly after another rearrangement of school districts.

Waving Goodbye

Driving through any city's residential neighborhoods between the hours of 8 a.m. and 4 p.m. can be a slow affair. When children are present, the speed limit usually tops out at 20 miles per hour. In Waverly, the school has been closed for a long time. Still, a hand-painted sign asks travelers to keep it under 25 mph. A father shepherds two children and a dog on the short walk from the park to their home. He holds the kids' hands and they stick to the sidewalk, though mine is the only car on the road.

Waverly is the smallest incorporated town in Spokane County, and it feels like it. Visitors to Waverly might be forgiven for looking around and asking, "What makes a town a town?" There is a fire department, a Grange, and evidence of agriculture. Other than that, there's a collection of houses, a controlled burn, a barking dog, a shuttered door, a babbling stream. There's history here, for sure. A future feels less certain.

Hangman Creek feels like more than a creek but not quite a river. Its waters flow serenely over green marshland, giving the effect of a road more than a river, as the bank is flush with the water level.

95

Population: 183
Founding: 1892

INSETS L to R: Latah (Hangman) Creek runs for 60 miles from the Rocky Mountains to the Spokane River. • The grounds of the old Latah School overlook the valley. • Many area families have farmed here for generations. • The business or service recorded in the Latah area is the post office built in 1873.

TOP: Just try to walk past this barn without thinking about the pursuit of happiness.

Latah

Coplen's Camping Ground

Benjamin Coplen took a claim on Hangman Creek in 1873, 10 years prior to the discovery of gold in nearby Idaho. Coplen knew the score. Mines meant railroads, and railroads meant towns. He platted the town of Latah near the site of Alpha, the existing post office. In Nez Perce, Latah is said to mean "camping ground" or "place well supplied with food." Three years later, the Oregon Railway and Navigation Company built through Latah. Before the turn of the century, the town had grown to nearly 500 people. In 1892, Latah incorporated.

As elsewhere on the Palouse, Latah-area farmers did well raising wheat and lentils. As urban centers grew in the early 20th century, small farms began to consolidate. In town, business was still booming. After its founder, Latah counts Edwin Ham and his son David among the town's most prominent early citizens.

The Hams came to Latah in 1883 and built the first general store. When the railroad came, Edwin and son found themselves in a position to compete with businesses miles away. Their proximity to Idaho's silver mines didn't hurt. Soon, father

and son began expanding the business. David got into land development and later became a politician. Perhaps because of his regional importance, the historical record contains detailed physical descriptions of David: "D. T. Ham grew from a handsome young man with a rather overwhelming walrus moustach [sic] to a distinguished figure marked by his grey King George V beard." David served as a US Marshal under Presidents Harding and Coolidge. His house, a two-story, heavily ornamented Queen Anne structure built in 1886, was placed on the National Register of Historic Places in 1978 and remains a well-kept example of the architectural style. In 1905, Ham sold the house to William McEachern, who opened Latah's first bank. McEachern's descendants still lived in the house when it went on the national register. Almeda McEachern Oatman willed the house to the local historical society.

In 1900, Latah had four general stores and one specializing in footwear, as well as a blacksmith, a livery, and a warehouse. An article from that time notes that "The rich agricultural country wherewith it is surrounded is a guarantee of continued growth and prosperity." Latah's population reached its apex as it incorporated and has gently declined in the century since.

A Mammoth Discovery

What links tiny Latah, Washington, to the big city of Chicago? In the early summer of 1876, Benjamin Coplen noticed that his cows kept getting stuck in the peat bog on his property. He started poking around in the bog and hit something. Coplen enlisted his brothers to help dig up whatever it was that he'd hit. The first thing to emerge was a vertebra, and then a scapula. These weren't cow bones. The brothers kept digging and unearthed two long, curved bones, one of which weighed 145 pounds. Maybe they were elephant bones, a teacher suggested. He was close.

The Coplens kept digging, and so did their neighbors. The little town filled with curious visitors and reporters. A photo made its way to Yale geologist James Dana, who settled the mystery: The Coplens had uncovered a mammoth. As the town of Latah turned itself into an archaeological site, more mammoth bones turned up, including an intact skull. The assembled skeleton resides today in Chicago's Field Museum of Natural History, which purchased the skeleton in 1914.

Latah's amateur archaeologists continued to find fossils, but the mammoth discoveries of 1876 never repeated themselves. The town hopes to create a full-size steel mammoth sculpture and position it next to the highway. They just have to dig up the funds.

Rejuvenating Latah

Route 27 traces the shape of the creek through Latah and isn't much wider. A roadside sign at the entrance to town points the way to the Latah School, though directions aren't necessary. The two-story brick building overlooks the town from the top of a hill.

The school dates to 1908 and gives Latah a second entry on the National Register of Historic Places. Left vacant from 1960 to 2000, the school received a makeover just in time for its 100th birthday, with new walls, flooring, and windows. When the school opened, only a handful of Americans in a given town completed high school each year. Having a school like Latah's demonstrated a community's commitment to education. Latah graduated its last class in 1958. Marie and Steve Widmyer bought the historic building in 1999 and, after further renovations, reopened the school as a special-events venue. Wedding packages start at about $3,000. Looking out from the gazebo on the school's lawn, the Palouse undulates in shades of green and yellow.

Latah's Public School was the first of its kind in the Palouse region. The class of 1958 was the last to graduate. Saved from demolition and placed on the National Register of Historic Places, the school now hosts weddings and other events.

As beautiful as the area is, Hangman Creek is the site of a major cleanup effort in the state. The creek is a tributary of the Spokane River. Soil erosion, increased temperatures, manure, and wastewater discharge have contributed to the water's bad condition. In some areas, a wide band of muddy water stretches several feet from the waterline. The state has committed $500 million to clean up the water's toxicity and improve habitat for the redband trout and other wildlife species. Though the quiet hillside in Latah feels a million miles from anywhere, the river insists on every community's interconnectedness.

Latah's Evergreen Cemetery, just outside of town, is the final resting place of many of Latah's earliest residents. On the land surrounding the cemetery, the agrarian lifestyle continues.

96

ENTERING
Rockford

TREE CITY USA

FIREWOOD

Population: 470
Founding: 1878

INSETS L to R: The foothills of the Selkirks rise around Rockford. • This cabin is near the entrance to Rockford. In town, visitors will find the Pioneer, Military, and Farm Museums. • Rockford's walkable downtown offers coffee shops, gifts, and a few lunch spots. • Though it looks like a low-lying town, Rockford is nearly 2,400 feet above sea level.

TOP: Rockford is a Tree City, denoting its success in urban forest management.

Rockford

Wild, Wild West

What we tell about history depends on when we tell it. At the turn of the 20th century, towns like Rockford had only been around for a few decades. Early histories are effusive and romantic, focusing on a town's likely prosperity as though boosting a town's reputation might guarantee it. Indeed, as towns sprang up along rail lines, promotion was seen as essential to a town's development.

A 1923 source notes that Rockford's founder, D. C. Farnsworth, named the town for "the many fords used in crossings over Rock Creek." Nearly a century later, the town's website is more specific: "Native Americans had a crossing over Rock Creek, which was very rocky and the water was shallow. They called it the 'Rocky Ford,' and that was the way our town got the name." The earlier version makes no mention of Native inhabitants; the latter, none of the town's founding settler.

Rockford began as a sawmill. Farnsworth and his partners, John Farnsworth and A. M. Worley, were the first business in town. Soon, Rockford had a flour mill, a newspaper, and nearly a 1,000

residents. In 1900, contemporary descriptions of Rockford noted its "pre-eminent" grain market, paying "top-notch" prices to local farmers utilizing the mill, "which has no superior in the state." Rockford's citizens "are industrious and progressive," and making an effort "to engage only the very best teachers in the public schools." Though Rockford surely maintains a sense of community pride, recent histories can afford to tell a more complex story.

Close on the heels of Farnsworth, et al., one of Rockford's early businessmen was German immigrant Bernard Bockemuehl. His Rockford brewery was such a success that he expanded, moving to Fort Spokane, where he opened a brewery, riding a sled to bring beer to the soldiers. Bockemuehl's great-grandson carried on the tradition, opening the Fort Spokane Brewery in 1988.

William Grubbe, Rockford's first doctor, reportedly landed in Rockford after escaping a group of Indigenous people who killed his traveling companion and horse. Luckily for Grubbe, Rockford needed a doctor at a time when "anyone could nail a diploma on the wall and begin treating patients."

Recent Rockford historians also highlight Rockford's reputation as a center of horse rustling. In 1882, Aldy Neal ran a horse-thieving ring composed of his entire family. When the Neals tried to flee, some Rockford citizens gathered to bring Aldy Neal to justice. On their way to the courthouse, they met a large group of men armed with guns who abducted Neal from the group and lynched him. No one present gave up the names of the perpetrators.

From a birds-eye view of Rockford in 1910, none of these stories are visible. One wonders what stories Rockford will remember in another 100 years.

The Children of the Sun And Those Who Are Found Here

The Spokane people once lived on 3 million acres of land centered on the Spokane River and were divided into three groups, the Upper, Middle, and Lower Spokane. They were hunter-gatherers, moving seasonally to follow resources. In 1855, the Spokane sent their chief, Slough-Keetcha, to observe negotiations between territorial governor Isaac Stevens and other tribal leaders. Missionaries at the Red River school baptized and renamed the chief Spokane Garry, after Nicholas Garry, a director of the Hudson's Bay Company which had sent Slough-Keetcha to an Anglican mission school as a boy. Spokane Garry returned to his tribe and became an influential leader and teacher.

The Spokane declined to participate in a treaty, though they retained federal recognition as a sovereign nation. In 1881, President Rutherford B. Hayes established the Spokane Indian Reservation in the northwest corner of the county. The reservation represents approximately 5% of the tribe's traditional homelands.

French fur trappers referred to the Indigenous people they encountered as the Coeur d'Alene, meaning "heart of the awl," in reference to the people's skillful trading practices. The people's name for themselves was *Schitsu-umsh:* "the discovered people," or "those who are found here." The Coeur d'Alene lived in permanent villages based around the three nearby lakes, Coeur d'Alene, Pend Oreille, and Hayden. Trade routes connect them with tribes on the Great Plains and all the way to the Pacific coast. The Coeur d'Alene signed a treaty in 1859, and President Ulysses S. Grant established the Coeur d'Alene Reservation by executive order in 1873. The reservation and subsequent treaties reduced the tribe's lands from 5 million acres to just 345,000 today. The town of Rockford lies between the Spokane and Coeur d'Alene Reservations.

Pioneer Corner depicts life in the earliest days of Rockford's settlement. The Rockford Women's Club maintains the park.

Stay for the Barn Party

Today, Rockford is home to three museums and several historic churches. Every year since 1943, Rockford has hosted the Southeast Spokane County Fair. In 2019 the festival celebrated with the theme "75 years of barn parties." Held the third weekend in September, the fair includes a soapbox derby and a basketball tournament in addition to the usual parade, Grange exhibits, and 4-H entries.

From the hills surrounding town, Rockford looks much as it did a century ago. Houses cluster in the valley around churches and the creek. Moving out from the center, the homes are increasingly distant from one another as the shape of the town quickly cedes to farmland. Route 278 makes a sharp corner through downtown as Emma and First Streets, Rockford's business district. The charming downtown area includes businesses like Hurd's Mercantile and Company and Banner Bank as well as a few taverns, Fredneck's and Harvest Moon.

Tiny Rockford was the subject of national headlines in 2017 after a 15-year-old sophomore at Freeman High School killed another student and injured three more, using his father's AR-15 and a .32-caliber pistol. Now, as always, the truth of what it's like to live in a place can't be shown in a single photograph, visit, or dive into archives. The incident at Freeman entered Rockford into a growing community that no one wants to join—those who know the grief of a school shooting.

Rockford nestles into a mostly dry Spokane River valley near low foothills. Mount Spokane ski resort is just a short drive north, and there are two large conservation areas between Rockford and Idaho to the east.

Hurd Mercantile & Company
A Unique & Thoughtful Gift Mall

97

Population: 612
Founding: 1891

INSETS L to R: Farfield's library is connected to its museum. Together, they're a powerhouse of resources and services. • Fairfield wraps up its annual Flag Day celebration at the Community Center. • Grain elevators tower over the town of Fairfield. • A paved walking path separates the industrial area of Fairfield from the playground.

TOP: Kentucky bluegrass grows in Fairfield under the management of Fusion Seed Company.

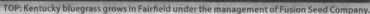

Fairfield

The Fairest in the Land

Colonel E. H. Morrison figures heavily into Fairfield's past. Born in 1848 in New Jersey, Morrison received a world-class education. By the age of 22, he'd studied and lived in Europe and Asia, specializing in mining and engineering; however, some records note his birth year as 1842 and in New York, not New Jersey. Describing history often involves repeating early errors, and maybe it doesn't matter whether Morrison was born in '48 or '42. Then again, it seems as worthwhile to note what we don't know as what we do. Morrison's obituary notes his birth year as 1848. In any case, in 1861, he enlisted in the infantry in Wisconsin and served during the entire Civil War, including the Red River campaign, the siege of Vicksburg, and other battles.

At 30—or 36—Morrison took a position in the Walla Walla land register office, working for the Oregon Railway & Navigation Company. In 1891—or 1888! —Morrison moved to Fairfield, where he seems to have succeeded in every available venture. He named the town, "on account of

the extensive grain fields and also to please Mrs. Morrison," whose hometown had the same name. Morrison's name appears in turn-of-the-century records for preferred swine and cattle breeders and purveyors of seed varieties alike. In 1905, the Department of Agriculture noted Morrison's Washington-grown beets as of the highest quality, yielding the most sugar, "not only much greater than the average, but $1\frac{1}{2}$ tons greater than any other variety." Morrison is credited with starting the sugar beet industry in the area, which led to explosive development in the nearby town of Waverly.

Morrison's death was noted in *The Spokesman-Review*'s "semi-weekly" in 1914: "He was one of the most widely known citizens of the Inland Empire and his business and social connections made him almost a national figure." A century later, the same paper remembered Morrison's passing. Journalist and historian Jim Kershner highlighted Morrison's reputation for hospitality and his agricultural skill, noting that Morrison had "sold his seed to every state in the Union," but that "his true gift was his 'spontaneous sympathy' with whoever was in his company, whether senator, governor, ranch hand, or wilderness guide."

Morrison was a skilled and educated farmer who served his country and cared about his community. He sounds like the kind of person you might still find in Fairfield today.

Fun Projects by the Local Press

Glen Adams grew up in Fairfield, graduating from high school there in 1931. A few years later, he established Ye Galleon Press, a publishing company specializing in history, especially the history of the Pacific Northwest. Ye Galleon is the oldest independent book publisher in the region. Adams published its first title in 1939. Over the years, he published firsthand accounts by pioneer women, whalers, and local people, as well as projects in the larger scope of migration and exploration. Until 1974, Adams set the type for each book by hand.

In awarding Adams a spot in the Washington State Centennial Hall of Honor, the state noted that Adams "preserved and made accessible many regionally important works which otherwise would be lost to historians." Adams took a personal interest in the work, publishing what he felt was important and helping writers find the right publisher when he thought someone else would handle a project better than he could.

The Washington State Library created a special collection of Ye Galleon's works, with 450 titles collected. At the end of most, readers will find a colophon, or a publisher's statement. The statement gives a sense of Adams' personality. "This was a fun project," it reads. "We had no special difficulty with the work." Adams died in 2003.

Fairfield's Favorite Holiday

On June 14, 1855, Wisconsin teacher B. J. Cigrand led his students in a birthday celebration for the American flag, 108 years after the country officially adopted the stars and stripes. Cigrand advocated widely for a Flag Day holiday. The sentiment was spreading. New York schools started celebrating the day a few years later, and soon the entire city of Philadelphia was in on the holiday. Fairfield started celebrating Flag Day in 1910, four decades before Truman signed legislation to enact National Flag Day in 1949. More than a century later, the holiday is still officially Fairfield's favorite day. Every year, the city hosts a Flag Day festival, featuring the usual mix of parades, pancake breakfasts, fun runs, and beer gardens.

Fairfield's library is open two days per week and is attached to the local historical society and museum. The museum has information on the genealogical history of many families in the area, including neighboring towns of Latah, Waverly, Spangle, and Mount Hope.

In 2018, the town launched a beautification project. The centerpiece of the project to date is a flag mural, painted on a wood-framed metal backdrop overhanging a wall of plaques honoring Fairfield's servicemen and women. This is Fairfield's Military Wall of Honor.

In town, a row of low buildings to either side of the Wall of Honor constitutes Fairfield's business district. At the top of a short incline, the light-filled brick library stands next to the museum. A welcome sign hangs under the museum's Ionic columns. On the side of the museum, a simple map outlines the small towns of Spokane County in relationship to each other. Rockford is represented with a sawmill, Waverly with a beet factory, and Fairfield with its museum. The museum is out of proportion on the map; it's larger than all of the other structures. In the same way, from any vantage point in Fairfield, the largest thing in sight is the row of grain elevators. They tower over downtown in a clear statement of the town's identity. If Fairfield is looking for more opportunities for beautification, all of that concrete seems like the perfect canvas.

Local industry looms large in Fairfield. Between the post office and the dental clinic, the recently started Military Wall of Honor bears a few plaques, below a painted flag.

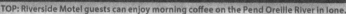

98

Population: 447
Founding: 1896

INSETS L to R: Downtown Ione looks like it would attract tourists, but some locals prefer not to market the town as a tourist destination. • Ione is in what's called the "forgotten corner" of the North Pend Oreille Scenic Byway. • This classic farmhouse near the river is for sale in Ione. • As the signs suggest, heritage markers and recreation trails are near the tidy downtown.

TOP: Riverside Motel guests can enjoy morning coffee on the Pend Oreille River in Ione.

Ione

One-Time River Queen

In the last decade of the 19th century, James Morrison and Elmer Hall settled in Ione, the most recently settled of the three interconnected mining towns in northern Pend Oreille County. In 1896, Hall established the first post office in town. It would be another 15 years before the town began to flourish, thanks to the confluence of two events. Frederick Blackwell's Idaho and Washington Northern Railroad reached the area in 1909, and the Panhandle Lumber Company, an electric sawmill, became a major employer. That same year, Ione incorporated.

Just before the railroad arrived, steamboats transported travelers and goods up the Pend Oreille River. The *Ione* was one such steamboat. Nicknamed the "Floating Palace" and the "River Queen," it was fully furnished and carpeted. Starting in 1892, travelers could take the train to Newport, board a steamboat like the *Ione*, and travel up the Pend Oreille. Summers saw as many as 500 people from Spokane out for a steamboat cruise.

Prior to settlement, the seminomadic Kalispel Tribe lived along the river. Part of a larger group,

the Pend Oreille, the Kalispel spoke Salish and were known as the "camas people," after the root that formed a staple of their diet. When the US formed treaties with many Native American nations, the Upper Kalispel ceded their homeland and moved to a reservation in Montana, while the Lower Kalispel refused. The nation's refusal to sign a treaty meant they retained their homelands; however, it also meant they lacked protection against settlers taking their land under the Homestead Act.

In 1914, the US established the Kalispel Reservation, today encompassing not quite 11 square miles. Not far from the Kalispel Reservation, the largest reservation in Washington is home to the Confederated Tribes of the Colville, under the terms of the treaty negotiated in 1872. As with every Indigenous population in the state, the Colville and Kalispel today inhabit an area that is a mere fraction of the size of their ancestral homelands.

In 1909, the newly incorporated town of Ione had nearly three dozen businesses and a population of around 300 people. Thirty years later, a fire destroyed most of the mill's property, and the town never fully recovered. The town's economy hung on until the final mill closure in 1995. Today, Ione faces an uncertain future.

The River Runs North

Fifty years before the gold rush brought prospectors to the far northwest, Canadian David Thompson became the first non-Indigenous person to reach what is now Pend Oreille County. Working for the North West Company, Thompson pushed the fur trade across the Rockies and mapped the Kootenai River. In 1809, Thompson began an expedition on the river flowing out of Pend Oreille Lake. He hoped it would empty into the Columbia and provide a route to the Pacific. The Pend Oreille is one of just a few rivers in the United States that flows north. Thompson encountered members of the Kalispel Tribe, marking perhaps their first point of contact with white people. The Kalispel traded with Thompson and helped him find his way. On that initial trip, the dangerous rapids at Box Canyon ended the expedition. Thompson visited the area again two years later, with the same result. The following year, he took another route and made it to the mouth of the Columbia.

Small-Town Still Life

Despite a sometimes divisive history, the small towns of Pend Oreille County have long been interdependent. Until a few years ago, the Ione Lions Club operated a 10-mile train ride taking tourists on a historical tour of northern Pend Oreille County. Ticket sales from 11,000 annual riders generated about $40,000 for the community annually. As part of the ride, actors from Metaline Falls' Cutter Theatre would take over the train and pretend to rob the guests; donations from the robbed riders generated as much as 10% of the theatre's annual operating budget. The ride closed in 2016 because the train tracks, no longer in commercial use, are too expensive to maintain per federal regulations. Funds went to support not just the theatre, a nonprofit arts organization, but also such key local services as the fire department and the school district, shared by all three area towns. The train had operated as a tourist attraction for 35 years, and the loss of income was a blow to the community. A few years later, the Lions Club came up with an alternative. Rail Riders utilizes a modern version of rail bikes and hand cars, a technology that dates back to the 1850s, when maintenance workers traveled up and down the rail on wood and steel wheeled platforms. Today's pedal-powered, four-seat rail bicycles offer visitors a 9-mile tour for $24 each, or $12 for kids.

The lakes and forests of Pend Oreille County are home to a great diversity of animal life. About 234 species of birds live or migrate through the area, as well as 16 species of reptiles and amphibians, and 73 species of mammals.

While the Lions Club continues its efforts to promote Ione, other residents want nothing to do with tourism. Marion, a retired hospice nurse, moved here a few years ago. She and her husband bought the Riverview Motel, a two-story affair on the shore of the Pend Oreille River. As they've worked to renovate the motel, they've noticed local resistance to development of any kind. It's a common sentiment in some small towns around the state: "We don't want to be another Leavenworth," people say. It's hard to know just what they mean, though: maybe it's the nuisance of traffic, or perhaps concerns that developers seeking to profit from tourist dollars will inflate property values. From a local's front porch, these might seem like reasons to resist change, but if Ione doesn't invest in development, it may die.

According to Marion, most of the town seems willing to let that happen. From the sunny porch of her riverside motel, the town feels anything but dead. Morning mist rests in the treetops. The lake is still and clear. Life vests hang next to kayak paddles on the motel wall. Marion is happy to lend travelers a boat for free.

Ione is home to a satellite campus of the Spokane Community College system, but the town's high school graduated its last class decades ago. Kids from Ione attend the Selkirk school on the highway between Ione and Metaline. The college campus in Ione is open just one day per week and focuses on preparing local students for jobs in locally based industries.

99

Population: 197
Founding: 1900

INSETS L to R: Blink, and you'll miss Metaline, but the North Pend Oreille Chamber of Commerce hopes you'll stop by. • The American Pie Drive-in picked up where Hoogy's left off. • Somehow this tiny town sustains a sizeable bar and grill in addition to the drive-in. • Hooknose, Eagle, and Sherlock Peaks in nearby Metaline Falls.

TOP: Once upon a time, Metaline had a steakhouse called Hoogy's.

Metaline

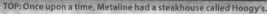

Golden Promises

Though the town of Metaline officially incorporated in 1948, its earliest non-Indigenous settlers came a century earlier, drawn by the discovery of quartz and hoping for gold. The earliest settlement of Metaline was the first gold camp in the far northeastern corner of the state. Pend Oreille County formed in 1911, the last county created in the state. Prior to that, the area called Metaline was part of Stevens County. By the 1890s, many of the early prospectors had left the area, but those who stayed formed a community strong enough to rebuild the town of Metaline after a devastating flood in 1894. The year 1904 brought a road from Metaline to nearby Ione. Around the same time, steamboat service expanded through the newly widened Box Canyon. The railroad came in 1910, and with it, the steamboats became obsolete. By then, the Metaline Mining District was in full swing.

In 1890, the Washington state geologist noted that the district held "an immense amount of metal." Lewis P. Larson and Jens Jensen began operations at the Metaline Lead and Zinc Company before the arrival of rail. In 1910, the first rail car full of lead, zinc, and silver made its way across the Pend Oreille River from Metaline to Metaline Falls, where the railway ran high above the river. Production increased steadily, taking off in 1928 when Larsen financed diamond drilling and discovered further significant ore deposits. Within a few decades, the Metaline area produced fully 20% of the nation's lead and more than 10% of its zinc.

One early visitor is on record noting Metaline as an "out-of-the-way place." Through its relocation post-flood and the rise and fall of the mining industry, Metaline remains out of the way, though Highway 31, better known as the International Selkirk Loop, runs right through it. The town's population has been in a steady decline since the 1950s, when about 500 people lived here. Today, there are 60% fewer. After a century spent building a town around the extraction of natural resources, today, nature seems to be taking the town back.

The Slash

In 2003, the federal government opened a border station in Metaline to stop terrorists and weapons from finding their way into the United States.

Thirty-eight agents staff the station, many of whom worked previously at the border between the US and Mexico, where arrests could number in the hundreds per shift, per agent. In Metaline, arrests are fewer and farther between. Agents patrol on horseback, ATV, and even on foot. With the authority to patrol as far away as the city of Spokane, agents have detained as many as 200 people at the bus depot there, despite a Spokane City Council ordinance requiring them to first obtain permission from the mayor. In Metaline, border patrol efforts center on "the slash," a 30-foot clear-cut through Colville National Forest. Electronic sensors and air patrol supplement the patrol effort on the ground. In the winter, the slash is a bright white line of snow cutting across mountaintops. On this side, us. On the other, them. The trees on both sides of the slash are the same.

An Uncertain Future

Like Metaline Falls and Ione, the town of Metaline will be greatly affected by the recent closure of the Teck Pend Oreille Mine. To all three communities, the closure means not only lost jobs but also, likely, the loss of population. At a job fair in the wake of the mine's closure, a Tennessee-based company offered as many as 57 jobs to miners willing to relocate. While the mine closure has had a major effect, it wasn't a surprise. Teck American opened the mine in 2014 after five years of maintenance-only operations. At the time, zinc and lead prices were rising after a steep falloff during the recent nationwide economic recession, and Teck American promised to triple the existing workforce at the mine. Teck said the mine had a five-year lifespan in 2014. In 2019, that prediction proved true.

As elsewhere in the county, Metaline's future may depend on tourism. The Gardner Caves are a primary attraction near town. In 1903, Ed Gardner discovered a cave system not far from his Metaline homestead. Soon after, mining magnate W. H. Crawford filed to preserve the area as a state park. Newspaper coverage at the time recorded the impressions of early visitors to the cave system. "Pulling our stomachs up against our hearts and our hearts into our mouths," visitors made their way through narrow passageways into what would eventually become known as one of the largest limestone caverns in the state. Visitors to Metaline can take a guided tour of the cavern.

A few crumbling establishments like Hoogy's Steakhouse greet visitors traveling through Metaline. Just down from Hoogy's, the well-kept Western Star Bar and American Pie Drive-in offer alternatives.

Other visitors may find interest in theories that the cult-classic TV show *Twin Peaks* is thought to be set in the Metaline area, in the way that another 1990s TV show, *Northern Exposure,* was set but not filmed in Alaska. Among other pieces of evidence, enthusiasts of the show cite the location given by FBI Special Agent Dale Cooper in the pilot episode, "5 miles south of the Canadian border and 12 miles west of the state line." Locals who may fear an influx of obnoxious tourists can probably rest easy. Whereas the *Twilight* series made a vampire seekers' haven of Forks, Washington, anyone interested in the real location of Twin Peaks is less likely to be on the hunt for Killer BOB and more for coffee and pie.

The Northern Pend Oreille County Chamber of Commerce hosts a tiny visitors center along the highway that serves as Metaline's main street. A few dozen houses line the residential streets of the riverside town, not quite a third of a mile square.

100

Population: 238
Founding: 1911

INSETS L to R: The old rail trestle cuts narrowly between the mountain and Box Canyon Dam. • Plans for a grand hotel fell through, but miners soon utilized the rooms as apartments. • The Cutter Theater, home to both a stage and a museum, provides many opportunities for community engagement. • The Cutter Theater and Community Center both serve as gathering spaces for events in Metaline Falls.

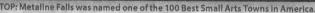

TOP: Metaline Falls was named one of the 100 Best Small Arts Towns in America.

Metaline Falls

Metal Miracles

Metaline Falls was born in the mines. The 1850s brought the first gold rush prospectors to the area. The placer mines they established required intensive labor for little yield. Chinese miners were among the first to extract minerals from the area; limited documentation exists about their contribution to mining, however, as dams have inundated archaeological sites and 19th-century discrimination against the Chinese seems to have excluded them from much of the area's historical record. Though the first miners were after gold and silver, lead and zinc would bring economic prosperity and large-scale development, hence the name, given by the earliest non-Indigenous settlers: the Metalines.

Before the railroad came through, a combination of pack trains and riverboats carried out the zinc and lead extracted from these early mines. In 1907, the government widened a difficult passage of the river at Box Canyon to make way for better transport. Shortly thereafter, Danish immigrant Lewis Larson and Frederick Blackwell of Maine initiated the greatest economic development in the region. With Blackwell's financial backing, Larson's

Lehigh Portland Cement Company began an operation that would employ the area for nearly a century.

While Larson focused on local development, Blackwell invested in rail. His Idaho & Washington Northern Railroad reached Metaline Falls in 1910. The next year, Metaline Falls incorporated. A bridge across the Pend Oreille connected Metaline Falls with the highway in 1919, and hydroelectric projects and logging contributed to the area's development. During the mid-20th century, the Metaline Mining District was the top producer in the state and a source of zinc and lead during WWII. As industry depleted the area's natural resources, rail lines diverted efforts away from Metaline Falls. Box Canyon and Boundary Dams still employ area residents, but logging and mining have run their course.

Basketball Courts for Battlefields

The loss of a school is one step in the decline of a town, and so it's unsurprising that a town would fight to keep its school district. Such is the case with Metaline, Metaline Falls, and Ione. At the Cutter Theatre in Metaline Falls, an exhibit on local school consolidations tells the story.

Homesteaders established school districts "as soon as the number of children could justify it." The first school went up in Metaline Falls in 1902. Without buses, children walked for miles, rode horses, and forded the river to get to school. By the time schools in northern Pend Oreille County were established, professional educators viewed rural schools with disdain. Many of these educators pushed for school consolidation to encourage rural families to move to more urbanized areas and participate in larger school districts.

During the Great Depression, teachers' wages fell for three years running in Metaline Falls. Companies started closing, and homesteaders left to find work. The Huckleberry School closed in 1936, followed closely by the Forest Home, Tiger, and Lost Creek Schools. Metaline Falls' schools consolidated with Metaline's, just half a mile down the road and over the river. Consolidation both united and divided the communities: just a few miles apart, the communities of Ione and Metaline Falls became bitter rivals, using basketball courts for battlefields.

In the 1960s, the county sought to consolidate schools once again. Neither town would concede to busing its students to school in the other. "Over my dead body," one resident remarked. In a compromise, the county built the new Selkirk High School halfway between. An exchange between a mother and her son, who'd begun attending the new school, illuminates the difficulty of assimilation. "How many on [the basketball team] are from Ione and how many from Metaline Falls?" she asked. "Mom," her son replied, "This is Selkirk now."

The old Metaline Falls school, designed by architect Kirtland Cutter, has been repurposed as the Cutter Theatre, a nonprofit performing arts center, home to a theatre, library, and exhibit space.

Lead's Legacy

Tucked between the Colville National Forest and the Pend Oreille River, Metaline Falls is stunningly beautiful. Rock climbers can access more than 70 routes on surrounding limestone cliffs. Sullivan Lake offers camping, fishing, and multiple hiking trails for all levels of ability. For the less outdoorsy types, Metaline Falls hosts several annual events, from arts festivals and car shows to theatrical productions. Now more than ever, Metaline Falls could use the economic benefits of responsible tourism.

The Box Canyon Dam, built in 1955, generates enough power to supply 36,000 homes. It is a "run of the river" dam, which means it doesn't have the capacity to store the energy it produces. Its reservoir is 56 miles long.

On July 31, 2019, the Pend Oreille mine in Metaline Falls closed after more than 100 years of fluctuating economic relevance. The mine reopened in 2014 after being open only for "care and maintenance" since 2009. With the most recent closure, Metaline Falls, as well as Pend Oreille County at large, lost more than 200 jobs. Just 40 workers will stay on to maintain the mine long-term.

Coverage of the mine closure notes the divide between urban and rural communities in the Pacific Northwest. Whereas urban centers thrive on a diversity of work opportunities, rural communities that have long depended on single industries based on natural resource extraction are suffering as those resources are depleted. Prior to the mine closure, Pend Oreille County's unemployment rate was 7.2%, compared with 4.6% across the state.

Other economic opportunities may lie in the opening of a new casino not far down the road, in Cusick. The casino anticipates offering up to 80 jobs to area workers. Residents of Metaline Falls reacted to the closure with expressions of grief and concern about population loss, and they also demonstrated hope. Pend Oreille County Commissioner Steve Kiss stayed focused on resilience, saying, "We will survive."

The Pend Oreille Apartments, better known as the Miner's Hotel, took 20 years to build. Started in 1929, work stalled during the Depression. Lewis Larsen had conceived of a grand hotel, but with mining booming, a shortage of worker housing turned the hotel into an apartment building for mine workers. Today, a 600-square-foot studio with one bathroom rents for $400 per month.

An old crow and a cute chick live here!

References

In an effort to save paper (and trees), we've opted to place the Works Cited section for each town online. To access it, please visit: https://advkeen.co/LittleWA_reference

Towns by Region and by County

PENINSULAS / COAST

SOUTHWEST

PUGET SOUND

NORTHWEST

CENTRAL CASCADES

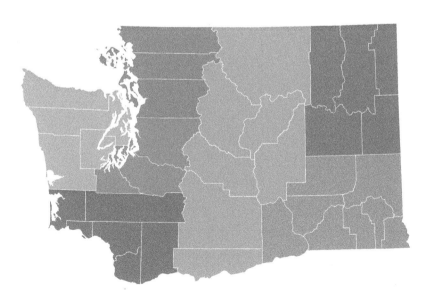

Photo credit: Audrey Zaragoza

About the Author

Nicole Hardina has lived in Washington for more than 20 years, in towns big and small. Alaska-grown, she is a Seattle-based writer who shares an apartment with two cats, a guitar, and several overflowing bookcases. Her writing has appeared in *Scope, Months to Years,* the *Bellingham Review, Proximity,* and elsewhere. She received a Grant for Artist Projects Award from Artist Trust in 2016 and is working on a memoir that is equal parts grief account and love letter to the Pacific Northwest. When not writing, she can be found on a flying trapeze or via her website, **www.nicolehardina.com.**